Muslims and Islam in U.S. Education

Muslims and Islam in U.S. Education explores the complex interface that exists between U.S. school curriculum, teaching practice about religion in public schools, societal and teacher attitudes toward Islam and Muslims, and multiculturalism as a framework for meeting the needs of minority group students. It presents multiculturalism as a concept that needs to be rethought and reformulated in the interest of creating a more democratic, inclusive, and informed society.

Islam is an under-considered religion in American education, due in part to the fact that Muslims represent a very small minority group in the population today (less than 1%). However, this group faces a crucial challenge of representation in United States society as a whole, as well as in its schools. Muslims in the United States are impacted by ignorance that news and opinion polls have demonstrated is widespread among the public in the last few decades. U.S. citizens who do not have a balanced, fair, and accurate view of Islam can make a variety of decisions: in the voting booth, in job hiring, and within their small-scale but important personal networks and spheres of influence that make a very negative impact on Muslims in the United States.

This book presents new information that has implications for curricula, religious education, and multicultural education today, examining the unique case of Islam in U.S. education over the last twenty years. Chapters include the following:

- Perspectives on multicultural education
- 9/11, the media, and the new need to know
- Islam and Muslims in public schools
- Blazing a path for intercultural education

This book is an essential resource for professors, researchers, and teachers of social studies, particularly those involved with multicultural issues, critical and sociocultural analysis of education and schools, as well as interdisciplinary scholars and students in anthropology and education.

Liz Jackson is Assistant Professor of Curriculum and Policy Studies at the University of Hong Kong Faculty of Education.

Muslims and Islam in U.S. Education
Reconsidering multiculturalism

Liz Jackson

LONDON AND NEW YORK

First published 2014
by Routledge
2 Park Square, Milton Park, Abingdon, Oxon OX14 4RN

and by Routledge
711 Third Avenue, New York, NY 10017

Routledge is an imprint of the Taylor & Francis Group, an informa business

© 2014 L. Jackson

The right of L. Jackson to be identified as author of this work has been asserted by her in accordance with sections 77 and 78 of the Copyright, Designs and Patents Act 1988.

All rights reserved. No part of this book may be reprinted or reproduced or utilised in any form or by any electronic, mechanical, or other means, now known or hereafter invented, including photocopying and recording, or in any information storage or retrieval system, without permission in writing from the publishers.

Trademark notice: Product or corporate names may be trademarks or registered trademarks, and are used only for identification and explanation without intent to infringe.

British Library Cataloguing in Publication Data
A catalogue record for this book is available from the British Library

Library of Congress Cataloging-in-Publication Data
Jackson, Liz.
   Muslims and Islam in U.S. education : reconsidering multiculturalism / Liz Jackson.
     pages cm
  1. Islamic education—United States. 2. Muslims—Education—United States. 3. Multiculturalism—United States. I. Title.
  LC913.U6J33 2014
  371.0770973—dc23
  2013046255

ISBN: 978-0-415-70504-2 (hbk)
ISBN: 978-1-315-81412-4 (ebk)

Typeset in Galliard
by Apex CoVantage, LLC

Contents

Foreword vii
Preface xi

1 Introduction 1
2 Perspectives on multicultural education 11
3 9/11, the media, and the new need to know 53
4 Islam and Muslims in public schools 76
5 A path forward: Interculturalism 113
6 Blazing a path for intercultural education 147
7 Conclusion 167

Index 173

Foreword

Liz Jackson provides two invaluable services in this book. The first is to identify, and begin to correct, the distorted and incomplete ways in which Muslims are represented in American popular culture and in American school materials (textbooks, state standards, and curricula). Her account is richly informative and provides a framework for rereading those materials through a more critical lens. Second, she discusses the importance of these problems in the context of a wider understanding of multicultural education, and in this context her argument frames a broader set of questions about the purposes and methods of education in a democratic society. Her analysis is critical, challenging, but also constructive in providing a more productive way forward in dealing with Islam – as well as other "controversial" cultural subjects – in schools.

There are at least 2.6 million Muslims in the United States (Neal 2012). Worldwide, they are projected to make up more than a quarter of the global population by 2030 (Neal 2012; Pew Research Center 2011). Yet, as Dr. Jackson makes clear, the public perceptions of this group – itself internally diverse in significant ways – is broadly misunderstood within the U.S. and viewed almost invariably through the lens of public perceptions and fears about terrorism. Worse than ignorance, this perception is colored by paranoia and intolerance, by religious bigotry, and by the ethos of a "clash of civilizations," as if we were in the middle of a new Crusades.

Public schools, which should be informing the public discussion and basing it on fact, offer a mixed bag of information and stereotypes about Muslims. One of Dr. Jackson's main contributions here is a close reading of textbooks and other curriculum materials used in the U.S. When Muslims are not being ignored entirely, they are often characterized through simplistic folk wisdom and conventional narratives. In many ways, she notes, the situation has improved since 9/11, as educators came to recognize their responsibilities to better inform students about Muslim culture and Muslim nations. Textbooks produced since that time are on the whole better than their predecessors. There are also supplementary materials educators can access to provide richer and more accurate information. But this desire has to contend with local community cultures, especially in some parts of the nation, that regard anything that seems to be too friendly or sympathetic to the Muslim point of view as somehow disloyal, unpatriotic, and/or unChristian.

Moreover, schools are not the only institutions that inform (or misinform) the public. Dr. Jackson also reviews a variety of films, television shows, and other artefacts of popular culture, which have done so much to shape the ways Muslims are portrayed in the public imagination. It is crucial for educators to recognize the power of these other influences, and to plan their teaching and curriculum with an eye toward counterbalancing and correcting their misimpressions. Dr. Jackson provides a compelling argument here for the need for critical media literacy and the importance of reading these elements of popular culture – and for that matter elements in the formal curriculum – at cross-purposes with how they might have been intended: questioning their silences or omissions, asking how certain versions of representation shape perception, and recognizing how even some attempts at "balance" can still reinforce deeper biases.

The other main contribution of this book is its review of different conceptions of multicultural education, and its development of an alternative view, *interculturalism*. It is striking that most accounts of multicultural education themselves gave slight attention to Islam, until recently, despite the size of the U.S. Muslim population and its clear importance on the world stage. Books like this one are helping to correct that neglect. But there is also the more general matter of how and why other cultures are introduced into the curriculum at all. Dr. Jackson reviews three dominant paradigms of multicultural education: assimilationist, pluralist, and critical, and shows how the content of curricula is shaped by the broader educational purpose behind each type of multicultural education. Is the purpose to incorporate other cultures into a melting-pot of mainstream U.S. culture and values; is it to promote tolerance and coexistence, despite persistent cultural differences; or is it to provide a reflective mirror through which to reexamine and problematize aspects of what is taken for granted in the dominant culture? Each of these approaches has some value, but Dr. Jackson contrasts them with a fourth approach, interculturalism, which emphasizes the active *preservation* of cultural differences, and the active *engagement* of learners and citizens across those differences, through respectful dialogical encounters. Dr. Jackson's arguments for interculturalism go much further in their educational implications than in the particular instance of learning about Islam.

And so this book poses a number of challenges to educators – and by extension to teacher educators. For educators, the case of teaching about Islam means being willing to go against local culture and conventional wisdom. It means being willing to engage controversy. It means being willing to address the always explosive topic of religion and religious tolerance. It means being willing to critically engage elements in popular culture, and even in school materials themselves, and to teach across the grain of popular ideas and stereotypes.

Put more positively, it means being willing to encourage an active intercultural engagement with ideas, values, and histories that are sharply unlike our own. It means being willing to foster respect in the face of difference, and to encourage hope in the face of paranoia and fear. This is no small order.

For teacher educators this means giving teachers the intellectual tools to engage and question received "truths." It means promoting a critical media *and* curriculum literacy. And it means encouraging in teachers the virtues of courage, a disposition to go against the grain, and a curiosity and openness toward the different – and modeling it ourselves. These are much broader educational concerns than apply simply to the case of Muslims; but precisely because the case of Muslims is so colored by widespread attitudes of suspicion and even hatred, it puts our commitment to these values to the test.

Nicholas C. Burbules
University of Illinois, Urbana–Champaign

References

Neal, Meghan. "Number of Muslims in the U.S. Doubles Since 9/11." *New York Daily News*, May 2, 2012. www.nydailynews.com/news/national/number-muslims-u-s-doubles-9-11-article-1.1071895 (accessed January 21, 2014).

Pew Research Center. "The Future of the Global Muslim Population." January 27, 2011. www.pewforum.org/2011/01/27/the-future-of-the-global-muslim-population/ (accessed January 21, 2014).

Preface

On September 11, 2001, I was a junior studying political science at Portland State University (Oregon). I was starting a new position as a "peer mentor," which was a cross between a teaching assistant and an upper-classman mentor for incoming freshmen. I would be teaching for the first time in tutorial sections of a course called Chaos and Community. Like many young Americans, I knew very little about Islam before that autumn. That academic year, I simply aimed to stay a few weeks ahead of my freshmen, who wanted me to teach them about terrorism and Islam, and comfort them, as they left home for the first time during this state of unprecedented (for them) national panic and insecurity.

Like many Americans, I became increasingly fascinated with Islam over the next several years. I had a few friends in Portland who were Muslim, and I noticed they seemed nothing like any Muslims I had ever seen in the news. They were from Southeast Asia and Northern Africa, wore blue jeans and t-shirts, and were quick with jokes and banter. In 2002, I spent the summer in Adana, Turkey, as a camp counselor for American children of U.S. Air Force personnel stationed at Incirlik, many of whom were involved in missions in Pakistan and Afghanistan. I found that Turkey was nothing like I had imagined it to be. Most of the women I met, even in eastern Turkey, wore blue jeans and worked and traveled outside the home by themselves. When Turkey beat Korea in the World Cup, I was at a beach bar eating pizza, and the place erupted in boisterous, topless men dancing to Turkish rock music. And there were Roman ruins and Christian historical sites everywhere. I experienced another Muslim country at the end of the summer, taking a brief historical and cultural tour of Egypt. There, I saw another side of Islam – another country where a diversity of peoples, cultures, traditions, ethnicities, and religions lived and worked together, despite this vague assumption I had prior to my trip, about entering a homogeneous "Muslim world."

After that, I contracted the travel bug and became a dedicated backpacker and budget tourist. I studied at the University of Cambridge for my master's degree and saw a new country every chance I got, viewing the world as my classroom. I began to concentrate my studies in philosophy of education, as I started querying how my values developed within particular cultural and political contexts, comparing my attitudes with those of my fellow postgraduate students and people I met in my travels. Despite warnings and a general sense in the United States that Americans would become unwelcome worldwide as the U.S.-led coalition in Iraq began to disintegrate, I found that no matter where I went, people rarely saw me as a "generic American," but rather as a nice, friendly person, a foreigner, etc.

I returned to the United States for my doctoral studies, attending the University of Illinois at Urbana-Champaign. As I was completing my coursework and field qualification requirements, I went to a conference in Malta. Fondly recalling my trip to Egypt as I located Malta on a map, I decided to extend my trip to travel by myself to Tunisia. Tunisia at that time was entirely peaceful and stable, though Algeria and Libya were American "no-go" zones. However, although I was armed with my trusty travel guide, I hit a few snags along the way.

First, my guidebook had warned me that Tunisia was a very conservative Muslim country, and as such, I would likely experience difficulties with men, as a single white Western female. Apparently, it was unusual for women to be in the public sphere, as there was a sharp segregation of the sexes. Upon seeing me, an exotic white woman breaking the taboos of society by taking part in public life, some men would feel compelled to try their luck. In this context the book advised that I neither talk to nor make eye contact with men. And if any men touched me, I should give the meanest response possible, shaming them in Arabic and giving a cruel glare. As I began wandering through the market in Tunis my first day, I kept this advice in mind. However, after a few hours without sexual harassment, I became less careful and cautious. Overwhelmed by the heat of the day and the spirit of the marketplace, I began drifting in a trancelike state, from incense and tea, to shoes and scarves. Suddenly I found myself in a major intersection of the medina, during a rush hour of sweaty bodies, bumping into me, jostling me, knocking my handbag.

As I snapped back into reality, my guidebook's words came back into my mind, and I began radiating a mean glare as recommended. Yet upon taking in the scene properly, I realized that there were men and women everywhere, not segregated, but integrated, and that all were equally sorry to bump into me, as they bumped into each other. In fact, I found that I was the only body in the alley that seemed ill at ease in the parade, and people were actually going out of their way not to disturb me, because *I* was being exceptionally sensitive. Perhaps my guidebook was correct in cautioning me not to wander into countryside villages, nonchalantly chatting up men. But such advice seemed alarmist and inappropriate in the Tunis medina, where the free mingling of sexes ended up bothering *me*, the American, much more than anyone else.

A second snag along my way through Tunisia came up after departing the city by public minivan taxi, as I found that service was not as consistent in some parts of the country as my book had led me to believe. Twice I was stranded in towns where I was the only person who wanted to go further on that day, and both times individual taxi men facilitated me taking private taxis to get to my final destination. Both cases I was practically hitchhiking, though I departed from central transportation hubs. At neither time did I feel particularly fearful.

Having nearly tossed out my travel book, I took it all in with more of a blank slate and found that these "traditional Muslim men" appeared to fear me, a young American woman, as much as I could fear them.

In one minivan taxi, I was surrounded by a French Tunisian family, who insisted I stay with them upon reaching the evening's destination. After my labors with my guidebook thus far, I gratefully consented. Our ability to communicate was quite poor, since I have little to any French or Arabic, and none of them had more than a few words of English. However the mother and daughters were so effusive, warm, and bubbling with love that it seemed cruel to decline their hospitality in order to search the village for any cheap, uncomfortable hostel. That evening, I was treated like an honored guest at their three-room house, given my own private room and electric fan, and periodically offered food and drink. My hosts were fascinated by my guidebook, and I showed them a picture of one of the tourist sites of their town. The next day, they called upon a male cousin my age and asked him to come over and escort me to the historic area, to the bank, and anywhere else I would like to go. He had some conversational English ability, and faithfully and dedicatedly escorted me, walking a few paces in front of me all over the small town. When he was not asking me about America and where I had traveled before, he was making sure I was not hungry or thirsty or tired or sad. I was, throughout the day, entirely overwhelmed with his hospitality and politeness. We took a taxi back to the house in the hot afternoon, and he refused to let me pay my share of the fare.

Though the mother begged me to stay longer, I had a flight back to Malta and the states approaching, so I bid the family farewell the best I could the following morning. This family had taken me in and treated me like a queen, when I was a dusty backpacker and they did not have running water or air conditioning. I had never been treated with such profound hospitality, and certainly never with such generosity by complete strangers. The mother only allowed me to leave upon taking many group pictures with my camera and stuffing my handbag with sweets and fruits. As she hugged me upon my departure back to the bus station, I began to cry, feeling so touched by the warmth I had been shown. At this outburst, the mother became alarmed and all the more desirous that I stay there. There seemed no way to communicate what I was feeling; she did not understand what good thing could move me to tears. She ran back in the house to grab another fistful of sweets and loaded my purse to bursting, as I struggled back to the bus station.

Upon returning to the United States, I started to feel personally alienated by rhetoric about Islam and its relationship to terrorism in the news media. The Muslims prominently featured on television were nothing like any Muslim I had ever met in the United States or in the Muslim countries I had visited. On the one hand, I met so many kind, smiling, generous, giving Muslims. Sure, there were some obnoxious, unfriendly, and rude ones, but unkindness can be found in any community or society. On the other hand, all the Muslims I met were unique one to the next, and across diverse societies; the only real connection among them was the belief in and submission to one god. Like Christians, agnostics, Jews, and so on, I felt it would be wrong to prejudge them based on some exceptional, infamous cases.

I also began to wonder why I had not known anything about Islam prior to traveling to Muslim-majority countries (and choosing to study Islam at university). Was I not taught anything about the religion or peoples in school? Why did I have the belief, prior to my travels, that Islam and Christianity were in some sense geographically separated, historically and today? How did I not know that there were Christians living in Muslim countries? Or Muslims living in East Asia, Western Europe, and the United Kingdom?

This text is the result of my trying to resolve some of these queries. It has been a challenging and fascinating journey. I am extremely grateful for the opportunity I have had to work with leading researchers in educational theory, cultural studies, and religious studies along the way. As this book involves a fresh examination and fuller analysis of many of the ideas and issues I explored and developed in my dissertation research, I am thankful first for the advice of my doctoral supervisors Nicholas Burbules, Fazal Rizvi, Walter Feinberg, Cameron McCarthy, and Valerie Hoffman. Without their careful readings, reasoned critiques, and years of lively and difficult questioning, I could not have developed the perspective I have today. I received additional valuable mentorship from Michael Peters while at the University of Illinois, and continue to enjoy debating issues of multiculturalism versus interculturalism with him and Tina Besley, both now at the University of Waikato, New Zealand.

I also wish to thank John Lang for careful and critical feedback on drafts, and Gerald Pfeifer and Suzy Elbow for additional comments and recommendations. Thanks also go to my colleagues at the University of Hong Kong, Mark Bray, Gerard Postligione, Law Wing-Wah, and Sarah Aiston for their support and encouragement. I am additionally grateful for indexing assistance by Jenneffer Sixkiller, and the support and feedback of Christina Low at Routledge. And thank you to my friend Dominic Biava for vital, last-minute research assistance.

On the day that I passed my preliminary dissertation examination, which was my first major research project about Islam and U.S. education, I met a physics doctoral student who was also at the University of Illinois, who later began to "assist" me in my research on the representation of Muslims in U.S. popular culture. He would call me and ask me what I was doing, and I would invite him over to my tiny apartment to watch movies like *True Lies*, *Babel*, *Iron Man*, and heavy political documentaries about Iraq and the Middle East. Since then, we have moved together to South Africa, the United Arab Emirates, and Hong Kong, and I still talk sometimes incessantly about Muslims and Islam in U.S. popular culture and public education. Thank you so much to my dear husband Timothy Wotherspoon, for supporting me through ongoing debate, patience, hours watching ludicrous films, and eating plenty of Thai food for the last five amazing, challenging, exciting years. Perhaps we can cut down our consumption of movies in the "Muslim terrorist" genre in the future.

1 Introduction

The relationship between religion and public education in the United States has always been controversial. In the past, debate has mainly concerned the respective priorities of teaching about, enabling, or promoting different faith traditions, as well as secularism, in schools. Whether schools have had an indoctrinatory Protestant or generally Christian social context has been a concern since the development of common schools to educate children across ethnic and class lines in the nineteenth century. However, in recent decades, Christians have also had good reasons to feel their views have sometimes been unreasonably excluded from public schools, by educators who may feel uncomfortable with any mention of religion in their classrooms. Such debates relate to larger questions in the society about whether the United States is a "Christian nation," multicultural, or "secular humanist," or ought to be neutral about religious belief and unbelief.

Islam has rarely been discussed in this context. Warren Nord's comprehensive 502-page (1995) volume titled *Religion and American Education* has but a handful of sentences discussing Islam and Muslims. Though religion became widely recognized as a multicultural education issue in the 1980s and 1990s, James Banks and Cherry McGee Banks discuss Islam and Muslims in curriculum for the first time in their 2004 guide to U.S. multicultural education, and then only within a special subsection of the chapter on religion and education. Education of American Muslims has emerged as a research topic akin to that of education of other religious groups in society today, who may opt for private education, often seen by parents as more in line with their faith commitment.

Yet how U.S. public schools should address Islam and Muslims, through curricular content and social context, has become its own distinct battleground since September 11, 2001 (9/11). In the days after the event, teachers across the country faced students who looked to them for answers. I was among these educators, and the students' need to know vividly impacted my first year of teaching. Across the decentralized educational system of the United States, some teachers were asked by administrators or school counselors before the next teaching day *not to dwell* on the day's events (Noppe et al. 2006). Others were told the opposite. In the weeks to come, parents and private interest groups for and against teaching about Muslim terrorists, ordinary Muslims, or related topics, emerged to criticize educators and textbooks for not teaching the right information or the right perspectives about Islam, 9/11, and Muslims in society or worldwide (Bennetta 2006; Hochman 2006; Sewall 2003). Today, many educators may feel uncertain of what or how to teach in relation to Muslims and Islam. Empowering educators is important in this context, if we see the role of public education in the United States as preparing young people to become informed participants in a religiously plural, liberal democratic society, where they will encounter diverse others, and make decisions with and alongside them, including Muslims in the United States and abroad.

This book starts from these assumptions: First, that U.S. public education has an important role to teach students about the social world around them. This is part of general acculturation, a main role of education as Horace Mann, founder of U.S. "common schools," argued (Messerli 1972). It is not enough to teach the "basic facts" of skills of literacy and numeracy. It is an important problem that some schools may be failing to teach such basic competencies to all schoolchildren. However, I start my examination here assuming that schools must do more than this in order to prepare students to become independent adults: independent in an intellectual sense, able to come to their own well-considered opinions and informed perspectives about issues, based upon their distinct experiences. My view here also supports a minimal form of assimilation, as I understand education to have a socializing role in preparing students to take part in democratic traditions of the country they are a part of. I believe that a nation-state must engage in providing such an education to prepare people to take up roles in society in the future, regardless of where their family comes from or what they believe – their culture, religion, or moral background. How to do so is no easy task; that is what this book is about.

Second, I assume here that the United States is a *religiously plural* country and a *liberal democratic* society. Let me unpack these terms and what I mean by them here. The first claim is about the actual makeup of the society today; it is not about what I, or anyone else, would like the country to be. The fact is that people from all religious traditions, as well as agnostics and atheists, live permanently in the United States, which promises in its constitution *religious toleration:* People have the right to practice their faith, so long as they do not cause unnecessary, substantial harm to others. From a historical or highly general perspective, one might say the country is a "Christian nation." The country has a strong, proud Christian presence, and the government has funded Christian organizations throughout its history, despite any so-called separation of church and state (Zinn 1995). However, this does not mean that the United States should be a country that is *only* for Christians, where only Christians can feel at home. The founding fathers did not feel this way, recognizing even within Christianity a pluralism of beliefs and practices, which can be at odds with one another in some practical circumstances (such as in public education). They concluded it was best to permit toleration of religious difference rather than to officially favor one religious community over another in the United States. In 2008, about 75% of U.S. adults identified as Christian (including Catholic), while 15% identified with no religion and 4% identified with other religions, namely Judaism, Islam, Eastern religions, and new religious movements (Kosmin & Keysar 2009). I follow this understanding of the United States as factually and constitutionally religiously plural here.

By "liberal democratic" in this text, I mean to refer not to partisan politics, but to the liberal tradition of individual freedom and equal rights that is held as foundational to U.S. citizenship across political parties and throughout society today. This is the tradition linked to liberal political philosophy, associated with thinkers such as John Locke, Jean-Jacques Rousseau, Immanuel Kant, and John Stuart Mill. In the essay "Answer to the Question: 'What Is Enlightenment?'" Kant (1970) argued that all men should be conceived as free and able to think and act independently. In relation, he elaborated *reason* as "like the vote of citizens of a free state, every member of which must have the privilege of giving expression to his doubts" (1993: A738/B766; Jackson 2007). "Liberal" philosophers, in this general sense, have for centuries linked personal freedom to democracy, within an ideal form of government. For a society to be ruled wisely, it should be ruled by people who come together to deliberate from their diverse perspectives, given their diverse talents. One might argue that this is an ideal rather than an actuality in the United States today. Politics has become a cynical domain. People are failing to "reach across the aisle" to shake hands, goes a common sentiment, and good decision making that helps the greatest number of people, or avoids the worst unnecessary harm, is in such a context a mere utopian vision.

This book nonetheless focuses on education to enable democratic flourishing, with awareness that this is a difficult time in U.S. political history; indeed, perhaps a new form of multicultural education can help to ameliorate some of today's challenges related to democratic dialogue. A final assumption I start this conversation with is that Muslims and non-Muslims alike are unintentionally harmed by educational tendencies today that preclude students learning much useful information about this religion and community. Since 9/11, some groups have begun to protest teaching any positive information about Islam and Muslims, which aims to debunk overly broad stereotypes, or give a view contradicting that of the "clash of civilizations" (Huntington 1993), of "despots, oil sheikhs, and terrorists" (Shaheen 2001). However, such views that reduce Muslims to threatening "bad guys" and oppressed women do not accurately portray the whole of the Muslim world. Most Muslims are not dangerous, terroristic, or anti-American; most are not Arab or Middle Eastern, but South and Southeast Asian. As I discuss in this text, some people feel that understanding the worldwide Muslim community comprehensively should be discarded for an education focused on preparing for terrorism. Yet who is helped by teaching the worst-case scenario as if it is a general fact about nearly one-fourth of the world's population?

Some argue that students' patriotic education is hindered by a focus on religious toleration or multiculturalism in schools (Finn 2002; Hirsch 2003). There are more abstract concerns, which have been raised by parents and some educators, that students need to learn about *right* and *wrong* and that education that discusses Muslims as diverse, good and bad people (like any others) since 9/11 contradicts or blurs this binary understanding (Hochman 2006). However, it is not right to teach students that 23% of the earth's population is bad, uncivilized, or anti-American. It is not right to teach prejudice, when friendship and peace may flourish to the benefit of Muslims and non-Muslims alike. It is not patriotic to teach religious intolerance in the United States.

Recent surveys have found that many Americans are ignorant about Islam and Muslims. According to the Council on American-Islamic Relations (CAIR 2006), 10% believe strange things about Muslims, such as that they worship a "moon god." Furthermore, 25% believe that Islam is a religion of hatred (CAIR 2006), and a majority believes that Muslims are disproportionately prone to violence (Deane & Fears 2006; Pew Research Center 2006). Such "understanding" makes sense, if we imagine that people do not learn about social diversity in formal education, but from the media. Indeed, 80% of those polled who indicated never having heard of Muslims leaders condemning terrorism (63%, overall) stated they got their information about Muslims from television (CAIR 2006: 7). Most Muslims in the news and in movies are extraordinarily violent, uncivil, and/or combative, however. This is no accident. There are violent, uncivil, and combative Muslims in the world. Though they are a small subsection of an unimaginably large cross-section of humanity, they are the most newsworthy in the United States, especially since 9/11, and given U.S. interests in the Middle East. It is not newsworthy when Muslims peacefully attend mosque for daily prayer, buy their friends cups of coffee, or discuss the tragic nature of international terrorism, including that wrongfully done under the name of Islam.

Education has a role to play here. Traditionally, it has had a role to minimally assimilate diverse populations, which includes in many educators' minds the need to debunk harmful, ignorant stereotypes and overgeneralizations. Historically, the media has presented Jews in a negative light (Shaheen 2001); one could argue that black Americans face representational challenges similar to those of Muslims today in mainstream news media (Hollinger 2008; McCarthy & Dimitriadis 2000). However, when a child meets another child who is black or Jewish, he or she learns a different side of the story. In the case of Islam and Muslims in U.S. public schools, educators are also charged with teaching social studies, which includes an understanding of the customs, norms, and rules of society, its social makeup, and those elsewhere in the world. In this context, students should learn more about Islam and Muslims than what they are learning from news media and popular culture; the worst ugly stereotypes should be at least contrasted with ordinary images of Muslims, in the United States and elsewhere, who, as one recent book was titled, "don't want to blow you up" (Cortés & Hastie 2007). Why this education is not always taking place, and why and how it should, are the main questions I examine in this text.

It is often a challenge for social studies educators to discuss controversial issues in their classrooms, and in the case of Islam, they face controversy related both to 9/11 and to teaching about religion more generally in public schools. They face related hurdles in finding good information, and evading criticism or punishment for teaching inappropriately from the views of diverse members of society. And it is no easy task to be a schoolteacher in the United States today without these obstacles. Public education's value is being questioned. Best educational practice has become controversial. The latest research gives few widely recognized, conclusive rules to follow when it comes to providing quality, effective education at the countrywide level, other than to ensure that every child comes from a good home, where he or she is intellectually stimulated within a family that lives in relative comfort (i.e., not in poverty or with a low-wage job that translates into economic insecurity). Different options are being explored, with little time for review before switching things around, when it comes to vouchers, charter schools, and so on. Teachers face a great deal of pressure, but no one is sure what should be expected of them, what they should be trained for, and what they should achieve and how. In this context, it can be a very insecure experience to be a public schoolteacher. Discussing Islam in the classroom becomes one more task on a to-do list filled with items related to professional development, student learning standards, high-stakes tests, and performance evaluations.

Against this larger backdrop, my task here is to examine the challenges teachers face and students experience in understanding Islam and Muslims, as part of U.S. and world communities. I understand the case of educating about Islam and Muslims as both a religious issue and a multicultural issue here, and I primarily use the latter frame to explore the major facets of the situation, though religious and multicultural challenges are intertwined.

There is also a challenge related to ignorance begetting ignorance in this case: How can teachers teach about Islam when they have not learned about it themselves – and when it can be very difficult to perpetually play "catch up"? This question is what makes this case interesting to those considering multicultural education more generally, whether they may be concerned with various world groups, within and outside the United States, such as Chinese people or Buddhists, or emerging internal minority groups, such as the homeless or new migrant communities. The approach to difference I promote here with regard to multicultural education is underpinned by the observation that educators in a democratic society are charged to teach about controversy and current events, which they may know little about to begin with, themselves. Thus, what I argue here may be less relevant to traditional multicultural challenges of U.S. society, having to do with historically recognized disadvantaged groups in the United States, than to considering how teachers can aid students to understand controversial social issues in an informed way generally. As I argue here, controversial issues should not be hidden from students, or regarded as not a proper part of the sphere of public education or social institutions. Rather, teachers must invite students to a public conversation about important social issues. My educational recommendations for teaching and learning about Islam and Muslims in U.S. public schools are thus helpful for reconsidering what is required to meet these larger political aims of education: how educators can be neutral but not promote relativism and how educators can help students grapple with important questions to empower themselves and others democratically in society.

In the next (second) chapter, I review the history of multicultural education in the United States. The discussion is oriented around an examination of the major traditional approaches for understanding and managing difference in society more generally, from conservative assimilationism to critical multiculturalism. This is a broad overview that also highlights the issue of religion in public education. I express some sympathy with each of the traditional approaches to diversity in education. From a historical and holistic viewpoint, they each have their place and usefulness, in terms of conceptualizations of the individual in society in relation to culture, and the role of public education. However, I argue that each also has limitations when it comes to certain social issues, including particularly the case of teaching and learning about Muslims and Islam in U.S. public schools. None supports an education about Islam and Muslims that meets the demands of religious toleration and educator neutrality, and each has flawed conceptions of cultural difference in society.

Although the framework of thinking about multicultural education elaborated in the second chapter will be referenced frequently throughout this text, some readers will no doubt be more fascinated by the analyses in subsequent chapters of today's post-9/11 climate of education about Muslims and Islam. The third and fourth chapters turn to this status quo. The third chapter considers the educative impact of the mass media and popular culture, focusing particularly on news journalism, movies, and television. It begins with an overview of the way that media can be viewed as educational. I argue that it is not simply the case that media directly influences understanding as indoctrination. Rather, media highlights and obscures certain perspectives and frameworks and suggests at the general level that some framings are normal and good, while others are simply absent; these can become unthinkable practically and ideologically. Muslims have a true disadvantage in representation in mass media. Good Muslims are largely absent. Normal, imperfect but ordinary Muslim individuals are infrequently visible. This is a historical trend, and I follow Edward Said (1997) and Jack Shaheen's (2001) analyses of news media and Hollywood films in my account, while also elaborating on contemporary context. Crucially, the stories are not all fiction, and even movies like *Iron Man* have an interesting and important relationship to fact, which can be drawn out in this case, in connection with 9/11. And we have some reason for optimism, as media can be seen to become more self-reflective in recent years, as popular films and other media often critically play with negative stereotypes, rather than uphold them. Yet this overall context highlights that the informal learning environment of the United States fails to educate effectively about Islam and Muslims in society and worldwide. It impresses upon readers the need for educators to intervene in this climate to enable students to learn and understand more.

The fourth chapter turns to formal (school) education. Though it is difficult to know what students are learning in U.S. public schools countrywide, lacking comprehensive mass examinations or cameras in every classroom (which I do not recommend), I start my analysis by considering educational standards at the state level in social studies education, which normally frame the way subjects such as world history and world geography are taught. Often, there are so many standards that they represent the *ideal* curriculum, while many components may be left out in practice (Kincheloe 2001). I examine how Islam and Muslims are included in these standards, before turning to "the situation" of world history and geography textbooks, where Muslims and Islam are also likely to appear in a student's education. The word choice, "situation of textbooks," is intentional here. I discuss the textbooks generally first, including a historical overview of how they have discussed Muslims and Islam. I then turn to today's textbook approval process in Texas, where decisions are made that impact the production of textbooks approved and sold across the country. This approval process can be seen as an ideological battleground (de Leon Mendiola 2007). In 2010, the Texas State Board of Education additionally acted on the issue of the coverage of Islam in textbooks sold across the country, resolving to ban textbooks that, it argued, included "lionizing" of Islam, at the expense of Christianity. This educational event has potentially significant implications and is worth examining in full.

I then consider the content of textbooks that portray and teach about Muslims and Islam, analyzing central themes emerging from the examination of over a dozen of the most popular world history and world geography textbooks used in the last two decades. I compare different orientations toward Muslims and Islam, such as discussions in the texts suggesting that Islam promotes sexism or gender equality, for instance, and the way they relate 9/11 and recent events, comparing books, and older and newer editions of single texts. My analysis finds that although text coverage is not, on the whole, horrifically negative and stereotypical, it is slight, and negative representations may be on the rise, aligned with educational movements in the country today to scrutinize and attack any textbook (or educator) that makes references to Muslims and Islam that are not overtly negative (Bennetta 2005; Sewall 2003). At any rate, students are not likely to learn a great deal from these texts, particularly about current affairs. I turn finally in the chapter to examine educator practice more generally in social studies, analyzing resources and pedagogies used particularly for dealing with 9/11 and Islam. On the whole, I find that there are likely many different kinds of teaching practices occurring across the country today when it comes to Islam and Muslims. Yet I also argue that it is likely that many teachers feel unprepared, as I discuss educator practice and needs since 9/11 in relation to a new "need to know" that 9/11 created, and the lack of good resources for teachers to use in learning and teaching about Islam.

In the fifth chapter, I introduce a new framework for approaching difference apart from those discussed in the second chapter. I label this new framework as *intercultural,* and I compare it favorably with major multicultural educational approaches in the United States, in its conceptualization of social difference and for its educational implications for teaching and learning about Islam and Muslims. The word *interculturalism* has roots in an early, mostly forgotten movement in

U.S. multicultural history in the mid-twentieth century, which was succeeded by what I describe as *pluralism* in the second chapter. Interculturalism is increasingly favored today in Europe and Australia in relation to multiculturalism and the need for peaceful, mutually beneficial integration of Muslims with non-Muslims in Western societies. I examine this orientation toward difference, before considering its educational implications, arguing for a more student-centered pedagogy dedicated to developing student skills for democratic deliberation and debate and critical media literacy.

In the sixth chapter, I continue to expand an understanding of interculturalism for thinking about education about Islam and Muslims in the United States today, asking the question of what would need to be done to implement my recommendations at the large scale and what other challenges, practical and ideological, might stand in the way. In this context, I promote a shift in the way we conceptualize the educator's role in U.S. society and related teacher education more aligned to an intercultural educational approach. I also consider some potential challenges to my recommendations, such as the educational implications of interculturalism for elementary school education. Though hurdles to my recommendations can be found, we fail to prepare students to participate in a diverse society as democratic decision makers without implementing changes that enable young people to clearly and critically see the (social) world around them.

I thus conclude that U.S. schools can do a great deal more when it comes to educating youth about the world around them. My arguments here do not revolve around what are the most appropriate attitudes for students to learn through education, apart, perhaps, from those attitudes I described earlier as my assumptions here: (1) that the United States is religiously diverse; (2) that Muslims are not categorically bad, and that it is wrong and harmful to teach that they are, as if this is a matter of fact; and (3) that U.S. schools should function in support of the flourishing of a liberal democratic society, where equal rights and individual freedoms are the responsibility of the collective whole to enable, protect, and preserve. The schools and the society are arguably imperfect, and more can always be done. This book then constitutes a proposal to follow reasoned practices over those founded on faulty reason, to improve U.S. schools as a vehicle for improving the society more generally. The U.S. educational system faces many challenges today, but this does not require that we must accept worst practices that disable citizens to participate in an informed way in society. Much more can be done so that ignorance about Islam does not continue to prevail.

References

Banks, James A., and Cherry A. McGee Banks, eds. *Multicultural Education: Issues and Perspectives.* Hoboken: John Wiley & Sons, 2004.

Bennetta, William J. "How a Public School in Scottsdale, Arizona, Subjected Students to Islamic Indoctrination." *The Textbook League.* 2005. www.textbookleague.org/tci-az.htm (accessed January 8, 2014).

Cortés, Ricardo, and F. Bowman Hastie III. *I Don't Want to Blow You Up!* New York City: Magic Propaganda Mill Books, 2007.
Council on American-Islamic Relations (CAIR). *American Public Opinion About Muslims and Islam, 2006.* Washington, DC: Council on American-Islamic Relations, 2006.
Deane, Claudia, and Darryl Fears. "Negative Perception of Islam Increasing." *Washington Post,* March 9, 2006.
de Leon Mendiola, Annalisa. "Traditionalists versus Multiculturalists: Discourses from the 2003 U.S. History Textbook Adoption in Texas." PhD diss., University of Texas at San Antonio, 2007.
Finn, Jr., Chester E. Introduction to *September 11: What Our Children Need to Know,* edited by the Fordham Foundation, 4–11. Washington, DC: Thomas B. Fordham Foundation, 2002. www.edexcellence.net/publications/sept11.html (accessed January 8, 2014).
Hirsch, Jr., E. D. "Moral Progress in History." In *Terrorists, Despots, and Democracy: What Our Children Need to Know,* edited by the Fordham Foundation, 72–73. Washington, DC: Thomas B. Fordham Foundation, 2003. www.edexcellence.net/publications/terrorists.html (accessed January 8, 2014).
Hochman, Dalia. "Hominid Development: On Being a Social Studies Teacher During September 11." In *Forever After: New York City Teachers on 9/11,* edited by Teachers College Press with Maureen Grolnick, 85–96. New York: Teachers College Press, 2002.
Hollinger, David A. "Obama, the Instability of Color Lines, and the Promise of a Postethnic Future." *Callaloo* 31 (2008): 1033–1037.
Huntington, Samuel P. "The Clash of Civilizations?" *Foreign Affairs,* Summer 1993.
Jackson, Liz. "The Individualist? The Autonomy of Reason in Kant's Philosophy and Educational Views." *Studies in Philosophy and Education* 26 (2007): 335–344.
Kant, Immanuel. "Answer to the Question: 'What is Enlightenment?'" In *Kant: Political Writings,* edited by H. S. Reiss. Translated by H. B. Nisbet. Cambridge: Cambridge University Press, 1970.
Kant, Immanuel. *Critique of Pure Reason.* Translated by Vasilis Politis. London: Orion, 1993.
Kincheloe, Joe L. *Getting Beyond the Facts: Teaching Social Studies/Social Sciences in the Twenty-First Century.* New York: Peter Lang, 2001.
Kosmin, Barry A., and Ariela Keysar. *American Religious Identification Survey (ARIS 2008): Summary Report.* Hartford: Trinity College Program on Public Values, 2008.
McCarthy, Cameron, and Greg Dimitriadis. "Globalizing Pedagogies: Power, Resentment, and the Renarration of Difference." In *Multicultural Curriculum: New Directions for Social Theory, Practice, and Policy,* edited by Ram Mahalingam and Cameron McCarthy, 70–83. New York: Routledge, 2000.
Messerli, Jonathan. *Horace Mann, A Biography.* New York: Alfred A. Knopf, 1972.
Noppe, Illene C., Lloyd D. Noppe, and Denise Bartell. "Terrorism and Resilience: Adolescents' and Teachers' Responses to September 11, 2001." *Death Studies* 30 (2006): 41–60.
Nord, Warren A. *Religion and American Education: Rethinking a National Dilemma.* Chapel Hill: University of North Carolina Press, 1995.
Pew Research Center. "The Great Divide: How Westerners and Muslims View Each Other." In *The Pew Global Attitudes Project.* Washington, DC: Pew Research Center, 2006.

Said, Edward W. *Covering Islam: How the Media and the Experts Determine How We See the Rest of the World.* New York: Vintage, 1997.

Sewall, Gilbert T. *Islam and the Textbooks: A Report of the American Textbook Council.* New York: American Textbook Council, 2003.

Shaheen, Jack G. *Reel Bad Arabs.* Brooklyn: Olive Branch Press, 2001.

Texas State Board of Education. *Resolution.* September 24, 2010.

Zinn, Howard. *A People's History of the United States, 1942–Present.* New York: HarperCollins, 1995.

2 Perspectives on multicultural education

Introduction

A distinctive feature of U.S. public education historically has been its deliberate aim to integrate young members of society, to develop a kind of unity across lines of ethnicity, religion, language, and socioeconomic status. Such an education supports a traditional goal of U.S. society: to ensure that any member has the opportunity to flourish materially and spiritually, regardless of potential disadvantages owing to birth and family background. In the United States, all people should have the chance to succeed, even though not all are born in equally prosperous settings. From a historical perspective, regardless of one's home culture, or membership or lack thereof in privileged communities, one should be welcomed into a broad public sphere, where possibilities are endless to think, speak, believe, affiliate, work, and enjoy life. This remains a popular sentiment and ideal in society today.

Though education's original role in integration of diverse youth can be seen to fade over time, public schools nonetheless remain symbols of democracy in our society. They have played a fundamental socializing role: teaching the rules and principles of the country, including legal traditions and contemporary civic norms and practices. In the United States, this means communicating with young people about the political commitment to individual freedom from tyranny undergirding the Constitution and Bill of Rights. Americans are generally proud to have the freedom to speak and believe differently from others. Part and parcel of learning to be a U.S. citizen is to recognize these personal freedoms as rights, which entails understanding that people are different from one another and have different beliefs, values, practices, and hopes within U.S. society.

What makes sense in theory becomes complicated in practice, however. Indeed, one might respond to the last few statements with incredulity. From Alexander Hamilton's doubts about "the masses" to the number of African descendants various founding fathers enslaved, it is not hard to paint a starkly contrasting image than what is proposed here: of a society marked in the past and today as having violent, legally entrenched inequalities, against African Americans, women, and the poor, homeless, and landless (Zinn 1995). Though today all citizens are granted formal equality in general, the society remains plagued with issues never resolved at its founding: how much to help the socioeconomically disadvantaged, the rights of religious communities within public institutions, how to treat students in public schools who do not learn English at home, and so on. It is doubtful we will ever answer these questions, once and for all.

In this chapter, I examine different perspectives on multicultural education, by which I mean a type of education that aims to respond to the presence of diversity and inequality in society. As this chapter shows, how to understand and manage diversity and inequality in society has been and remains a hotly debated question, with different general solutions implying divergent paths forward in education. And in many cases, the ideal situations of political theories contrast with concrete realities of what is possible and effective in education practice. Additionally, what makes sense in one context may be inappropriate in another, within a sweeping survey of historical perspectives.

There is no universal schema for understanding the many different perspectives people hold on multicultural education, outside or inside the United States. We all have a slightly different opinion on each particular issue, and there are not readily identifiable, monolithic camps of educational or political theorists. However, there are two basic, easily contrastable positions that have been influential in U.S. history, which I focus on here as *assimilationism* and *pluralism*. I further distinguish within these two basic perspectives between *conservative* and *liberal assimilationism* and between traditional *pluralism* and *critical multiculturalism*.

Assimilationism is understood here as a disposition that regards the social differences that can be linked to inequality as barriers to participation in society, regardless of their possible value in the private sphere, such as within the family, church, or in other private organizations. Under assimilationism, difference is seen as *deficiency*, and possible victims of inequality – such as black Americans or Latinos – should adapt to mainstream or majority values and practices in order to succeed in society, and leave at home practices, orientations, and mannerisms that make them stand out in the broader society or public sphere. Education should therefore initiate those disadvantaged by their background to embrace majority cultural values and practices.

This view is sometimes called "conservative multiculturalism" or "monoculturalism" (Steinberg & Kincheloe 2001), as some theorists in the tradition defend the superiority of mainstream cultural ways and norms in society. Yet while some proponents of assimilationism view U.S. culture and society as universally exceptional and distinctive, others focus more on learning U.S. dominant-culture norms as a practical, useful matter today. These respective views can be distinguished as "conservative assimilationism" and "liberal assimilationism," with the former valuing mainstream culture as superior to others and the latter dismissing talk of culture in favor of a focus on individuals as presumably equal in a culturally neutral public sphere (Kincheloe & Steinberg 2001: 3–4). Banks (2009: 11) similarly describes assimilationism as a political liberal ideology, because individual equality is prioritized over the preservation of traditional cultures and communities in this latter view. As I will discuss, what is culture, and the nature of social disadvantage – as systemic or individually based – are important questions to consider in evaluating these perspectives (though I will often discuss assimilation at the more general level in this chapter, especially in relation to its implications for teaching and learning about Muslims and Islam).

By *pluralism* I mean to describe what many people in U.S. society today understand as "multiculturalism": a perspective that emphasizes that difference in society is good and that cultures, views, or practices that diverge from mainstream norms are generally worthy of equal toleration and/or positive recognition in the public sphere society, rather than barriers to equality. While assimilationism was often the de facto attitude of educators at earlier times in U.S. history, pluralism became popular and widespread during the twentieth century, and many different views can be elucidated that fall within this general approach, particularly in relation to educational aims and practices. Pluralist perspectives can be contrasted clearly with assimilationist views, as pluralism argues that assimilation unnecessarily harms sociopolitical minorities by dismissing cultural origins, a potentially important source of self-esteem and identity. Pluralists thus want educators to positively regard social difference to increase equality.

In the last paragraph, I mentioned *sociopolitical minorities*, by which I mean groups who face social or political disadvantage in society. Yet there are those who feel the term *minority* should be banished from our language, speech, and writing. This includes some liberal assimilationists, as I mentioned, who do not see the society as having majority and minority cultures, but center on each individual's equal opportunity (e.g., Ravitch 1990). They may want educators to be color-blind or culture-blind, focusing on differences within such "minority groups," such as Latinos or black Americans, and similarities across groups. Diane Ravitch (1990) has argued that viewing individual people as parts of minority groups is in itself a divisive act.

Some multiculturalists do not see society as inherently equal across different social groups but caution against "minoritization" on related conceptual grounds (Davis 2009: 127). *Critical multiculturalists* focus on understanding how inequality and oppression in society are structured and organized at a large-scale and result in the widespread belief in the inferiority of disadvantaged groups. The word *critical* here invokes the Frankfurt School of Critical Theory of the early-twentieth century, in its foregrounding of the way attitudes and beliefs circulate within societies, resulting in advantages for some and harm to others (Kincheloe & Steinberg 1997: 23). Critical multiculturalists problematize the way that minority status is socially constructed, arguing that the active labeling and naming process, even done with the intention of benefiting disadvantaged groups, harms these groups and continues to block their pursuit of genuine social freedom and equality.

Table 2.1 Conceptual differences across multicultural perspectives

	Assimilationist Conservative	Assimilationist Liberal	Pluralist (Multiculturalist)	Critical Multiculturalist
"Society is just."	*	*		
"Society is neutral."		*		
"Minority 'culture' is misconstructed."		*		*

Table 2.1 gives a brief overview of some of the major points of dissention across these perspectives, as discussed here.

The rest of this chapter explores these perspectives on multicultural education, considering how each approaches difference in society generally, and examines their educational implications in relation to teaching and learning about Islam and Muslims in public schools today. Each perspective has strengths and weaknesses. None should be discounted out of hand, but should be considered within a social context, to understand its utility, what makes it compelling, and where it falls short. However, I do focus here on the limitations of each, for approaching the educational need to respond to the case of social difference in regard to Islam and Muslims, in U.S. society and worldwide, today.

Assimilationism

Assimilationism is an important trend in U.S. history in relation to the country's early self-image as a land of immigrants. The metaphor of the melting pot has commonly been used, which suggests that out of different materials a new essence is created. In Israel Zangwill's 1909 play *The Melting Pot*, the lead character applauds "how the great Alchemist melts" various national and ethnic groups, "and fuses them with his purging flame" (1921; Akam 2002). This metaphor illustrates the liberal assimilationist stance, in viewing society as integrative and neutral, lacking a specific kind of soup base. All equally melt in this view, continually creating something new from disparate elements.

However, in reality, the pot had a base immediately evident, in the form of an originally dominant group that hardly required acculturation, but constituted the norm to which all other groups were expected to conform and adapt. Throughout much of the nation's early history, Anglo-Saxon men (men of English ancestry, and usually with historical ties to the British Empire) were commonly held as intellectually superior to all other groups, and being a white man was essential to full and equal participation in early politics and society (Akam 2002).

Howard Zinn argues that the founding fathers, most of whom were former colonial officers of the British Empire, aimed at a compromise between maintaining a vastly unequal distribution of wealth and power in the new country, and mobilizing the majority of poorer colonial residents to defeat England, by declaring "all men are created equal" in the Declaration of Independence (1995: 73–75). In this context, the phrase aimed to conceptually enlarge the view of what was required to be a free and equal new American. While one might cynically argue the phrase was thus somewhat disingenuously used, since the founding fathers were not interested in changing the balance in the economic structure of the early society, the political guarantee of equality among white men nonetheless paved the way to an increasingly inclusive and democratic country.

However, Social Darwinism was a prominent stance in Europe and the United States until well into the twentieth century. It presumed essential biological and mental differences between ethnic and/or racial groups and saw them as running on parallel tracks on the same field toward development, civilization, and political leadership and domination. Western Europeans in the Old World and British Empire contexts, and Anglo-Saxon Protestants in the United States, were seen under Social Darwinism as being "in the lead." Such attitudes remained commonplace in the early-twentieth century, impacting the treatment of immigrants to the United States from Ireland and southern, central, and eastern Europe. Theodore Roosevelt cautioned against "race suicide" of Anglo-Saxons in the face of growing minority groups, while in the *Saturday Evening Post,* one could find discussions of Polish Jews as "human parasites" and hypotheses on the extinction of various peoples of color around the world (Akam 2002: 46).

In this context, liberal thinkers in the young country nonetheless believed in the potential capacities of a broader cross-section of people, regardless of their ethnic or national origins. They argued that despite the natural (or widely recognized) social hierarchy among groups, it was mutually beneficial to live in diverse communities, and aid new immigrant groups on their path to social advancement, rather than to preemptively bar their full inclusion in society due to their difference. As politician and proponent of Irish immigration Edward Everett Hale put it in the mid-nineteenth century, "their inferiority as a race compels them to go to the bottom, and the consequence is that we are all, all of us, the higher lifted because they are here" (quoted in Gutman 1989: 265). Progressive thinkers like Hale were joined by others in society, concerned that minority norms were disruptive or threatening to overall peace and social flourishing, in promoting assimilation to enable minorities to more easily weave themselves into the fabric of mainstream culture and society.

Assimilation was undertaken through common schools, and other social institutions for adult newcomer groups, such as settlement houses. It involved changes in norms and moral standards and the development of pragmatic tools to increase immigrants' chances for prosperity in the New World. Settlement houses assisted new immigrants in developing practices better aligned with those of mainstream society, such as speaking and writing English, child rearing according to contemporary "American" norms, and abstaining from alcohol or visiting saloons. Both mainstream society and minority members within it were said to benefit from such assimilation. Among its lead advocates were some of the recipients of this sort of social welfare, such as Italian immigrant Rosa, who stayed at the Chicago Commons settlement house in the 1890s.

> They used to tell us that it's not nice to drink beer, and we must not let the baby do this and this. . . . Pretty soon they started the classes to teach us poor people to talk and write in English. . . . I used to love the American people, and I was listening and listening how they talked. That's how I learned to talk such good English. Oh, I was glad when I learned enough English to go to the priest in the Irish church and confess myself and make the priest understand what was the sin! . . . I have to tell another good thing the settlement house did for me . . .
> (quoted in Gutmann 1989: 218)

Common schools aimed in part to assimilate children from diverse religious, linguistic, national, and ethnic (European) backgrounds. Horace Mann, the founder of the common school movement in the United States in the early-nineteenth century, argued that compulsory mass education could eliminate widespread poverty among recent immigrant communities, as well as increase morality and appropriate social conduct, by teaching the "common elements" of the country's culture, including nonsectarian "great Christian truths," to be read *about* in the Bible, but not as topics of proselytization (Messerli 1972; Nord 2010; Tozer et al. 2006). Among other concerns (such as the feasibility of the government pulling poor and working-class youth out of factories for academic learning), the religious content of this moral education was an immediate source of public debate. In John Stuart Mill's eyes, this minimal Christian foundation of Mann's moral education "effected nothing more but a compact among the more powerful bodies to cease fighting among themselves and join in trampling the weaker . . . The Jew and the unbeliever," as well as Catholics and Calvinists who felt discriminated against by the "common" Christianity approach (Lasky 1924: 327–329; Tozer et al. 2006: 66). Nonetheless this vaguely Protestant foundation (Bible reading without authoritative interpretation) remained common in public schools throughout most of American history. The prominence even today of Catholic private schools in the United States stems from this legacy of exclusive Christian teaching in public schools, which was common and faced few major challenges until the 1960s, when the Supreme Court held that devotional Bible reading in public schools was unconstitutional (Nord 2010).

Some were systematically, officially excluded from common schools and related assimilation efforts, due to perceived racial difference. The continuous enslavement and oppression of black people in the United States until the mid-nineteenth century was often defended in terms of their supposed incapacity for civilization or peaceful coexistence within the majority white culture (Gutman 1989). Many viewed culturally oppressive assimilationism through federally facilitated schooling as the only way for Native Americans to live, in significant numbers, peacefully and prosperously within the new European-oriented nation-state (Akam 2002). Whether one was thought able to assimilate or be educated depended in part on perceptions of whether his or her more free and equal inclusion in society could constitute a national security risk. In relation, during times when national security was of increased concern, public xenophobia can be seen to rise, even against European Americans who had recently immigrated, or were seen as resistant to comprehensive assimilation. The European "hyphenated American," identifying, for instance, as "Italian-American," was seen as a threat during the First World War, carrying with his hyphen "a dagger that he is ready to plunge into the vitals of this Republic," according to Woodrow Wilson (quoted in Akam 2002: 47).

Critical responses to such prejudicial and stigmatizing attitudes emerged and developed over time. Known in the early-twentieth century as "pluralists," defenders of European ethnic or national minorities argued that hyphenated Americans were not dangerous, if unwilling or unable to dismiss their cultural traditions to access equal opportunities and political representation. Randolph Bourne and Horace Kallen were chief among those who argued that Americans should regard immigrants from southern and eastern Europe as patriots, even if they preserved some aspects of their cultural distinctiveness from U.S. norms (Akam 2002). Bourne proposed a view of society as an orchestra of tones, wherein difference is advantageous to the whole and each of its parts, rather than as a melting pot, in which minority groups conformed to maintain an Anglo-Saxon American culture:

> We have had to listen to publicists who express themselves as stunned by the evidence of vigorous nationalistic and cultural movements in this country among Germans, Scandinavians, Bohemians, and Poles, while in the same breath they insist that the aliens all be forcibly assimilated to that Anglo-Saxon tradition which they unquestioningly label "American." . . . America is a unique sociological fabric, and it bespeaks poverty of imagination to not be thrilled at the incalculable potentialities of so novel a union of men. . . . We have to give up the search for our native "American" culture. . . . It is our lot rather to be a federation of cultures.
>
> (1997: 16–17)

Kallen argued relatedly that it harmed minorities to encourage their "cultural amnesia," a forgetting or dismissing of their cultural origins:

> Men may change their clothes, their politics, their wives, their religions, their philosophies, to a greater or lesser extent [but] they cannot change their grandfathers. . . . Jews or Poles or Anglo-Saxons, in order to cease being Jews or Poles or Anglo-Saxons, would have to cease to be.
>
> (1915: 220; Akam 2002: 59)

Viewing pride in and affiliation with one's cultural origins as essential to one's sense of self, Kallen argued that one's disconnection from his or her heritage could be devastating at the personal level. He argued further that differences between groups were not as severe or irreconcilable as some argued and that immigrant groups could hold onto their traditional cultural orientation, while also participating, the political majority willing, in a pluralistic society, where more than one path could lead to individual and collective flourishing and prosperity.

A similar view was put forward by John Collier in the 1920s for Native Americans, who argued passionately for the acceptance of "American Indians" alongside "white civilization":

> These tiny communities of the red man . . . [it] seems a wild if a luring fantasy that they might live on, that they might use the devices of modern economic life, and pragmatically take over the concepts of modern science, and yet might keep that strange past of theirs, that psychic and social present as it truly is . . . so great with color, flooded with body-rhythm and song . . . And if the Pueblo lives on, could white civilization acquire anything from them?
>
> (1922: 16; Akam 2002: 115).

These early pluralists thus argued for respect and toleration of minority cultures, envisioning society as more of a "mixed salad" than a melting pot, wherein stability, peace, and social flourishing did not require the unequal expectation of assimilation based upon family background or cultural heritage.

Assimilationists were not without defenses for their stance, however, that likewise emphasized the plights of disadvantaged members of the society. Against cries of unfairness and injustice, many maintained – and continue to maintain today – that principal markers of difference from the de facto political majority needlessly stigmatize minority-group members, regardless of the desires or interests of the majority population. They argue that this (seemingly inevitable or reasonable) stigmatizing process, rather than any individual's intentions, is responsible for disabling the equal opportunities of disadvantaged people in society. Because symbols of difference from mainstream norms trace or imply historical or existing boundaries of sameness and difference, assimilationists countered that it benefited not just the political majority but minorities as well to gradually diminish signs of cultural difference, to enable greater minority equality. William Thomas and Florian Znanieck's analysis of Polish immigrants in the early-twentieth century is an early, ethnocentric version of this framing of the issues.

> Even if the Polish-American society should maintain in general that separation which its leaders have wished, the cultural level of *Polonia Americana* would always remain lower than that of American society, since its best men are and always will be attracted by the wider and richer field. . . . But as to the Polish-American institutions already created, their destruction would mean the removal of the only barrier which now stands between the

mass of Polish immigrants and complete wildness. The only method which can check demoralization and make of the immigrants – and particularly their descendants – valuable and culturally productive members of the American society, and imperceptibly and without violence lead to their real Americanization is to supplement the existing Polish-American institutions by others – many others – built on a similar foundation but in closer contact with American society.

(1999: 250)

Here, assimilationism is distinguishable from pluralism in emphasizing that society, including its most and least advantaged, benefits more from bringing minorities into the mainstream than from tolerating or recognizing their traditional ways as acceptable or significant, which they view as futile to enabling equality and maintaining social harmony. Like Kallen, Thomas and Znanieck do not deny the significance of culture in people's (Polish Americans') lives. Thomas and Znanieck view Polish institutions as essential to Polish Americans' personhood and their destruction as devastating. Yet they shift their concern from the need for minority toleration and recognition to that for assimilation, *Americanization,* to diminish differences and make them more similar, and thus more able to access equal opportunities. They focus particularly on those individual Polish Americans "attracted by" assimilation in their argument, who have the potential for equality, and they appear to measure other Polish Americans' capacities for assimilation by this standard. And they see the multicultural, mainstream society as a "richer" and "wider" field, toward which Poles must step to gain equal footing. Thus, even if Polish immigrants' cultural traditions might be tolerable, Thomas and Znanieck argue that the Polish immigrant still cannot truly succeed in America, lacking practical Americanization, recognized more exclusively as Polish.

While comparisons of cultures' relative worth or value are not uncommon among thinkers in this tradition today, or in the past, one need not use ethnocentric arguments to observe the de facto politically particular nature of contemporary society, which naturally precludes the participation of unassimilated people in its midst. Here, assimilationism can be split into two branches, as Social Darwinist thinking fades in the twentieth century: between those monocultural, conservative assimilationists who argue that the base American culture is inherently superior to that of newcomers, and liberal assimilationists, who argue that it is not about cultural difference, but about tools that make a difference in any individual's ability to succeed in U.S. society, or any other. Thus, liberal assimilationists emphasize that, for example, English is simply the major language of the society, and needed for success within it, regardless of its merit alongside other languages, or other interests that might be expressed by minority-language-speaking groups (Feinberg 1998). From a pragmatic standpoint, schools have as one major role assimilation as socialization into the public sphere of society: a "wider field" from that of one's family or neighborhood community. This requires giving some students new tools that other students might already have, such as English literacy, and an understanding of the norms and traditions of mainstream society. It seems undeniable that schools have a minimal role, at least, in this kind of assimilation. What is at debate is what assimilationism as an educational framework demands, entails, and excludes, in the context of pushes for other kinds of multicultural education.

For liberal assimilationists, society is culturally neutral, though it has particular political norms and understandings, while for more traditional, conservative assimilationists, the society has a distinct and distinctive American culture. However, at a basic level, both variants of assimilationism see society at large as a place that is *just*. Indeed, the basic assumption that the society effectively serves the public good is implicit to assimilationism, for social change, reintegration, and revision would be in order, if it was not good for newcomers to integrate with the base. Thus, another way of considering the debate between assimilationists and pluralists is to examine what these views hold for society at large, rather than for disadvantaged individuals, as pluralism implies that the status quo in society is not just, but actually ethically deficient in relation to the treatment of social difference.

Apart from challenging the specific implications of assimilation for minorities in U.S. society, pluralists have argued, in the past and today, that mainstream society's values, norms, and practices are lacking, focusing on inequality as a fundamental characteristic of the United States, despite the popular ideology of the American Dream and universal meritocracy (see Giroux 1993; Hacker 2003; hooks 1995; MacLeod 1997; Zinn 1995). In this case assimilation should not be favored over a vision of education for social reconstruction, or the sanctioning of a pluralist society where different communities and cultures are preserved and can live side by side.

In this contemporary context, those promoting assimilation of disadvantaged members of society can be seen to defend U.S. mainstream society as worthy of preservation and imitation, for its toleration, equality, democracy, and so on. Traditional conservative or monocultural assimilationists defend this stance in a "thick," substantial sense, while liberal assimilationists do so more minimally, focusing on a "thin" political culture. However, in either case arguments rest upon cross-cultural comparison. Arthur Schlesinger (1998) can be seen to follow the line of thinking of defending a thick sense of American culture over others. He argues, in response to charges of cultural oppression via assimilationism, that "Western hegemony ... can be the source of protest as well as power," as the "crimes of the West have produced their own antidotes." He contends that Western Europe remains,

> the source – the *unique* source – of those liberating ideas of individual liberty, political democracy, the rule of law, human rights, and cultural freedom [and] there is surely no reason for Western civilization to have guilt trips laid on it by champions of cultures based on despotism, superstition, tribalism, and fanaticism.
>
> (1998: 129; emphasis in the original)

The educational implications of the view of U.S. society as distinct, or at least comparatively good and acceptable, are limiting, however. Similarly defensive of mainstream norms and American "traditional" cultural foundations, the (relatively more liberal) Ravitch (1990) has denounced what she labels "ethnic cheerleading" – the more substantive cultural recognition pluralists demand – as undermining social stability, by needlessly perpetuating a politics of divisiveness over an emphasis on what makes U.S. society and its public school students universally distinctive, in a thinner, more procedural sense. She disdains, for instance, pluralist educators who have "seized upon the Mayan contribution to mathematics as key to . . . boosting the ethnic pride of Hispanic children," in favor of teachers "attempting to change the teaching of their subject so that children can see its uses in everyday life" (1990: 344–345).

Ravitch's "everyday life" here is neither Mayan nor Hispanic, but *essentially American*, assuming a "melting" of minority identities into the base as ideal. Regarding the European majority culture as sufficiently pluralistic in its toleration toward difference, Ravitch holds that pluralists conflate student confidence building with alienating minority youth from a relatively neutral mainstream society, to their detriment, and against the social goals of equality and stability. She further illustrates her critique of "ethnic cheerleading" by referencing an interview with a black female runner who claimed to be most inspired by the discipline of Russian (male, white) ballet dancer Mikhail Baryshnikov (Ravitch 1990). That one need not share a minority-group identity with another in order to identify with them on their individual quest toward achievement is Ravitch's point here. As in Thomas and Znanieck's defense of Polish assimilationism, Ravitch illustrates with the use of an individual instance of successful, harmless integration that there is nothing wrong with assimilationism, while pluralism remains problematic.

Ravitch's defense of each person's individual potential and equal opportunity in U.S. society is compelling. U.S. schools should aim to increase student opportunities, not limit them, and so to regard "minority" youth as extensions of cultural groups rather than as individuals, or the society as one that is inevitably unequal or unjust toward its minorities, goes against a worthwhile educational aim. However, a false dichotomy can also be observed in such rhetoric, which suggests that valuing and supporting America's commitment to individual freedom and equality requires forsaking minority cultural heritage and affiliation. Ravitch uses a binary, either/or logic, dismissing the possibility of one strengthening their sense of distinctive cultural heritage through patriotic or nationalist commitment within a pluralist national context, or of one cultivating patriotism through pride about his or her continued ability to commune with others based on ethnic or cultural heritage (Feinberg 1998).

Against assimilationists' claims that recognition of personal origins and group identities is a potential source of harm to minorities and/or the larger society, one can identity meaningfully as female, or black, for instance, without brandishing in any substantial sense his or her commitment to or inclusion in a broader social field. And teachers need not participate either in "ethnic cheerleading," or nation building, but can do both, at least in a minimal sense, without fear of incomprehensibility or incoherence, as Walter Feinberg suggests in his discussion of minimal multicultural recognition:

> If a student felt bad because classmates looked down on her because of cultural or racial affiliation, the teacher may become more active in promoting the self-esteem of the child. This could entail encouraging her to bring in cultural items that speak to the accomplishments of the group. Recognition here is still minimal, however. It is provided in order to aid the child's performance or comfort in the classroom, and it may or may not have any importance for the culture itself.
>
> (Feinberg 1998: 169)

While it is possible that Schlesinger, Ravitch, and other assimilationists would not see the harm in teachers boosting students' self-esteem in this sense, their texts often suggest that this sort of recognition could hardly take place in classroom settings without wasting time that could be devoted to *more important* matters: of social reproduction (teaching the skills needed to participate in society), assimilation (teaching students to identify with the larger, U.S. society), and nation building (teaching students to support the nation-state). They thus paint "ethnic cheerleading," or any sort of positive minority recognition, and learning what is needed to participate in society as mutually exclusive choices.

This tendency is well illustrated in recent assimilationist discussions of education about Muslims and Islam. Examples abound particularly since 9/11 of assimilationists framing pluralist toleration and recognition of Islam and Muslims as coming at the cost of teaching what is needed for social reproduction and nation building in public schools. Many instances can be found in an edited collection for educators produced by the Thomas B. Fordham Foundation, *September 11: What Children Need to Know* (2002). The editorial statement describes the collection as a critical response to pluralist pedagogy that emphasizes after 9/11 the equality and toleration the United States can afford its minority citizens, including Muslims, some of whom were attacked and victims of hate crimes after 9/11 (Council on American-Islamic Relations 2005; Wing 2005). As Fordham Institute President Chester Finn puts it, such pluralistic advice "was long on multiculturalism, feelings, relativism and tolerance but short on history, civics, and patriotism," and demands the presence of voices whose "reverence for tolerance [does not dwarf] their appreciation of other compelling civic values" (2002: 10). Finn indicates the civic values he finds more important, by choosing Al Shanker's "side of this pedagogical divide," and his commitment, "to teach the common culture, the history of democracy and centrality of freedom and its defense against aggressors" (2002: 11). One must take a side, suggests Finn: either promote multicultural toleration of diversity, *or* nation building and patriotism in the classroom. Finn implies that if one is oriented toward the latter, as he is, then inculcating toleration and the like are little more than a waste of energy – a detractor from education for nation building.

Likewise, Ravitch (2004: 147) has suggested that history textbooks' financially based concessions to pro-Muslim and Islamic groups desiring positive recognition of Muslims in schools have led to "their omission of anything that would enable students to understand conflicts between Islamic fundamentalism and Western liberalism." As in Finn's editorial, teaching tolerance of minorities is cast as at odds with teaching "anything that would enable understanding," or "what children need to know," to develop an appreciation for (among other things) their distinctively *American* identity. What makes Muslims too different to be viewed as a tolerable, rather than threatening, part of the U.S. or world story is not explicated; it is simply assumed they should not be treated as an internal or *similar* group, but as an outside, *different* group, that threatens and conflicts with the Western liberal tradition Ravitch sees undergirding society. Any potential harms done to Muslims through representing their beliefs in this basically negative way is not carefully considered, in light of the desire to educate about a distinct American ideal that Islam is seen as brushing up against.

Proponent of common core educational standards E. D. Hirsch has also argued against pluralistic approaches to educating about Islam and Muslims, that the "critical issue" since 9/11 is "intolerant medievalism versus the tolerant Enlightenment" (2003: 72). Once again mainstream American society is emphasized as tolerant and generally good, hardly worthy of critical reflection in the course of a classroom discussion, and positive educational tolerance or recognition of Muslims is framed as (paradoxically) contradictory to this message, establishing the aforementioned binary: *We can either recognize/tolerate Islam or recognize (tolerant) America, but not both.* The implication is that any treatment of Islam that aims to more positively recognize Muslims, as pluralists would advocate (as will be discussed more fully in the next section), contradicts the more general goal, in assimilationist writings, of instilling appreciation for majority norms through education. American Muslims seem to have to falsely choose between their religious and national identities in this educational framework, as Islam and the United States seem to be regarded by assimilationists here as mutually exclusive entities.

When it comes to educating about Muslims, assimilationists thus pit against each other positively recognizing difference and developing and sustaining a distinctive and coherent U.S. society, seeing the former as unnecessary for, if not disruptive to, the latter goal. In accepting the premise that the difference Islam makes is too great for toleration to be tenable, assimilationists echo the argument crystallized today as Samuel Huntington's (1993) "clash of civilizations" thesis (though clash of civilizations is a phrase attributable to Bernard Lewis [1990]). Huntington's view is that Western, secular societies face significant challenges today particularly from a fundamentalist, pre-liberal "Islamic civilization," which developed in relative isolation from Western civilization, and is thus a world apart socially, culturally, and ideologically (1993). Likewise suggesting that the development of Islam and the norms of Muslims are simply too dramatically different from those of U.S. mainstream society to be positively recognized in the classroom without distracting from concerns related to assimilationism and national socialization, Ravitch, Hirsch, and Finn promote an education about Muslims and Islam that is cautionary, rather than pluralistic or tolerant.

Yet as critics of the "clash of civilizations" view point out, there is no real or empirical boundary between these civilizations, between Muslims or Islam and the West, to justify the view that these groups are separate and cannot coexist peacefully. Demographically, Muslims reside and are citizens of countries of the West, Europe, and the United States, as well as of the East, the Arab or Islamic "world." Historically, Muslim cultures have developed side by side with those of "Westerners." And the challenges some particular contemporary Muslim groups pose within Western societies and internationally need not cause wide-scale prejudice or bias toward a larger and more diverse cross section of the world's population:

> The Islamic world accommodates diverse, talented, and hospitable citizens: lawyers, bankers, doctors, engineers, bricklayers, store managers, waiters, construction workers, writers, musicians, chefs, architects, hairdressers, psychologists, plastic surgeons, pilots, and environmentalists . . . traditional and Western . . . peaceful, not violent. . . . Their lifestyles defy stereotyping. . . . In fact, most of the world's 1.1 billion Muslims are Indonesian, Indian, or Malaysian. Only 12 percent of the world's Muslims are Arab.
> (Shaheen 2001: 34)

When one considers the diversity of Muslims worldwide today, and that many live peacefully within Western societies, interacting in secular public spheres effectively, the "clash of civilizations" argument about their basic cultural difference is unconvincing, and hardly seems to require an educational response. Huntington writes at length of the "fundamental differences" between Western and Muslim societies: of "different views of the relations between God and man, the individual and the group . . . husband and wife . . . the relative importance of rights and responsibilities, liberty and authority, equality and hierarchy," and so on (1993: 25). However, others highlight similarities of Western and Islamic beliefs, and a diversity of Islamic perspectives, as well:

> As a tradition of inquiry, liberalism is committed to ideals of openness and equality. But these commitments are to be found within many segments of traditional cultures as well. There is a healthy dialogue in many groups between those who are wedded to hierarchal traditions and those who seek textual authority to advance new ways of understanding and organizing themselves. For example, feminist scholars in Islamic societies use sacred Islamic texts to counter the interpretation that supports male domination. Challenges such as these come from within traditional culture and yet call on concerns that are mirrored in liberal thought as well.
> (Feinberg 1998: 242)

Here Feinberg challenges the view, shared by "clash" theorists and educational assimilationists, that Western and Muslim societies are basically different from each other and internally coherent/stable: as Huntington writes, "differentiated . . . by history, language, culture, tradition and, most important, religion . . . the product of centuries" (1993: 25). Others critiquing the "clash" thesis more generally argue that its perspective on cultural difference is limited by its reliance upon methodologically suspect and outdated anthropological conceptions of culture. Specifically, critics of Huntington's work and of traditional cultural anthropology argue that their focus on data useful for cross-cultural comparisons precludes more comprehensive understandings of cultures or societies, possibly also betraying a less than objective or neutral stance toward objects of study.

As Said (1979) and Rosaldo (1989) observe, Western European and North American cultural anthropologists have historically studied particular aspects of a group – common language and behavior, physical artifacts, and religious and other beliefs – to compare and contrast features between groups, describing the sum of contrastable things as the group's culture. (Of course, Eastern societies have likewise developed cultural understandings or representations of "outside" Western peoples; see Clark [1997]) As self-identified traditional cultural anthropologist H. Sidky writes, cultural anthropology's "key distinguishing feature . . . is to present a holistic, evolutionary and *comparative* view of humans in which the . . . cultural aspects . . . are deemed to be relevant and significant" (2003: 5).

Said and Rosaldo have identified two major problems with this traditional approach. First, the scholar's position relative to his or her object of study is not irrelevant, but potentially central to findings, as the scholar approaches the object of study seeking specific knowledge of use to, or benefiting, his or her sponsors. They argue that this research method, carried out invariably by scholars who stand to gain personally from their findings, can obscure a more internally accurate, or mutually beneficial, understanding of a group or community (Rosaldo 1989). Additionally, as Said wrote of Orientalist scholars, frequently observations are made in the context of unequal power relations that can obscure more objective findings:

> There is very little consent to be found, for example, in the fact that Flaubert's encounter with an Egyptian courtesan produced a widely influential model of the Oriental woman; she never spoke of herself, she never represented her emotions, presence, or history. *He* spoke for and represented her. He was foreign, comparatively wealthy, male, and these historic facts of domination that allows him not only to possess Kuchuk Hanem physically but to speak for her and tells his readers in what way she was "typically Oriental." My argument is that Flaubert's situation of strength in relation to Kuchuk Hanem was not an isolated instance. It fairly stands for the pattern of relative strength between East and West, and the discourse about the Orient that it enabled.
> (1979: 6)

Said argues that unequal power relations can bias studies toward the researcher's point of view on the subject, disabling him or her from properly taking into account the object of study on its (or his or her) own terms. Likewise, Said views Huntington's gloomy perspective on Islam today as not based in deliberation or investigations taking place in a context of equal respect, but as those of a poorly informed outsider, who himself stands to gain by putting forward provocative and alarming, but poorly justified, views.

Such methodological issues can be reasonably avoided through refining one's research practices in various ways – triangulating evidence, engaging in reflective analyses, and so on (Rosaldo 1989). Yet a second, related problem remains: Even if unequal power dynamics and personal interests need not present serious problems for scholarly objectivity, the continued emphasis on discovering cross-cultural patterns and points for comparison can obscure other important group characteristics and dynamics. Franz Boas thus criticized anthropology for seeking cross-cultural patterns rather than an understanding of a groups' internal dynamics generally, arguing that "forcing phenomena into the straightjacket of a theory is opposed to the inductive process by which the actual relations of definite phenomena may be derived" (1940). Rosaldo thus concludes regarding traditional anthropological research that

> Although the classic vision of unique cultural patterns has proven merit, it also has serious limitations. It emphasizes shared patterns at the expense of processes of change and internal consistencies, conflicts, and contradictions. By defining culture as a set of shared meanings, classic norms of analysis make it difficult to study zones of difference within and between culture . . . cultural borderlands appear to be annoying exceptions rather than central areas of inquiry.
>
> Encounters with cultural and related differences belong to all of us in our mundane experiences, not to a specialized domain of inquiry housed in an anthropology department. Yet the classic norms of anthropology have attended more to the unity of cultural wholes than to the myriad crossroads and borderlands.
>
> (1989: 278)

Like Feinberg on the perceived differences between Western and Muslim philosophies, critics of traditional cross-cultural research view it as emphasizing contrastable whole entities at the cost of the recognition of internal divisions, diversity, and dynamism. The "clash of civilizations" is thus seen as an extension of biased logic in support of otherwise unfounded political arguments about the inevitability of cross-cultural conflict. While Huntington provides a historical overview of cross-cultural conflicts between the West and Muslims to bolster his view, a different focus – say, on historical cross-cultural unions, or on cross-cultural commonalities, as were mentioned by Feinberg – would yield different conclusions for a political theory than that these groups are destined to violently clash.

Educational assimilationists in the United States today nonetheless follow the logic of the "clash" view when it comes to educating about Muslims and Islam, concluding that Muslims are too different from and threatening to U.S. society to be positively recognized in schools – that pluralist or multicultural recognition in this case undermines education for social reproduction and national preservation, which they view as more fundamental than the inculcation of pluralist values such as toleration, empathy, and understanding. Yet there is no compelling justification for this logic, or for this educational approach – no reason to ignore the possibility of tolerance toward Muslims, but teach instead of "conflicts between Islamic fundamentalism and Western liberalism," and nothing of what Muslims and Westerners share, or of the vast majority of Muslims, who are moderate and peaceful, and who may be U.S. citizens, with conservative ideologies and family values strikingly similar to those of their so-called opponents (Shaheen 2001).

It may make more sense to doubt Muslims' capacities to assimilate if we view the United States as a "Christian nation." This is not the tactic used by most people who support the "clash" view. That Western countries have been made up largely by Christians is usually deemphasized by thinkers such as those mentioned here, in the context of modern secularism, and even rampant, immoral capitalism, as in Benjamin Barber's conception of the clash of "Jihad vs. McWorld" (1996). However, others argue that in education and elsewhere in U.S. society, there are hidden components of Christianity that continually force non-Christians to choose between their religion (or lack thereof) and a Christian public sphere.

Clark notes that in recent polls, equal proportions of the U.S. public agreed with statements that the United States was a "Christian" or "Biblical nation, defined by the Judeo-Christian tradition," and that it was a "secular nation" (2006: 169). Though from a different perspective, Christians may argue that public schools exclude their voices – and indeed, I will argue something similar here – Clark highlights in relation numerous instances of Christian privilege over other religious and non-religious groups in U.S. society and its public institutions, including the schools.

> I can talk openly about my religious practices without concern for how it will be received by others . . .
>
> I can be sure to hear music on the radio and watch specials on television that celebrate the holidays of my religion . . .
>
> I am largely unencumbered by having to explain why I am or am not doing things related to my religious norms on a daily basis . . .
>
> I am not judged by the improper actions of others in my religious group . . .
>
> My religion and religious holidays are so completely *normal* that, in many ways, they may appear to no longer have any religious significance at all; further, having been legally constructed as *secular*, my religious holidays can be openly practiced in public institutional settings without a thought to the violation of the separation of religion and state . . .
>
> (Clark 2006: 177–179)

Public school teachers today generally do not substantively recognize Christianity (or any other religions) as part of their daily work. Indeed, many Christians, like many Muslims and Catholics, educate their children in private rather than public schools, to ensure that their education has a significant religious component and is aligned with their religious belief and practice. However, consider the case of Muslim students in public schools versus that of Christian students: Ramadan is not recognized or even necessarily understood by many educators; nor are Muslim dietary needs, or the preferred prayer schedule, though making allowances for Christian prayer in school has had strong public support (Nord 2010). Surely, it is the prevalence of Christian traditions and norms that Muslims might struggle to assimilate to in the United States, rather than to its thin secular norms and practices – *if* Muslims significantly struggle to assimilate to the culture of the United States.

However, most Muslim Americans share that it is not anything essential about the United States, its culture or its schools, that makes integration difficult, but rather discriminatory attitudes and behavior many reasonably fear, especially after 9/11, by people who do not understand their religion and ignorantly conflate it with anti-Americanism, violence, misogyny, and terrorism. In this context, pluralists' counter-argument that it is the act of stigmatizing difference that leads to inequality and discrimination in society, rather than the mere presence of difference, seems more compelling. As Jim Zogby, a Maronite Christian who presides at the Arab American Institute, asks, "What does [suspicion and prejudice] do to their development and psyche, if they're thinking, 'They don't want me here?'" (quoted in Fifield 2013).

People learn to understand difference as superiority and inferiority, but this is not necessary knowledge. In the history of the United States, the understanding of what is essential and distinct about American identity and nationality has continually broadened, as groups who were at one time regarded as too different to integrate – Native Americans, black Americans, Jews and Catholics, and so on – have increasingly been conceived as equal in capacity and potential. Assimilationists contend that a key component of Western liberalism and U.S. political culture is tolerance toward difference; this message is often emphasized by those defending American exceptionalism in comparison with Islamic culture or Muslim societies. Yet in the case of those American Muslims who live respectfully and peacefully, in abidance with laws and norms of a secular (and sometimes pro-Christian) public sphere, these professed commitments of assimilationist educators to American liberal traditions ring hollow.

Assimilation no doubt has its role in public schools and other institutions within a liberal democratic society that tolerates religious and other forms of social and cultural difference. And Muslims can and do assimilate in U.S. society (Haddad 2004; Haddad & Lummis 1987; Leonard 2003). Arguably, in an abstract sense, there is nothing wrong with assimilation as an approach to the presence of Muslims in U.S. society. Yet contemporary assimilationists' prioritization of negative stereotypical views and fears about Islam over toleration fails to consider both the needs of Muslims for public understanding and toleration and the needs of non-Muslim students to understand difference in society reasonably, rather than with suspicion and fear – assuming violent clashes where there can be handshakes. Muslims are not simply "out there" to "get us," but they also commonly live in relative peace in U.S. society, and educators who obscure this information do their students no great service. Thus, in regarding social difference as something that should be dismissed and ignored, or worse, in the case of Islam, assimilationism fails to respond to the need for understanding and tolerance, conceiving Islam simplistically as an inferior tradition, though like Christianity and secularism, it frames diverse cultures and ways of life.

Pluralism

As with assimilationism, it is hard to characterize all proponents of a general perspective as having the same vision of society and the aims of education. However, some major areas of contrast on points discussed previously can be identified within the theories of another group of social and educational thinkers I describe as pluralists here. Though we saw in the last section that pluralists like Kallen, Bourne, and Collier criticized assimilationist policies early in U.S. history, more substantial pluralist educational theories and pedagogies developed during and after the Civil Rights Movement of the latter half of the twentieth century (Banks 2004). African American, Latino, and women's struggles for equality in schools and other public institutions increased public concern about society and its institutions not regarding all of people equally, with some requiring protection and actions done on their behalf to enable their full equality. Different traditions and variants of pluralist education, for minority culture recognition and preservation, were part of a larger project for greater equality in diversity.

After it was observed in 1954's *Brown vs. Board of Education* (which prohibited racial segregation in schooling) that black children were psychologically harmed by a lack of positive representations of black people in educational materials and in mainstream society, educators became aware that classroom strategies for including ethnic and racial minority groups more meaningfully into curricula would help enable ethnic and racial minority youth to access equal educational opportunities, thereby enhancing the groups' positions in society more generally. As leading pluralist educator Banks observes, however, initial efforts to include minorities in curricula were often unsystematic curricular add-ons:

> The first responses of schools and educators to the ethnic movements of the 1960s were hurried. Courses and programs were developed without the thought and careful planning needed to make them educationally sound or to institutionalize them within the educational system. Holidays and other special days, ethnic celebrations, and courses that focused on one ethnic group were the dominant characteristics of school reforms related to ethnic and cultural diversity during the 1960s and early 1970s.
>
> (2004: 6)

Banks saw these programs as ineffective for portraying minorities as a significant part of society, and he has been instrumental in pushes for more comprehensive inclusion of minorities in schools' curricula (i.e., content). By exploring ethnic and racial diversity as significant factors throughout the curriculum, Banks argued that ethnic and racial minorities in the society would be able to access universal cultural knowledge without alienating themselves from their cultures of origin, while white students could learn to appreciate the essentially racially and ethnically diverse nature of their society. The society is therefore viewed not as Anglo-Saxon or white, but as a kind of rainbow nation. "Multiethnic" education, as it was originally called, was thus promoted as beneficial to all members of society and the classroom:

> Individuals who only know, participate in, and see the world from their unique cultural and ethnic perspectives are denied important parts of the human experience and are culturally and ethnically encapsulated. . . . However, we should not alienate students from their ethnic cultures or force them to experience self-alienation and desocialization. Ethnic youths should not be required to deny their ethnic identity, ethnic heritage, and family in order to attain school success. Human beings are quite capable of being bicultural and to some extent multicultural. . . . Students are more likely to master skills when the teacher uses content which deals with significant human issues, such as race and ethnicity in our society. Multiethnic literature can help students master important writing, listening, and other communication skills. Data about ethnic settlement patterns in our cities, their immigrations and migrations, and vital statistics about ethnic groups can be used to help students learn essential mathematical skills and understandings. . . . Multiethnic content should thus become an integral part of the total school curriculum.
>
> (Banks 1993: 106–107)

Initially Banks included in his scope of concern ethnic and racial groups in society, including African Americans, Hispanics, and Italian Americans, regarding each community as a significant part of the American story that was left out of the formal curriculum and, in relation, subject to unfair prejudice and stereotypes. However, his "multiethnic" approach was soon renamed "multicultural," as he observed that members of other groups also "perceive themselves as oppressed [and] echo the grievances of ethnic groups and thus broaden the scope of the reform movement" (Banks 1993: 24). Groups advocating for the rights of women, religious minorities, sexual minorities, and people with disabilities expressed that they too had faced historical misrepresentation and discrimination in American society and thus should also receive positive recognition in the curriculum as distinctive members of society, whose perspectives and knowledge were worth better understanding, respecting, and/or preserving. Formal and informal educational elements, such as the posters on the walls and the food in the cafeteria, and disciplinary knowledge were examined and revised in this context, to portray a world and society that were open and culturally neutral, inherently diverse, and active in pursuing greater and more universal social justice, democracy, and equality.

A related but distinct trend occurring on a much smaller scale in the mid-twentieth century was *intercultural* education. As Cherry McGee Banks (2012) notes, intercultural education in the United States aimed at assimilation as well as prejudice reduction, through intergroup communication and dialogue inside and outside of school settings. Such projects "were based on the assumption that there were more similarities than differences among people and that when people from different racial, ethnic, and religious groups had an opportunity to get to know each other they would learn acceptance and respect" (Banks 2012: 79). Interculturalism can be distinguished from pluralism in its focus on interaction across groups, rather than the messages or lessons of education. The Springfield Plan of 1939 was one of the best-known and earliest models of the U.S. intercultural approach, which involved classes for adults and children (based in Springfield, Massachusetts), wherein people "from different ethnic groups, religious groups, social class groups, and other groups could critically discuss social, economic, and political issues" (Banks 2012: 83). Such programs flourished alongside multiethnic education until the mid-1960s but decreased in favor of pluralistic and multicultural approaches with a more teacher-centered and/or knowledge-centered orientation since that time.

Today pluralist educators may focus on including second-language learners, gay and lesbian students and those with alternative gender orientations, and students with special learning needs (among others) meaningfully in schools' curricula and social environment. Many also continue to focus on race and ethnicity, gender, and social class. Banks and Banks's 2004 textbook on pluralist multicultural education advocated, for the first time, special educational attention to Muslims, a group that pluralists, unlike assimilationists, view as worthy of (or requiring) positive educational recognition and representation. As the text states:

> These understandings can assist [teachers] in helping Muslim students to function in the traditional cultures of their parents and their American peer culture [and] also serve as a departure point for teaching students to know, to care, and to act against discrimination directed toward Muslims and other religious, cultural, ethnic, and language groups.
> (Banks & Banks 2004: A-1).

Here, the preservation of parents' "traditional" cultures, Muslim students' self-esteem, and equal opportunity for Muslims in society are all highlighted as important ends of educators approaching Islam in a positive way in the classroom. In contrast to Schlesinger and Hirsch's focus on American toleration triumphing over the fanaticism, fundamentalism, and intolerance in relation to Islam, Banks and Banks's chapter begins with a discussion of "one of the most oft-cited verses of the Qur'an: 'Do you not know, O people, that I have made you into tribes and nations that you may know each other?'" – elaborating, contrary to assimilationist rhetoric, that Islam sanctions positive recognition of difference.

Sections of the chapter titled "Islam in America," "The Middle East in the Midwest," and "America as Part of the Muslim World" further frame Muslims as an *integrated* religious group in the United States today, rather than as a group apart from the nation-state, or the West. The case of Muslims facing discrimination in mainstream American society is also discussed, contradicting the assimilationist tendency to discuss U.S. society in predominantly positive terms, as a basically just society. Here, the society is not perfectly just, and social difference need not be viewed as deficiency, in contrast with the assimilationist view.

Teaching About Islam and Muslims in the Public School Classroom: A Handbook for Educators, produced by the Council on Islamic Education, similarly promotes a pluralist interpretation of Muslims' place in U.S. society, stressing that all students should learn about Muslims and Islam in a more celebratory than derogatory manner, in order to recognize minority citizens adequately and increase equality and justice throughout the diverse society:

> Dr. Martin Luther King, in his famous 1963 "I Have a Dream" speech, talked about "my people who stand on the warm threshold which leads into the palace of justice." Indeed, possibly the last barrier to the "palace of justice" lies in our lack of understanding and tolerance of religions other than our own. It is through material such as this *Handbook* that we can celebrate our diversity, eliminate stereotypes, and build respect for our fellow humans.
>
> (1995: vii)

One sees a dramatic contrast between assimilationist and pluralist approaches to teaching about Muslims and Islam in U.S. education. While the former tend to frame Muslims as separate from the American story, vividly portray Islam and the United States as mutually exclusive realms, and regard the teaching of tolerance toward Muslims as exclusive to education for developing patriotic civic values, the latter would promote positive recognition of Muslims in public schools, to debunk stereotypes, celebrate national and international diversity, and decrease injustice in education and elsewhere in society toward Muslims. The pluralist approach certainly seems preferable in this instance, as Muslims need not be portrayed as anti-American, unworthy of empathy, or in some way separate from America or the West, in order to promote civic values such as patriotism, tolerance, equality, and personal freedom in public schools.

Yet some remain more cautious in representing minority groups, including Muslims, substantively and positively in the schools. Concerns remain for pluralist discourses in relation to their expressed aims of boosting minority self-esteem, increasing social equality, and preserving minority cultures. Although, as I argued previously, few people benefit from excluding or precluding understanding of minority groups in society through education, on the other hand, it is not always clear that substantive positive recognition of difference in the aim of these goals is effective, conceptually or educationally sound, or beneficial to minority-group or majority-group students in society, particularly in considering the case of teaching about Muslims and Islam.

I previously discussed how Ravitch criticizes pluralism for implying that one must identify ethnically or racially with educational representations – with the pictures in a story, or the people being studied – to have their self-esteem needs met and effectively learn. She argues that this perspective is narrow-minded, and as a liberal assimilationist, she observes that children's self-esteem "comes not from hearing about the monuments of their ancestors but as a consequence of what they are able to do and accomplish through their own efforts" (1990: 347). I counter here that one can do both: recognize (in a "thin," pedagogical sense) diverse cultures and orientations, as well as "their own efforts," and mainstream American norms. However, her point regarding the utility of multicultural self-esteem building and its logic about cultural difference nonetheless remains helpful. (Indeed, Ravitch might consider incorporating such a perspective on cultural difference into her understanding of Islam and Muslim identity, to complicate a simplistic view bordering on overgeneralization.)

Ravitch believes that the assumption that minority self-esteem is built through minority cultural recognition is wrong-headed in its implications for (1) sociological analysis and (2) personal identity formation. First, like those critics of cultural anthropology and "clash of civilizations" I discussed in the last section, Ravitch views the categories pluralists often use to frame difference as limited, tending to favor racial and ethnic categories over other important categories, and despite similarities of individuals across groups:

> In the particularist analysis, the nation has five cultures: African American, Asian American, European American, Latino/Hispanic, and Native American. The huge cultural, historical, religious, and linguistic differences within these categories are ignored, as is the considerable intermarriage among these groups, as are the linkages (like gender, class, sexual orientation, and religion) that cut across these five groups. No serious scholar would claim that all Europeans and white Americans are part of the same culture, or that all Asians are part of the same culture, or that all people of African descent are of the same culture. *Any categorization this broad is essentially meaningless and useless.*
>
> (1990: 342; emphasis added)

In Banks's early defenses of pluralist education, he wrote that students might be "culturally and ethnically encapsulated" without it, while more recently he wrote of Muslim students' "traditional cultures of their parents." Both of these ways of framing diversity as cultural difference suggest the existence of contrastable, monolithic cultural entities, while obscuring individuals as meaning makers, who function in many social and identity spheres simultaneously, often at ease. Thus, Ravitch's concern with pluralist educators' emphasis on ethnic and racial categorization is similar to the cultural critique of assimilationism and the "clash of civilizations," as she argues for an understanding of cultures as integrated and dynamic, rather than as clusters of segregated, static relics.

This counterpoint to pluralism is also shared by structuralist scholars working from within a critical theory tradition, also concerned with cultural identity formation and representation. I label these thinkers as "critical multiculturalists" here. Despite race and ethnicity's intimate tie to historical injustice, Cameron McCarthy writes that "racial factors are complicated by dynamics of gender . . . and dynamics of class," so that "[m]inority identities are therefore defined in the context of inter- and intragroup conflicts, encounters, and struggles between minorities and dominant white groups" – they are hardly encapsulated by racial or ethnic terms (2003: 290; 293). While one's racial identity does make a difference in one's life, there is no single black identity. Not all black people share similar experiences, because gender, class, and other factors are also crucial to one's outcomes and to an accurate sociological analysis. These other lines of difference and similarity come into play in everyday social life and should be accounted for, in social research and educational practice.

Pluralist educators who hold race and ethnicity as prominent in sociological analyses apart from other factors risk inflating their significance in social life to their students. As Joe Kincheloe and Shirley Steinberg point out, this can provide outsiders to a culture with an unrealistic understanding of how culture operates in everyday life:

> It is not uncommon for white visitors to come to the reservation excited to see authentic Native American culture. After returning from sight-seeing ventures, such visitors would be glum and disappointed, confiding that the Indian community they visited was littered with ramshackle houses and old cars on blocks in front yards. We didn't see any real Indian culture, they concluded. Such tourists, whether on the reservation or in the classroom, are unprepared to deal with contemporary problems resulting from racism, class bias and sexism. As they honour cultural difference outside of a historical, power-literate context, they trivialize the lived realities of exotic others and relegate them to a netherland of political isolation.
>
> (1997: 18)

Thus, a framing of cultural difference whose goal is to promote and celebrate difference in the broadest strokes of race and ethnicity actually hinders understanding of different "cultural" groups accurately, or what makes cultural differences matter in public life – the politics of difference – leaving students within and outside minority cultural traditions uninformed, if not misinformed, as participants in a diverse society where history, culture, class, gender, and other factors matter.

This problem of bias in depicting different traditions in terms of race or ethnicity, or by other markers of minority status, becomes personal, when minority individuals are expected or encouraged to treat their race, ethnicity, or other minority status as most essential to their sense of self. Ravitch's second problem with pluralism is thus that it simplistically treats historical markers of injustice, like race and ethnicity, whose meaning or significance varies across different social and historical contexts, as positive, important aspects of the "minority" individual, regardless of his or her other potentially salient characteristics and sources of self-perception. Treating individual students as distinguished in relation particularly to minority affiliation does not necessarily aid self-esteem.

For one, personal identity is not a mere product of birth, skin color, or demographic analysis, but is developed by individuals out of diverse, unique, personal experiences of engaging in the world around them. As Kwame Anthony Appiah (1994) observes, a pluralist education that aims to develop personal cultural, racial, and/or ethnic pride about things that identify individuals as minorities can limit one's options for self-understanding, tying one's sense of self needlessly to markers of historical stigma, rather than opening up new possibilities for growth and development, another worthy end of education:

> The large collective identities that call for recognition come with notions of how a proper person of that kind behaves: it is not that there is *one* way that gays or blacks should behave, but that there are gay and black modes of behavior. These notions provide loose norms or models, which play a role in shaping the life plans of those who make their collective identities central to their individual identities. . . .
>
> Demanding respect for people as blacks and as gays requires that there are some scripts that go with being an African-American or having same-sex desires. There will be proper ways of being black and gay, there will be expectations to be met, demands will be made. It is at this point that someone who takes autonomy seriously will ask whether we have not replaced one kind of tyranny with another. If I had to choose between the world of the closet and the world of gay liberation, or between the world of *Uncle Tom's Cabin* and Black Power, I would, of course, choose in each case the latter. But I would like not to have to choose. I would like other options.
>
> (Appiah 1994: 159; 163)

Being taught with regard to one's presumed, apparent or actual ethnic or minority identity does not simply fail to secure that all students' self-esteem needs are met, but can restrict one's sense of his or her options, by emphasizing one as a member of a minority group over other sources of selfhood. Thus, despite Banks's concern with minority students suffering alienation from not seeing people like themselves in the formal curriculum, Appiah fears instead minorities being alienated from broader views of identity by pluralistic presentations of the normalized "minority" self. As Thomas and Znanieck wrote of the Polish immigrant and Ravitch of the black runner admiring Baryshnikov, Appiah alludes to a richer, wider field than that commonly associated with being African American or homosexual, arguing that a pluralist education can obscure rich possibilities from individual view.

Others charge that positive recognition of minorities in the classroom hardly leads to meeting their complex needs for greater equality and social justice, a second major intended outcome of pluralistic education, and that attending more to structural sources of inequality is warranted if one wishes to make these larger goals ends in sight. As Bhikhu Parekh writes, educational recognition and social equality are different things, which require different processes:

> Misrecognition has both a cultural and a material basis. White Americans, for example, take a demeaning view of African Americans partly under the influence of the racist culture, partly because this legitimized prevailing systems of domination, and partly because the deeply disadvantaged blacks do sometimes exhibit some of the features that confirm white stereotypes. Misrecognition, therefore, can only be countered by both undertaking a rigorous critique of the dominant culture and radically restructuring the prevailing inequalities of economic and political power. . . . Cultural self-esteem cannot be developed and sustained in a vacuum and requires appropriate changes in all the major areas of life.
>
> (2000: 343)

Here Parekh articulates a divide between the inequalities of classroom representation and recognition and those of economic and political power, to caution against conflating the two in the hopes of resolving macro social injustice through micro classroom interventions. McCarthy similarly argues that "[t]he assumption that higher educational attainment and achievement via a more sensitive curriculum would lead to a necessary conversion into jobs for black and other minority youth is frustrated by existing racial practices in the job market itself," while "[v]arious studies have shown that the drive toward the elimination of prejudice though exposing white teachers and students to sensitivity training has not produced the intended result of the prejudiceless goal" (2003: 293). These critiques remind educators that injustice is not based merely in ideology, and so, it cannot be fought effectively with only ideology. Likewise with the case of Muslims, I will argue here that people have learned facts about Muslims being terrorists, in news media and elsewhere, and many social factors outside of public school grounds reinforce this popular but biased stereotypical representation. In such a context, teachers encouraging toleration among individual children is insufficient by itself to counteract the impact of the rest.

The critique of pluralism as a means toward self-esteem building and increasing equality both hit home in the case of Muslims, who often express a desire for maintaining a normal, rather than *different*, classroom identity in public schools (Rizvi 2005), and whose religious identities are represented elsewhere, in the media in ways that can undermine pluralist pro-Muslim classroom recognition as a means toward decreasing social stigmatization. But the final goal of pluralism, cultural or social preservation of parents' "traditional culture," is particularly problematic when considering religious cases, including that of Islam. Positive recognition for preservation implies that the schools should not remain neutral toward religion, but support religion(s) substantively, which precludes the commitment to neutrality regarding religion in public spaces such as schools.

Charles Taylor's influential view of the politics of recognition in Canada features the aim of cultural preservation prominently. Examining the case of Quebec, Taylor argues that the distinctly U.S.-based view that "individual rights much always come first . . . over collective goals," conflicts with the collectivist orientation of Quebec, which warrants an approach that focuses on the differences of groups over the procedural equal treatment of people as individuals within society.

> It is axiomatic for Quebec governments that the survival and flourishing of French culture in Quebec is good. Political society is not neutral between those who value remaining true to the culture of our ancestors and those who might want to cut loose in the name of some individual goal of self-development. It might be argued that one could after all capture a goal like *survivance* for a proceduralist liberal society. One could consider the French language, for instance, as a collective resource that individuals might want to make use of, and act for its preservation, just as one does for clean air or green spaces. . . . It is not just a matter of having the French language available for those who might choose it. . . . But it also involves making sure that there is a community of people here in the future that will want to avail itself of the opportunity to use the French language.
> (1992: 58; emphasis in the original)

Taylor argues that without a public intervention on the part of social institutions, an important part of a historical minority culture in the society, Quebec's Francophone culture, will fade away, as collective interests in a particular form of flourishing give way to individual liberal rights and opportunities for mainstream assimilation. Indeed, as we have seen here, assimilationists are compelling in arguing from an individual standpoint that students should gain access to a wider field and that this should be prioritized over any such group rights. This has clearly entailed the fading away of minority ethnic cultures in many cases in the United States over time, through schooling.

Yet while one's home community and ability to learn may be linked, making discriminatory or ethnocentric representations of minorities ineffective when teaching minority students, educators are not charged with preserving or maintaining different groups in society, but with educating youth to function autonomously in a public sphere that aims to be neutral and politically impartial, in support of substantive pluralist freedom and democracy. As Feinberg writes,

> Public schools often have good educational and political reasons to acknowledge a child's cultural meanings. For example, many children learn better where they feel they are respected and their background honored. . . . The obligation, however, involves the instructional aid required to enable the student to become a functioning citizen of this country. The obligation is not primarily to the child's original community.
> (Feinberg 1998: 122)

Teachers that respect their students' backgrounds, including religious backgrounds, and honor their students' cultural meanings, rather than deny, dismiss, or mock these, move rightfully away from the assimilationist approach to difference in order to more effectively teach students, in ways that do not burden them as members of the classroom community. Such education may include developing some recognition and understanding throughout the classroom community of different groups in society, to sanction classroom differences and inform about social differences. As I argued in the last section, education can assimilate and tolerate at the same time; one need not choose a side here.

However, such educational adaptations must be distinguished from more strongly promoting particular cultural or religious groups in the classroom, which neither serves the minority student's autonomy and development, nor that of other members of the classroom community. And when the student comes from a community whose norms and values may be commonly seen as going against the grain of mainstream U.S. society, such as a fundamentalist religious community, one must emphasize the individual's interests in autonomy over the group's interests in cultural preservation, to maintain commitment to education for equal opportunity. As Feinberg reminds, "We do not respect a tradition as such. We respect the availability of a tradition given a situation in which the individual has the ability to choose otherwise" (1998: 143).

That individual choice must be prioritized above substantive recognition of cultural groups within a liberal democratic society is compellingly articulated by Susan Moller Okin (2003), who argues that pluralist tolerance of minority groups in a society can preclude individuals' access to equal opportunities, particularly women's. Noting that in many traditional groups, "women are far less likely than men to be able to exercise the right of exit," respecting the groups' educational interests in self-promotion or preservation over that of the liberal societies' can diminish girls' and women's rights. To protect individual rights in line with the foundations of a liberal society, Okin concludes, "The liberal state . . . should not only *not* give special rights or exemptions to cultural and religious groups that discriminate. . . . It should also enforce individual rights against such groups" (2003: 346). A group's interest in self-preservation or cultural recognition does not justify an illiberal, substantively pro-religion education by public institutions, or an education that promotes a specific group's values to students, over their own right to pursue their own destinies.

This is a contentious claim particularly with regard to religion in the United States. While in the United States criticisms of the treatment of women in Muslim societies and communities are well known, the "right of exit" issue also impacts non-Muslim youth who are not educated in public schools, but in private religious schools in the United States, in ways that may preclude them being equally able to participate in secular higher education or professions in later life. This goes beyond the case of Quebec, in that students in Quebec still learn English – though they function in public in French – while those without a right to exit at a young age may not learn secular scientific understandings of evolution, for example, or advanced math or valuable technological skills. Though some members of religious communities, such as some evangelical Christian groups, the Amish, and Quakers, view it as their right to continue their faith tradition and practice within their families and communities without undue interruption or interference from the state (presuming no clear and demonstrable harm is incurred to their children as a result), they make a choice on behalf of their children when they exclude them from public education. Their children may exit their culture later in life, but they are likely to face more challenges doing so, without common schooling at earlier periods of development.

As public institutions, U.S. schools are charged with teaching all students equally, which requires teaching for a thin, common culture, in line with liberal assimilationism, in a sense, rather than teaching in a way that results in the promotion or privileging of any particular groups in society. In the last few decades, assimilationists have scoured school texts and resources for positive portrayals of Islam and Muslims, which they frequently regard as evidence of a pro-Islamic bias, in support of the goal of pro-Islamic indoctrination: converting public school students to Islam (see Sewall 2003; Stillwell 2008). Given American public school educators' general wariness regarding charges of religious indoctrination of any kind, it is unlikely there is such an effort toward conversion to Islam at work today. Yet critiques of pro-Islamic educational bias are nonetheless undergirded by an important point: Instruction that is substantially supportive toward religious traditions is not neutral with regard to ways of life and can be seen to inappropriately encourage particular religious views in the classroom. Assimilationists are therefore justifiably concerned when pluralist educational materials seem to teach in support of the beliefs of Muslims, rather than teach *about* them, for instance, by frequent references to religious beliefs not prefaced by "Muslims believe . . ." (Kunzman 2006). While it is doubtful that any child introduced to Islam this way will be converted by such implied consensus with Muslim views, one must distinguish between teaching *about* a religion in a public school classroom, to increase understanding and knowledge among non-believers, and teaching religious information partially, in ways that imply more than a minimal type of support for that particular faith over others.

For instance, controversial traditions or practices of minority groups – such as the wearing of hijab, or head covering ("veiling"), by many Muslim females upon entering adulthood, which is held by some as oppressive (and by others as a positive expression of individual and/or cultural autonomy) – should be the subject of *minimal* rather than *substantial* recognition, regarded in the case of the covered students as worthy of minimal recognition and toleration, but otherwise with neutrality – recognized, but not promoted, in the context of non-covered students. None should be expected to wear or to not wear hijab, and educators may discuss various perspectives on hijab in upper-level classes, as relevant, but not favor one side or another as fundamentally "right" or "correct" regarding its significance. This issue has implications not only for certain forms of secularism versus religious identification, but also for diverse ways of being a Muslim woman. Otherwise, the preservation of particular cultural traditions may be prioritized over individuals' educational interests, future autonomy in society, and personal practices and beliefs, and the educator fails to be neutral toward religion and the diversity of religious expression.

Pluralism, like assimilationism, is thus limited in dealing with diversity, particularly when one considers its effectiveness toward its professed aims and its cross-cultural orientation, which risks oversimplification in the same way that assimilationism does. Though its focus on the need for greater equality of diverse students and members in an imperfect society is compelling, its strategies of positive recognition can be nearly as problematic as assimilationist dismissals of social difference. When one considers that self-esteem needs of students, and their needs for greater social equality are not necessarily met through substantive positive recognition, it seems unlikely that Muslims' challenges in society with discrimination and prejudice can be effectively resolved through mere pluralistic classroom recognition. Additionally, neither approach seems to meet the need of minorities, as well as majority students, for adequately broad educational representations of difference. Educators should not paint their diverse students' cultural, ethnic, and/or religious backgrounds in boldly negative or positive strokes, when it comes to what makes them different, but approach the differences that matter in a more neutral but tolerant light.

Critical multiculturalism aims to respond to these criticisms, as a variant of pluralism. As discussed previously, assimilationists typically regard expressions or signs of difference from mainstream society as barriers to social success, thereby accepting a view of difference as stigma, while pluralists view differences from majority norms common in minority communities more positively, as a priori legitimate and worthy of recognition and inclusion. Thus assimilationists and pluralists take different perspectives on the difference that divergences from mainstream majority norms make. Yet neither stance encourages students to see social differences as context based and socially constructed, or equips them to effectively make up their own minds about what differences matter and the situations of different groups in society. Instead, they obscure the process of framing social difference from students, expecting or desiring that students take *their* perspective on minorities and difference in society, regardless of the availability of, or student intuitions regarding, alternative plausible views. In the case of Muslims, assimilationists expect students to view Islam with a critical eye, while pluralists sanction their toleration or appreciation – neither presents the alternative view as worthy of serious consideration.

Critical multiculturalists do not position themselves as substantively for or against minority norms or particular expressions of difference in society, but emphasize instead how social differences and norms are actively constructed, accepted, and maintained by meaning-making individuals, including their students. Ultimately, each person, and each student, is held as responsible for the views they accept, support, or promote. As accountable members of society, students must learn how to be skeptical toward others' claims, especially those that seem basic or easily able to take for granted.

The educational strategies of this approach can be seen to diverge from those of assimilationism and pluralism when it comes to teaching and learning about race and other kinds of social difference, the mass media, and the nature of the nation-state and patriotic commitment. In the case of racial identity, for instance, critical multiculturalists emphasize that a choice is involved in many people – including assimilationists and pluralists – commonly regarding or demarcating black people as not part of Western or American culture or civilization, emphasizing the contingent, but consequential, nature of this judgment:

> It is to be remembered that at the end of the last century the English cultural critic Matthew Arnold did not find it fit to include in the "the best that has been thought and said" any existing American writer. This powerfully reminds us that what is "Western" is not synonymous with what is "American," no matter how hard some people may try . . . the notion of Westernness is a powerful ideological construct – one thoroughly infused with ongoing struggle over meaning and values. . . . How is it that African Americans who have been in the Americas for at least as long as whites – how is it that the history, and writings, and culture of African Americans are non-Western? Who is demarcating the West? . . . Multiculturalists have tended to counter the Western civilization movement by insisting on "diversity" and cultural pluralism. But this approach leaves untouched the very premise of interchangeability of the culture of the U.S. and Europe and the notion that there is an easy fit between white America, the West, and Europe. It is this easy fit that needs to be questioned.
>
> (McCarthy 2003: 295)

Central to McCarthy's analysis of racial identity in America are the *processes* by which American whites and white America are demarcated as Western (part of the political majority), and African Americans and black America are demarcated as non-Western. In reaction to the normalized perspective, McCarthy recalls challenges or limitations to the view: Matthew Arnold not recognizing any American arts as significant to Western heritage, and black and white Americans (as constructed today) living in the Americas for approximately the same length of time.

Critical multiculturalists thus challenge commonly accepted understandings of social categories of difference by offering alternative points of view, perceiving the social construction of difference as an active process, rather than a passive act of merely observing external phenomena. Normalized conceptions of difference within society are chief among those warranting critical investigation, rather than acceptance or reaction, highlighting possibilities for ideological and social change as the products of individual critical thinking processes, and the contingency of today's norms, which are obscured by both assimilationist and pluralist treatments of difference as more concrete phenomenon, or facts, to be disseminated.

In McCarthy's analysis, mainstream beliefs or perspectives (such as that black Americans are non-Western) are contrasted with other sorts of evidence (such as that American blacks and whites have lived together outside of Europe for the same amount of time), introducing the possibility that beliefs that are often regarded as facts are not necessarily based in fact but in their interpretation by authoritative voices. Huntington's "clash" view is another prevailing ideology critical multiculturalists would evaluate alongside various sorts of evidence used both to support and to challenge the view, such as the terrorist attacks of 9/11, and the peaceful integration of many Muslims in America, respectively. Regarding their students first as meaning-making individuals, then, critical multiculturalists seek to enable their students to see the bases of their own beliefs about difference, and hold them up to a critical analysis of related evidence, counter-evidence, and additional perspectives. This is a very different approach than that of pluralists, as McCarthy writes:

> Multicultural changes in the curriculum . . . must be founded in the recognition that knowledge is socially produced and . . . relational and heterogeneous. . . . Efforts to redefine the curriculum in the name of multiculturalism must get beyond the narrow prescription of content addition and replacement. A critical approach to curriculum reform must make salient connections between knowledge and power. . . . Such an approach would bring the entire range of traditional and contemporary material . . . in the school curriculum into focus for examination.
>
> (2003: 302)

Here McCarthy suggests that educational knowledge claims should be examined by students reflectively, rather than passively received. Fellow proponents of critical multiculturalism Kincheloe and Steinberg similarly note that

> Critical theorists want to promote an individual's consciousness of himself or herself as a social being. . . . how and why his or her political opinions, socio-economic class, role, religious beliefs, gender role and racial self-image are shaped by dominant perspectives.
>
> (1997: 23)

As the mass media and popular culture are seen by many critical educators as significant influences on personal opinions among American youth, a sort of critical media literacy that encourages critical inquiries into representations within media and popular culture is one important part of a critical multicultural approach to understanding difference in society. Examining how and why dominant and influential media producers put forward particular representations of minorities, such as Muslims, rather than others, helps young people understand how their knowledge of others and different cultures in society is shaped by means and interests distinct from those of disinterested researchers, or even their personal or community's interest in knowledge and empowerment:

> In many cases our students depend on the media, more so than on textbooks or the classroom, for their understanding of existing social relations. . . . We must therefore find some way dynamically to interrogate the current

production of images in the popular culture; we must find some way critically to examine film, TV, newspaper, and popular music in the classroom.

(McCarthy 2003: 297)

The modern nation-state constitutes for critical multiculturalists another influence on popular perception that they advocate students' critical distance toward, as a socially constructed, or "imagined," culture or community, whose essence or nature is subject to debate and scrutiny, rather than unquestioning, passive acceptance. Here, critical multiculturalism can be seen to confront assimilationism directly, seeing it as having detrimental effects on minority group youth, rather than merely being an ideology of practical socialization. Critical multiculturalism follows Benedict Anderson's "imagined communities," view in this context, conceiving of the nation-state as the latest, most powerful successor of a series of hierarchal structures vying for people's loyalties, by framing them in terms of a larger, theoretical collectivity. In the following quotation, Anderson stresses the contingency of nationalism as a primary means for self-identification today:

> The very possibility of imagining the nation only arose historically when, and where, three fundamental cultural conceptions, all of great antiquity, lost their axiomatic grip on men's minds. The first . . . was the idea that a particular script-language offered privileged access to ontological truth. . . . Second was the belief that society was naturally organized around and under higher centres – monarchs who were persons apart from other human beings and who ruled by some form of cosmological (divine) dispensation. . . . Third was the conception of temporality in which cosmology and history were indistinguishable, the origins of the world and of men essentially identical.

(2001: 36)

As Anderson continues, without absolute faith in any higher order or structure to everyday human life, New World people began to think of themselves as patriots or nationals – members of limited plots of land who could collectively act to achieve more than they could as individuals – who could through this framework challenge European political-economic control of their lives and fortunes. Additionally, Anderson emphasizes the significance of the printing press and mass news production as key components of the rise of nationalism, teaching people informally to see themselves as part of a nation or a society, rather than as part of a global empire or world community. This historical context indicates that modern nation-states are not natural or essential groups, but are themselves the product of individuals' collective actions and interests, and subject, as well, to multiple perspectives – that their truthfulness or validity as social facts or markers of social difference is but one way of looking at the social world. Alternatives are also possible, from tribal, religious, or civilizational views, to international or cosmopolitan perspectives.

With regard to the nation-state then, critical multiculturalists advocate a historical approach that sees it as the product of specific acts, choices, and events, whose implications for students as autonomous actors today are not set in stone, but subject to divergent points of view, which should ideally be explored, deliberated upon, analyzed, and actively chosen. Thus, what it means to be a good American is framed as a matter of perspective rather than as a list of behaviors (say, the wearing of American flag lapel pins, or applying pro-America bumper stickers to one's car), enabling students to decide for themselves how to act out of civic duty, and to whom they owe civic loyalty or feel fellowship. Each is responsible for developing an informed and defensible, rather than merely intuitive, position on the so-called demands of patriotism or citizenship.

This perspective directly opposes that of many people who after 9/11 conceive patriotism as broad strokes and gestures of loyalty to the government and military. Yet as Michael Apple argues in response to the increased prevalence of this view in the public sphere in the last decade, "No national narrative that excludes the rich history of dissent as a constitutive part of the nation can ever be considered legitimate" (2003: 307). Patriotism is controversial today rather than fixed in U.S. society, and so it is not objectively informative or historically accurate to regard certain particular patriotic duties as compulsory, or require student displays of patriotic commitment (see also Hand 2011). Thus, critical multiculturalism favors neither a particular variant of patriotism, nor a single type of non-patriotism, universalism, or cosmopolitanism, over student development of reflective and autonomous points of view in relation to dominant perspectives and messages.

Critical multiculturalists see the assimilationist emphasis on nationalism and patriotic duty as *not* serving students as independent thinkers and actors, who must weigh out various options personally in order to autonomously make effective decisions, rather than merely support the political majority's perspective or interests. Approaching the case of national difference as they would any other sort of social difference – as open to multiple interpretations and understandings – critical multiculturalists thus open up investigations of national allegiance in the classroom, enabling students to weigh in on evidence for and against various perspectives on the meaning and nature of U.S. identity today, and express themselves autonomously. This approach thus frames social/political education as education for democracy. As Feinberg writes:

> Learning to express the concerns and values that arise from one's own standpoint . . . is clearly one of the avenues for the evolution of new forms of affiliation and association that the liberal multicultural nation stands to protect and that constitutes an important component of its moral identity. It is within and across the medley of difference that the common school continues the dialogue begun during the American Revolution about the nature of national unity and the character of national identity.
>
> (1998: 245)

As another large-scale group, Muslims would likewise be *explored* as they are socially constructed in the society, rather than *taught about*, by the critical multiculturalist. Unlike assimilationists, they would expose students to views counter to the "clash" view regarding their difference from majority American norms, in order to bolster student objectivity, but unlike pluralists, they would not sanction a priori positive assessments of Muslim beliefs and practices, but remain more neutral, to emphasize students' active role in choosing reference points for understanding others in society. Reactive to both idealistic and romantic and negatively stereotypical portrayals of Muslims, the end of critical multiculturalists' examinations of Islam would be to provide students with experience evaluating predicaments involving difference in society, by analyzing a variety of evidence, rather than to provide one-sided information or a preferred perspective, which may seem to students far removed from the information they receive elsewhere about Islam, as we will see in the next chapter.

In aiming to respond to limitations observed within assimilationist and pluralist discourses, critical multiculturalism is promising in highlighting the contingent nature of social knowledge and learning, and the way ideology can interact with attitudes and beliefs in exploring issues of social difference. Its focus on giving students intellectual tools for personal autonomy and for participation in democracy is also compelling. Schools should not merely share mainstream majority beliefs, norms, and practices, or the best and latest articulation of these, but pave the way for the next generation to make their own decisions and choices, as they face new situations and possibilities.

However, as an approach to difference, it is also limited by its common, "critical" framing of the world in terms of winners and losers. As Steinberg and Kincheloe write, "critical multiculturalism names the power wielders who contribute to the structuring of knowledge, values, and identity – a trait, we might add, that makes the position quite unpopular in some circles" (2009: 5). As they go on, they identify "power blocs" in U.S. society, of white supremacy, of patriarchy, capitalist exploitation, and social classism, and they identify individuals and groups within these blocs as responsible for injustice and inequality in society. They suggest that these groups intentionally aim to oppress and harm others because it is in their interest. In education, Kincheloe and Steinberg thus make it their task to particularly share with students this way of looking at the world.

Like Huntington's "clash of civilizations" view, this approach casts people too broadly as good and bad. One may identify selfish, hateful, biased evildoers among the elite in U.S. society, and it is also helpful to observe the way that disadvantage in society is structural, implying that some gain while others lose within a system that can be seen to maintain and exacerbate, in some instances, gaps between rich and poor, powerful and powerless. Providing a perspective apart from individual meritocracy can also be valuable, so that students recognize that the playing field across society is not today equal or fair at the start: that some people have privileges in education and elsewhere in society, while others face hurdles.

However, as Michael Peters argues, "by dividing up cultures into two separate, discrete classes (oppressed and oppressor), [such theory] implies a false homogeneity of both parts, reifying them, and thus tends to downplay their interconnections, the links, the fluid boundaries and exchanges" (2012: 35). As discussed previously, to label people as privileged and responsible or oppressed and powerless based on categories such as sex/gender, race, and class does not clarify well how inequality and oppression circulate and impact people's lives in society, or how different groups and individuals interact and develop their identities dialogically, in interdependence with each other, as Peter McLaren notes.

> Whiteness can be considered as a conscription of the process of positive self-identification into the service of domination through inscribing identity into an onto-epistemological framework of "us" and "them." . . . So we find that it is impossible to separate the identities of both oppressor and oppressed. They depend upon each other.
>
> (McLaren 2001: xv)

Additionally, talk of "power blocs" is not a helpful way of developing understanding of society, where there are not simply harmful, powerful people and weak, beneficent people, but power shifts circuitously within diverse social contexts, from the family to the workplace, and so on. A view of society that frames it as good and bad obscures rather than highlights for students how systemic oppression operates in different people's lives.

Critical multiculturalism's focus on the powerful and powerless suggests that by virtue of birth some people are not oppressed in society, but are free to define themselves and the world as they choose. Such a framing of power and oppression masks how concepts of white supremacy and other notions of superiority and inferiority make demands and place restrictions on all people. Understanding how people incidentally rather than intentionally gain advantages at a cost to others is an important social justice project precluded by this binary thinking, by this naming or accusing of some people and groups as in some useful way "responsible" for social injustice and inequality at large.

The pedagogical and psychological implications of such dualistic thinking are also problematic. Critical multiculturalism aims to develop in students a critical consciousness based on a bold notion of how oppression occurs in society. For students who are identifiable with the "power blocs," this often means an education on their white privilege, and how they are responsible for racial oppression because of their skin color and their unwitting acceptance of privilege and advantage throughout their lives (Applebaum 2009). However, such an approach is rarely pedagogically effective. McCarthy (2003), among others, has observed such messages are not often effectively received by white students, and it is morally ineffective to ask students to accept responsibility for processes and events they are hardly autonomous in participating in, but that they should actually be *learning about* in the classroom (Jackson 2009). Educators' role should be to help students understand how privilege and disadvantage operate and circulate, rather than to blame or shame privileged students, simplifying morality and ethics, and redistributing power and privilege against historical or systematic frameworks, rather than individual or contextual information (i.e., "white students, look what you've done to the poor black students").

In this context, it also seems disingenuous to frame critical multiculturalism as without a direction other than student autonomy, for student learning seems tied into developing a critical consciousness about power blocs. Given this aim, critical multicultural educators' choices about which alternative perspectives to expose students to and how are likely to be highly partial, not choosing perspectives based on their popularity or inherent reasonableness, but with the goal of assigning blame to power blocs in mind. Critical multiculturalists' black/white (good/bad) world should be considered among others, but not sanctioned. From a practical standpoint, many students may not understand such bold, political statements as legitimate classroom knowledge – particularly those with a critical orientation to educational authority.

Steinberg and Kincheloe seem to accept many of these challenges in part, as they describe the power blocs as dynamic historical formations rather than set in stone, and note the ways in which one can be identified as more or less powerful in relation to race, class, gender, and so on (2009: 9). Yet their elaboration of how multiculturalists might "out" the "power wielders" in practice remains too simplistic, given their aim of developing student critical thinking capacities. As examples, they note that "when George W. Bush, Dick Cheney, and William Bennett refer to family values, they are speaking of a white entity" and that in U.S. education, ancient Egyptian history is white-washed, "debilitating . . . contemporary blacks and other non-whites, teaching them to believe that they are intellectually inferior to whites" (2009: 14; 15). Though elsewhere they also note that "the power bloc works consistently to obscure such appreciations" (2009: 9), they do not sufficiently connect the dots to explain these bold opinions about "white" family values and "white" Egyptian history. Given the seriousness of their claims, it would be helpful for Steinberg and Kincheloe to explain these views in more detail; otherwise, their recommended pedagogy about power blocs seems more ideological than research based, though there is evidence for their more empirical claims, regarding the systemic nature of socioeconomic inequality in relation to historical racial and gender inequality in U.S. society.

As with assimilationism and pluralism, critical multiculturalism has promise in its focus on teaching students to think about and consider multiple perspectives. It is true that poor people can be seen to have supported politics in the United States that have not been in their own best interest due to ideological factors (Steinberg & Kincheloe 2009). And many disadvantaged members of society experience a personal sense of inferiority that should be forcefully countered in schools, through an education that enables them to see themselves as part of a restructured democratic society of the future. It is also worthwhile to understand the extent and complex organization of inequality in U.S. society today. Yet critical multiculturalism risks the same oversimplification and binary good/bad thinking it blames assimilationism for, holding it as unproblematic to state, for instance, that "the white power bloc develops a bag of tricks to mask its social location, making use of disguises, euphemisms, silences, and avoidances"

(Steinberg & Kincheloe 2009: 16). Such statements may be useful to ponder or explore in a university sociology class, or in an advanced placement English literature or philosophy class, but as an understanding of the world or of U.S. society, they are not likely to be useful or helpful to promote in public schools.

Conclusion

U.S. society and its public schools have a rich history of multiculturalism, of tolerating and even celebrating difference, and it is worth appreciating the strengths of the prominent positions on multicultural education that have developed over its course in their historical contexts, while at the same time understanding that each has outer limits to its usefulness. Assimilation, as discussed here, remains an important role of public education in the United States. In order for democracy to flourish and enable the next generation to increase equality and prosperity across society, students need a common understanding of the country they live in: its rules and norms. Yet assimilationism cannot fully characterize our approach to difference, as schools need not support homogeneity and dismiss minority cultural (or ethnic or religious, etc.) orientations to socialize youth. The extreme end of dismissing difference as a stigma or marginalizing force a priori is unnecessary. We may require a common language, generally speaking; this does not mean one accent is superior to another, or one religion, manner of dress, or private belief.

Pluralism also has its strengths, notably in demanding positive recognition in place of dismissal, suspicion, or prejudice. Yet it also has limitations to its effectiveness. Schools should not be places of partiality toward any of the country's diverse ways of life, but must continue to uphold the ideal of a rich field for students to enter, not teaching how to be part of a faith tradition, but how to live together within diverse communities. Critical multiculturalism also has significant benefits as an approach to difference, in emphasizing how our perspectives are intentionally and unintentionally shaped by partial influences, urging students to think for themselves, using their own experience as a base for comparison, among other alternatives. It usefully highlights the dynamic nature of popular perceptions of difference, and a potential to reorganize society in line with ideals rather than the contemporary status quo. However in its extreme educational aims, it can be unhelpful to students, as teachers' notions of critical consciousness and power blocs can imply a moral education with overly broad conceptualizations of individuals as groups of oppressed and oppressor.

However, I remain somewhat sympathetic toward critical multiculturalism, as its understanding of how popular knowledge is constructed can be illustrated by examining public knowledge and awareness (and lack thereof) about Muslims and Islam in U.S. society today in relation to historically dominant media messages. Since 9/11, media has often bolstered voices echoing a history of harmful U.S. ethnocentrism toward Muslims and Islam, obscuring other voices and perspectives. As mentioned, since 9/11, some educators within the assimilationist tradition have relatedly equated all Muslims with terrorism, framing toleration of Islam and learning what students "need to know" as dichotomous options. This is unnecessary, inaccurate, and unhelpful. It does not serve the country in increasing toleration, democracy, or equality, as it obscures a great deal.

On the other hand, the case of Muslims since 9/11 in the media and in schools also suggests that critical multiculturalism is not entirely helpful in playing the blame game, as journalists and teachers may sincerely struggle in this context to understand a group about which misinformation and negative information is rampant today – but are not part of any "power bloc," which purposefully harms Muslims for their own clear advantage. 9/11 complicates things for understanding Muslims and Islam in public education, and not simply because non-Muslims can be seen to gain from Muslims' loss. In the next chapter, I examine 9/11, U.S. media, and the new "need to know," as important factors related to developing a multicultural education for teaching and learning about Islam and Muslims in the society today.

References

Akam, Everett Helmut. *Transnational America: Cultural Pluralist Thought in the Twentieth Century.* Lanham: Rowman & Littlefield, 2002.

Anderson, Benedict. *Imagined Communities.* New York: Verso, 2001.

Appiah, K. Anthony. "Identity, Authenticity, Survival: Multicultural Societies and Social Reproduction." In *Multiculturalism: Examining the Politics of Recognition*, edited by Amy Gutmann, 149–164. Princeton: Princeton University Press, 1994.

Apple, Michael. "Politics of Compulsory Patriotism." In *Education as Enforcement: The Militarization and Corporatization of Schools*, edited by Kenneth J. Saltman and David A. Gabbard, 291–300. London: RoutledgeFalmer, 2003.

Applebaum, Barbara. "White Privilege/White Complicity: Connecting 'Benefiting From' to 'Contributing To'." In *Philosophy of Education 2008*, edited by Ronald David Glass, 292–300. Urbana, IL: Philosophy of Education Society, 2009.

Banks, Cherry A. McGee. "A Historical Perspective on Intercultural/Multicultural Education in the United States." In *Mapping the Broad Field of Multicultural and Intercultural Education Worldwide: Towards the Development of a New Citizen*, edited by Nektaria Palaiologou and Gunther Dietz, 78–92. Newcastle upon Tyne: Cambridge Scholars Publishing, 2012.

Banks, James A. *Multiethnic Education: Theory and Practice.* Upper Saddle: Allyn & Bacon, 1993.

Banks, James A. "Multicultural Education: Characteristics and Goals." In *Multicultural Education: Issues and Perspectives*, edited by James A. Banks and Cherry A. McGee Banks, 3–30. Hoboken: John Wiley & Sons, 2004.

Banks, James A. "Multicultural Education: Dimensions and Paradigms." In *The Routledge International Companion to Multicultural Education*, edited by James A. Banks, 9–32. New York: Routledge, 2009.

Banks, James A., and Cherry A. McGee Banks, eds. *Multicultural Education: Issues and Perspectives.* Hoboken: John Wiley & Sons, 2004.

Barber, Benjamin R. *Jihad Versus McWorld: Terrorism's Challenge to Democracy.* New York: Random House, 1996.

Boas, Franz. *Race, Language and Culture.* Chicago: University of Chicago Press, 1940.

Bourne, Randolph. "Cultural Pluralism: Randolph Bourne's Vision of America as a Confederation of Distinct Peoples, 1916." In *Identity, Community, and Pluralism in American Life*, edited by William Fischer and David Gerber, 14–19. New York: Oxford University Press, 1997.

Clark, Christine. "Unburning the Cross – Lifting the Veil on Christian Privilege and White Supremacy in the United States and Abroad: Building Multicultural Understanding of Religion, Spirituality, Faith, and Secularity in Educational and Workplace Settings." In *Religion in Multicultural Education*, edited by Farideh Salili and Rumjahn Hoosain, 167–214. Charlotte, NC: Information Age Publishing, 2006.

Clark, J. J. *Oriental Enlightenment: The Encounter Between Asian and Western Thought*. New York: Routledge, 1997.

Collier, John. "The Red Atlantis." *Survey* 49 (1922): 15–20, 63.

Council on American-Islamic Relations. *Unequal Protection: The Status of Muslim Civil Rights in the United States, 2005*. Washington, DC: Council on American-Islamic Relations, 2005.

Council on Islamic Education. *Teaching About Islam and Muslims in the Public School Classroom: A Handbook for Educators*. Fountain Valley: Council on Islamic Education, 1995.

Davis, R. Deborah. "Minorities vs. Minority Groups: How Language Defines, Defiles and Denigrates Life." In *Multi/Intercultural Conversations: A Reader*, edited by Shirley R. Steinberg, 123–130. New York: Peter Lang, 2001.

Feinberg, Walter. *Common Schools/Uncommon Identities: National Unity and Cultural Difference*. New Haven: Yale University Press, 1998.

Fifield, Anna. "Growing Up Muslims in America." *Financial Times*, July 19, 2013.

Finn, Jr., Chester E. Introduction to *September 11: What Our Children Need to Know*, edited by the Fordham Foundation, 4–11. Washington, DC: Thomas B. Fordham Foundation, 2002. www.edexcellence.net/publications/sept11.html (accessed January 8, 2014).

Fordham Foundation, ed. *September 11: What Our Children Need to Know*. Washington, DC: Thomas B. Fordham Foundation, 2002. www.edexcellence.net/publications/sept11.html (accessed January 8, 2014).

Giroux, Henry A. *Living Dangerously: Multiculturalism and the Politics of Difference*. New York: Peter Lang, 1993.

Gutman, Herbert G. *Who Built America? Working People and the Nation's Economy, Politics, Culture and Society*. New York: Pantheon, 1989.

Hacker, Andrew. *Two Nations: Black and White, Separate, Hostile, Unequal*. New York: Scribner, 2003.

Haddad, Yvonne Yazbeck. *Not Quite American? The Shaping of Arab and Muslim Identity in the United States*. Waco: Baylor University Press, 2004.

Haddad, Yvonne Yazbeck, and Adair T. Lummis. *Islamic Values in the United States: A Comparative Study*. New York: Oxford University Press, 1987.

Hand, Michael. "Should We Promote Patriotism in Schools?" *Political Studies* 59 (2011): 328–347.

Hirsch, Jr., E. D. [2]"Moral Progress in History." In *Terrorists, Despots, and Democracy: What Our Children Need to Know*, edited by the Fordham Foundation, 72–73. Washington, DC: Thomas B. Fordham Foundation, 2003. www.edexcellence.net/publications/terrorists.html (accessed January 8, 2014).

hooks, bell. *Killing Rage: Ending Racism*. New York: Henry Holt, 1995.

Huntington, Samuel P. "The Clash of Civilizations?" *Foreign Affairs*, Summer 1993.

Jackson, Liz. "Reevaluating White Privileged Ignorance and Its Implications for Antiracist Education." In *Philosophy of Education 2008*, edited by Ronald David Glass, 301–304. Urbana, IL: Philosophy of Education Society, 2009.

Kallen, Horace. "Democracy versus the Melting Pot." *Nation* 100 (1915): 190–194; 217–220.

Kincheloe, Joe L., and Shirley R. Steinberg. *Changing Multiculturalism*. Buckingham: Open Court Press, 1997.

Kunzman, Robert. "Imaginative Engagement with Religious Diversity in Public School Classrooms." *Religious Education* 101 (2006): 516–533.

Lasky, Harold J., ed. *Autobiography of J. S. Mill with an Appendix of Hitherto Unpublished Speeches and a Preface by Harold J. Lasky*. London: Oxford University Press, 1924.

Leonard, Karen Isaksen. *Muslims in the United States: The State of Research*. New York: Russell Sage, 2003.

Lewis, Bernard. "The Roots of Muslim Rage." *The Atlantic Monthly*, September 1990.

MacLeod, Jay. *Ain't No Makin' It: Aspirations and Attainment in a Low-Income Neighborhood*. Boulder: Westview, 1997.

McCarthy, Cameron. "After the Canon: Knowledge and Ideological Representation in the Multicultural Discourse on Curriculum Reform." In *Race, Identity, and Representation in Education*, edited by Cameron McCarthy and Warren Crichlow, 289–305. New York: Routledge, 2003.

McLaren, Peter J. Preface to *Multi/Intercultural Conversations: A Reader*, edited by Shirley R. Steinberg, xi–xix. New York: Peter Lang, 2001.

Messerli, Jonathan. *Horace Mann, A Biography*. New York: Alfred A. Knopf, 1972.

Nord, Warren A. *Does God Make a Difference? Taking Religion Seriously in Our Schools and Universities*. Oxford: Oxford University Press, 2010.

Okin, Susan Moller. "'Mistresses of Their Own Destiny': Group Rights, Gender, and Realistic Rights of Exit." In *Citizenship and Education in Liberal Democratic Societies: Teaching for Cosmopolitan Values and Collective Identities*, edited by Kevin McDonough and Walter Feinberg, 325–350. Oxford: Oxford University Press, 2003.

Parekh, Bhikhu. *Rethinking Multiculturalism: Cultural Diversity and Political Theory*. Cambridge: Harvard University Press, 2000.

Peters, Michael A. "Western Models of Intercultural Philosophy." In *Interculturalism, Education and Dialogue*, edited by Tina Besley and Michael A. Peters. New York: Peter Lang, 2012.

Ravitch, Diane. "Multiculturalism: E Pluribus Plures." *American Scholar* 59 (1990): 337–354.

Ravitch, Diane. *The Language Police: How Pressure Groups Restrict What Students Learn*. New York: Vintage, 2004.

Rizvi, Fazal. "Representations of Islam and Education for Social Justice." In *Race, Identity, and Representation in Education*, edited by Cameron McCarthy and Warren Crichlow, 167–178. New York: Routledge, 2005.

Rosaldo, Renato. *Culture and Truth: The Remaking of Social Analysis*. Boston: Beacon Press, 1989.

Said, Edward W. *Orientalism*. New York: Vintage, 1979.

Schlesinger, Jr., Arthur M. *The Disuniting of America: Reflections on a Multicultural Society*. New York: W.W. Norton, 1998.

Sewall, Gilbert T. *Islam and the Textbooks: A Report of the American Textbook Council.* New York: American Textbook Council, 2003.

Shaheen, Jack G. *Reel Bad Arabs.* Brooklyn: Olive Branch Press, 2001.

Sidky, H. *A Critique of Postmodern Anthropology: In Defense of Disciplinary Origins and Traditions.* Lewison: The Edwin Mellen Press, 2003.

Steinberg, Shirley R., and Joe L. Kincheloe. "Setting the Context for Critical Multi/Interculturalism: The Power Blocs of Class Elitism, White Supremacy, and Patriarchy." In *Multi/Intercultural Conversations: A Reader,* edited by Shirley R. Steinberg, 1–30. New York: Peter Lang, 2001.

Steinberg, Shirley R., and Joe L. Kincheloe. "Smoke and Mirrors: More Than One Way to Be Diverse and Multicultural." In *Diversity and Multiculturalism: A Reader,* edited by Shirley R. Steinberg, 3–22. New York: Peter Lang, 2009.

Stillwell, Cinnamon, "Islam in America's Public Schools: Education or Indoctrination?" *SFGate,* June 11, 2008. www.sfgate.com/politics/article/Islam-in-America-s-public-schools-Education-or-2482820.php (accessed January 8, 2014).

Taylor, Charles. *Multiculturalism and "The Politics of Recognition."* Edited by Amy Gutmann. Princeton: Princeton University Press, 1992.

Thomas, William I., and Florian Znanieck. "Disorganization of the Polish Immigrant." In *Social Theory: The Multicultural and Classic Readings,* edited by Charles Lemert, 248–252. Boulder: Westview, 1999.

Tozer, Steven E., Guy Senese, and Paul C. Violas. *School and Society: Historical and Contemporary Perspectives.* New York: McGraw Hill, 2006.

Wing, Meredith. "Post 9/11 Hate Crime Trends: Muslims, Sikhs, Hindus and Jews in the U.S. (2005)." *The Pluralism Project.* Cambridge: Harvard University, 2005. www.pluralism.org/reports/view/104 (accessed January 8, 2014).

Zangwill, Israel. *The Melting Pot.* New York: American Jewish Book Company, 1921.

Zinn, Howard. *A People's History of the United States, 1492–Present.* New York: HarperCollins, 1995.

3 9/11, the media, and the new need to know

Introduction

In the last chapter, I contrasted major perspectives on social difference in the history of U.S. education, considering each in relation to teaching and learning about Islam and Muslims. There is another important way that people learn about social issues and diversity in our society today apart from in school settings, however, particularly regarding controversial issues that teachers can be nervous to discuss, such as religion and politics: through the mass media. Indeed, teachers may also learn about contemporary political issues, as students and the general public do, through mass media and popular culture. This includes news journalism of television, printed media, and on the internet, "edu-tainment," as well as entirely fictional accounts that often resemble historical or contemporary realities in part, such as television serial programs, movies, and books.

These more informal educational venues are a concern to educators of many different persuasions, as their impact on students is difficult to deny and can be hard to counter. Whether one views representations of social difference in the mass media as directly educational, or as reflective of common beliefs and attitudes deemed acceptable or normal in society, Muslims are particularly vulnerable to damaging stereotypes in this domain that have at least an indirect influence on young people. This should be taken into account by educators as partly constitutive of students' background knowledge and experience, which plays a significant role in shaping their reception to school knowledge (official and unofficial).

This chapter considers informal education about Islam and Muslims in U.S. society: what is taught and learned in the public sphere outside the field of education, of schools and universities. First I elaborate two major approaches to understanding the educational influence of media and popular culture, relating them to the major perspectives on multicultural education that I discussed in the last chapter. No matter what perspective one takes on how to navigate social difference in education, teachers tend to agree that the force of the media is something to be reckoned with, and even challenged in the classroom. I give few indications of how educators can do so in this section, but give a fuller, practical discussion of this issue in terms of teaching for critical media literacy, after presenting evidence in this chapter and the next one about what students are likely to learn and know about Islam and Muslims today, from mass media and contemporary public education.

After considering these approaches to media and education, I elaborate the claim that Muslims are subject to harmful, disproportionately negative representations in contemporary media, including news and related nonfiction journalism, and popular culture, fictional stories we tell in movies and television. This claim is somewhat unexceptional, as many people have examined our "popular" knowledge of Islam and Muslims before me: most notably Shaheen, who has maintained a comprehensive list of Hollywood films' portrayal of Arabs (1984; 2001), and Said, who has considered the way academics and journalists have considered the Muslim and Arab worlds in U.S. society throughout decades (1979; 1997). However, what I am interested in here is how facts, fictions, and overgeneralized stereotypes about Muslims and Islam have fused together since 9/11, giving credence in many people's minds to the "clash of civilizations" view, fleshing out an ideological image of international relations. According to some prominent voices in U.S. society today, 9/11 evidenced the view that Muslims are violent, irrational, and hate the United States, through the actions of a small group of extremists, despite the fact that their interpretation of Islam is viewed by great numbers of Muslims as an aberration or perversion of their faith (Palmer & Palmer 2008; Shaheen 2001).

There is an interesting connection between ideology and reality in relation to 9/11, which can be traced in moving from the world of facts to the world of fictions in mass media: from news journalism to popular culture and entertainment. The real event of 9/11 bolstered stereotypes already existent that Muslims are violent, irrational, and uncivilized. Furthermore, it has led to more emboldened defenses of biased representations, and related defenses of excluding alternative points of view about Islam and Muslims in the U.S. public sphere. This is a dangerous trend with important implications for public education for democracy. It fuels assimilationist rhetoric that you can either assimilate children, or appreciate diversity when it comes to social difference in this case, but not both, as I discussed in the last chapter. Here, the critical multiculturalists seem to have it right when they argue that outside forces play a significant role in teaching people about difference in society and that media do so for their own interests, in profit making through storytelling, rather than for the sake of democracy or social justice. Yet media did not simply create a horrific story of Muslims and violence; one occurred in real life. And journalists did not and do not communicate such stories to harm Muslims or democracy, but rather view it as their duty to inform about the worst of (self-identified) Muslims. It is important to understand the relationship between fact and fiction in this case, to set the stage for an understanding of what educators have done and are doing in public schools since 9/11.

Media as education

There are two common ways in which news and entertainment media can be viewed as educational. First, they can be viewed as *directly instructional:* We learn information and values from media sources, viewing news as truthful, or behaviors in entertainment media as acceptable or normal. News media aims to be instructional in this way, showing and telling about events happening locally and around the world, expanding the kinds of information and areas of the world one knows about from the narrower confines of everyday life. People view media as educational in this way when they argue against alcohol and cigarette advertisers targeting young people, or against violent videogames. In this case, they assume children and youth will do what commercials tell them to do, or see video games as guidelines for their own behavior.

Many people consider children more susceptible to media messaging – particularly in entertainment or advertising media – than adults. Schrag and Javidi (1997) argue that children's "first stories" teach them about the world around them and that children frame future information received against this foundational backdrop, regardless of whether it is based in fact or fiction. Particularly this possibility resonates when one considers how children's stories often take them to previously unknown areas of the real world, like China in *Mulan* (1998), and the Middle Eastern or Arab world in *Aladdin* (1992).

Indeed, various people concerned with stereotyping in children's films challenged portrayals of Arab people and culture in *Aladdin*, when the Walt Disney animated feature film was released in 1992. A fairytale story, *Aladdin* primarily wishes to entertain while telling a moral story about "good guys" and "bad guys." Yet it does not moralize merely through plot devices, but expresses, in the eyes of critics, qualities of good and bad through physical and other aspects of the characters. The good characters – Aladdin, the genie, the princess, and her father – have little to no foreign accent, lighter skin (except the genie, who has blue skin), and more average, *human* facial features and body structures. Characters at odds with Aladdin, such as palace guards, greedy vendors, and villains, have accents, darker skin, and absurdly large noses: "bad teeth, large hooked noses, and unclean tunics, caftans, and headgear that are just a tad too exaggerated" (Steinberg 2004: 178). Islam's dictates toward aiding the poor are ignored by vendors who chase Aladdin through the city swinging swords, for his stealing one piece of fruit (Shaheen 2001). The picture painted is of a dangerous and inhospitable place where, as the introductory song states, "they cut off your ear if they don't like your face – it's barbaric, but hey, its home." Due to public pressures after being released, Disney removed the two lines, "they cut off your ear, if they don't like your face," but retained the last line, prompting a *New York Times* editorial to state that "[t]o characterize an entire region with this sort of tongue-in-cheek bigotry, especially in a movie aimed at children, borders on the barbaric" (Editorial 1993; Shaheen 2001).

Others argue that such a view of media – news journalism and entertainment sources – as directly educational is too simplistic. Older children can distinguish cartoons from reality, and it would be hard to conclusively prove that young children always conflate the two, or base their developing sense of reality on fictional sources of information about events and people far removed from their everyday lives. People may also engage in a critical way with nonfiction media, understanding that news journalism and reality television are cultural productions rather than wide windows portraying the world as it is. Thus, a second way people view media as educational conceives media not as a direct, straightforward teacher of information, but as a dynamic and self-referential marketplace of ideas, beliefs, values, and perceptions that people navigate, at times unwittingly but other times quite critically, in continually revising their understanding of the world.

As Stuart Hall argued (1973), people participate in an engagement process with media, as members or non-members of its target audience, and may passively receive ideas and attitudes from media, or respond more critically to its messages (see also Morley 1980). Producers of media can be seen to accept this framing of media's impact, as they study audience behavior and response through marketing and consumer research today, which they recognize as an investment in knowing and predicting their target audience's response to their product (a movie, television show, cartoon, etc.). Thus, representations in media and popular culture are fleeting moments in a continuous feedback loop, wherein media producers use research on the values, norms, and attitudes of their target audience to develop products and continually refine their understanding of their audience in relationship to their past success. This picture is further complicated by realizing that not all people receive media messages the same way, even within a target demographic. As some conspiracy theorists doubted the Moon landing, there are those today who believe 9/11 was not a surprise attack by international terrorists. People are thus active, rather than passive, recipients of even apparently straightforward media information.

Most researchers focusing on media's impact recognize its educational nature in this more complicated way. They find that even when media intends to put forward certain kinds of attitudes and perspectives, it is not always successful, owing to the complex ways different individuals "read" media messaging. For instance, as Cortés (2005: 70) points out with regard to pluralist representation of social diversity in media,

> Some critical theorists argue that media fostering of "nonchange" – or at least a reduction in the speed of change – may constitute the most important behavior-related aspect of the media. From this perspective, interracial buddy movies and desegregated TV news teams may actually retard the process of social change. Rather than role modeling integration, they may surreptitiously suggest that social change is occurring so rapidly and normally that additional special efforts are unnecessary.
>
> Then there is the issue of disinhibiting effects. . . . Do movies that celebrate vigilantism contribute to societal violence by removing inhibitions to imitative behavior? Or do they reduce violence by providing viewers a catharsis for pent-up frustrations? Do films with teenage sex disinhibit such activity by making it appear normative and "safe," . . . [o]r do they provide a vicarious substitute for the real thing?

The sorts of attitudes media messages reinforce are not necessarily what was intended, despite some people's interests in using the media to shape behavior.

In my analysis of how Islam and Muslims are represented in U.S. media, I understand media's educational impact more in this second sense: as a source material which people interact with in various ways, passively accepting data received in some cases, but often negotiating its various direct and implicit messages and perspectives. As mainstream media is also produced with this framework in mind, the perspectives, views, and representations it puts forward are educated best guesses about the a priori values and attitudes of the general population, as news media and popular culture producers generally try to gain as large an audience as possible among the media-consuming public.

It is also important to recognize the relationships between different media to each other and real-world events in the case of representations of Islam and Muslims. The association of Muslims with terrorism or violence in contemporary media does not come strictly from individual or collective fantasy or imagination. In relation, writers and producers of dramatic stories told in television sitcoms and major films must look to real life, as it is mediated for those who do not witness for themselves real-world dramatic events, to create realistic tales that captivate audiences, without upsetting cross-sections of it, by contradicting their previous beliefs or background assumptions about reality. Thus, news media and popular culture have different relationships to reality – the former is charged with framing it (that is, significant or extraordinary events within it) with some accuracy, while the latter must mix real elements with fantasy in a way that does not disorient or offend large parts of their target audience (the U.S. consuming public at large), to successfully entertain.

That Muslims remain a popular scapegoat in Hollywood, a placeholder for evil elements in realistic fictions, lacking serious public scrutiny, then reflects, at the very least, a perceived lack of mainstream, public concern with protecting the image of Muslims – in other words, public acceptance of associating Muslims with terrorism. Media producers' informed hypothesis about media consumers is that they will not change the channel or refuse to buy movie tickets because stereotypical portrayals of Muslims offend them. Rather, they are *attracted* to news coverage of anything related to Muslim terrorists, and to fictional plots centered on Muslim villains, in place of negative representation of other groups that the public and media audiences are more sensitive about today: for instance, Jews or Catholics.

In the United States, it is expected that one can find in media a wide range of points of view on any given topic, and unsurprisingly in this context, basic media literacy is promoted by educators of many different stripes. Such media literacy emphasizes at least minimally that not all journalistic information should be passively received, but critically considered, in light of evidence available from the source and elsewhere. Assimilationist educational groups such as the Fordham Institute and the Common Core State Standards Initiative (2012) promote media literacy in terms of "evaluating credibility and accuracy" of sources. Pluralist educators aim to reduce public prejudice and understand media literacy by implication as important for teaching that commonly held stereotypes can be harmful. Critical multiculturalism emphasizes media literacy as skepticism toward mainstream media sources, which work for profit and are therefore not entirely impartial, as one might wish them to be. (That is, they do not neutrally or impartially open a window to the world, but may only reveal that which will keep audiences "tuned in.")

However, while educators of many different stripes may in principle value media literacy, in practice, it means different things to people. Among major U.S. news sources, Fox News programs tend to encourage skepticism toward the *New York Times* and MSNBC as too "liberal," while on Comedy Central's popular news commentary program *The Daily Show with Jon Stewart*, Fox News journalists are regularly mocked as being inept and overly ideological, sending the message that Fox News is untrustworthy. Educators similarly represent a range of positions regarding what should be held as valid media messages and what should be subject to scrutiny.

Recent polls show that Americans see each other, the general public, as too gullible toward media messages (Smith & Rainie 2008), but what this means also depends on who is asked, and in what context. In a 2012 study of election advertising, it was found that 80% of Democrats and 20% of Republicans felt an anti-Obama advertisement was unfair, with approximately the same ratio reversed in reception of an anti-Republican ad (Levine 2013). Americans believe in the need for media literacy to develop the ability to critically receive biased or imbalanced messages that (they feel) are wrongly portrayed as factual. Yet what is fact versus fiction is controversial when it comes to political issues today. Ordinary or average teachers' views tend to reflect across the general population, indicating that what they think is critical media literacy in practice can also vary widely from one to the next.

How educators should represent diversity in society, and Muslims particularly, are likewise increasingly controversial questions today, as I discussed in the last chapter. Assimilationists tend to think that the right thing to do is to teach about Muslim terrorism exclusively, and highlight negative topics in relation to Islam. Pluralists and critical multiculturalists would do the opposite, sharing information about Muslims who are ordinary (and good) citizens in the United States and around the world, and responding critically to the more prevalent, discriminatory view of the faith and community. When one considers media's educational impact in relation to learning about Islam and Muslims, it seems worthwhile to supply students with a different message than that which prevails in the media, as I show in the next section. Without formal education, Americans "know" about Muslim terrorism, violent Muslims, that jihad is a "holy war." . . . It is hard to imagine in this context that schoolchildren need to know more that *supports* these points, but nothing about alternative perspectives, though the assimilationist view remains popular today. The rest of this chapter considers the "evidence" and "data" given in mainstream media and U.S.-based popular culture, particularly since 9/11, about Islam and Muslims.

Just the facts versus what sells

Researchers have elaborated the systemic, structural character of Muslim misrepresentation in Western and particularly U.S. news media throughout the latter half of the twentieth century (Kamalipour 1997; Karim 2003; Mousa 1984; Said 1997; Shaheen 2001). As Shaheen (2001) and Said (1997) extensively document, during this time period, Muslims have typically been framed as dangerous and violent by news media and popular culture. Though more mixed, good and bad representations of Muslims have also emerged, since September 11, 2001, representations of Muslims in relation to terrorism and conflict have remained highly prevalent. Such representations have focused on real-life Muslim villains such as Osama bin Laden and Saddam Hussein, have framed 9/11 and related events such as the "Arab Spring" in terms of a clash of civilizations, and have positioned more ordinary Muslims as "bad guys" within domestic news stories. Though we see fictional accounts of Muslim "bad guys" becoming more complex, movies and television still tend to bolster as much as they might debunk negative perspectives, enabling people to continue to read that Muslims are uncivilized, violent, and dangerous as a dominant message.

The 9/11 event – the attacks and their aftermath of investigation – brought real fear and a real villain, who identified himself as a Muslim fundamentalist and anti-American crusader, bin Laden, to ordinary households in a dramatic, for many, unforgettable, way. President George W. Bush (2001) emphasized in pinpointing bin Laden and al-Qaeda as the likely culprits of the attacks that "the enemy of America is not our many Muslim friends," but "traitors to their faith, trying, in effect, to hijack Islam itself." In this context, Abid Amiri observes that in the first six months after 9/11, media coverage related to Muslim Americans was more positive than it was during the six months before the 9/11 attacks:

> While 42 percent of the total segments/articles in CNN, Fox News, *New York Times* and *Washington Post* were categorized as positive/supportive in the first six months after 9/11, only 25 percent of the news was supportive of Muslim Americans in the six months before 9/11.
>
> (2012: 5)

In relation, some surveys indicated a slightly more positive attitude toward Muslims and Muslim Americans within the six-month period after 9/11 than in periods before and after, as 9/11 created a new need to know about Islam and Muslims, "which forced the media to cover Muslims more frequently," with more airtime given to diverse Muslims' voices and views (Amiri 2012: 6).

Yet from the time of the first anniversary of 9/11, a dramatic shift in media representation and in mainstream views of Islam and Muslims can be observed. As Amiri notes, "positive news articles and news clips . . . declined from 42 percent in the 6 months after 9/11 to 21 percent after the first anniversary [while] negative coverage . . . increased by 21 percent," as "unlike the first six months after the 9/11 incidents, many leaders and politicians did not come out to ask the public for unity with the Muslim communities" (2012: 8). During this time, the news media took on the role of informing the public about bin Laden, and related terrorist suspects and groups, often in alarmist tones. As negative coverage has increased, favorable perceptions of Islam in opinion polls decreased, from 41% in 2005 to 30% in 2010 (Pew 2010).

Since 9/11 and up until his death in 2011, bin Laden became a living symbol for concepts of Muslim terrorism and Islamic extremism. Textual and pictorial media analyses show how bin Laden was portrayed increasingly over time as a villain, a monstrous face in the shadows, in alignment with the public understanding of him as a clear, embodied form of the threat of Islam apparent since 9/11 to U.S. society (Borradori 2003; Jackson 2010; Kellner 2004). This is not an unreasonable or unpredictable result: Bin Laden claimed responsibility for destroying hundreds of innocent American lives, and he himself emphasized (in part) that he was on a jihad toward the United States. Yet as a consequence of this state of affairs and its popular, public mediation, the single most common representation of a Muslim has been of a scary, shady character: an unlikable, intolerable enemy of society. Although one might hope that the most common representation of Islam in American mass media is of an ordinary, good man, woman, or group of believers, a leader or group that represents a larger cross-section of the community, instead it is of a dark presence, out to "get" Americans. The most recognizable Muslim in America has been an actual (self-professed) menace to U.S. society, a real-life villain, and his stature as such has led to a proliferation of imagery connecting Islam and Muslims with terrorism and fear.

After bin Laden, Saddam Hussein has been the second-most famous (or rather, infamous) Muslim in the United States. He, like bin Laden, is hardly a positive or representative example of a Muslim, whether we think from within a U.S.-based perspective, or a global view. In an article published the day after the 9/11 attacks (with the somewhat skewed headline), "Attacks Draw Mixed Response in Mideast," Hussein is highlighted as the single Middle Eastern leader who did not condemn the 9/11 attacks, appearing in alignment with bin Laden in stating that "the American cowboys are reaping the fruit of their crimes" (CNN 2001). As one compares the headline with the coverage, it seems that one inappropriate, unreasonable Middle Eastern response is seen as equivalent to nearly a dozen compassionate ones, in terms of its significance within the framing of this text. Since the time of the first American gulf war, Hussein has been an infamous enemy in many Americans' eyes, and most likely was the most well-known Muslim in the United States before 9/11. At his execution in 2007, President Bush was quoted stating that Hussein's death "is an important milestone on Iraq's course to becoming a democracy" (Fallows 2007). Such a statement indicates the significance of Hussein as an individual – another infamous Muslims enemy of the United States.

In U.S. news portrayals of 9/11 and international and domestic terrorism, the "clash of civilizations" thesis is often echoed in place of more contextual accounts of events and settings. Ervand Abrahamian (2003: 531) notes that for several months after 9/11 the *New York Times* printed a specials news section continually emphasizing 9/11 as Islamic jihad, with articles with titles like

> 'Yes, this is about Islam', 'This *is* a religious war', 'Jihad 101', 'The one true faith', 'Dictates of faith', 'Defusing the holy bomb', 'Barbarians at the

gates', 'The force of Islam', 'Divine inspiration', 'The core of Muslim rage', 'Dreams of holy war' . . . 'The age of Muslim wars', 'A head-on collision of alien cultures', 'Feverish protests against the West', 'How Islam and politics mixed' . . .

Newspapers additionally featured extended interviews and statements of Huntington, as well as any indications that his critics had changed their views and now supported his thesis (Abrahamian 2003). Much research has documented in this context how *cultural* arguments and conversations took center stage, obscuring analyses of *political* relations between the United States and Muslim societies, as bin Laden himself emphasized, as possibly relevant factors and issues, such as the Arab-Israeli conflict. Indeed, while promoting positive views of "our Muslim friends" and allies, the Bush administration at the same time strongly discouraged mainstream news media from rebroadcasting any of bin Laden's words about 9/11 (disseminated by Al Jazeera News), apparently to preclude any transmission of "coded instructions from the 'terrorist-in-chief'" (Carey 2002: 74). Bush also discouraged any reflective consideration that 9/11 may be related to blowback from U.S. foreign policy, by emphasizing upon hearing a bin Laden broadcast that "Americans will not be influenced by any enemy of our country . . . we're at war with these terrorists," conflating dialogue about political rather than cultural factors with concurring with the enemy (Bush 2005). As Abrahamian notes, in this context,

> Few dared to mention Palestine within the context of September 11. When a lone Georgia congresswoman raised the possibility that US support for Israel in the Palestinian conflict might have something to do with September 11, she was promptly denounced [and] swept out of office by a massive influx of out-of-state campaign money. . . . When Tony Blair emphasizes the importance of dealing with the Palestinian problem while waging the war against terrorism, US papers ignored his statements or buried them in the inside pages. The *New York Times* claimed without irony that the US media, unlike the British, could not deal with both issues at the same time because it would be "equivalent to walking and chewing gum at the same time."
>
> (2003: 536)

As Abrahamian argues, the development of a taboo against analyzing the Middle East and 9/11 with a political or historical rather than cultural mindset would have longstanding implications for U.S. democratic culture, as practical, critical arguments about historical and political-economic interactions would be held as unethical, compared to dogmatic reasoning about inevitable Islamic terrorism and culture clash. Regardless of where one stands in relation to the claim that U.S. international affairs and foreign policy were related to 9/11, media headlines that focus only on the cultural argument about a civilizational clash obscure other possible factors, as well as the importance of treating

Muslims not as representatives of a violent or barbaric culture, but as diverse, good and bad, individuals.

Other headline events related to Muslims and Islam concern political changes occurring across some of the Arab world over the last few years. Though often described as an "Arab Spring," as Ehab Galal and Riem Spielhaus note, the prevalent use of this term to describe "disparate events that originated in vastly differing historical circumstances within separate Arab countries" enables "homogenizing the Arab world to a common region, hiding the different histories, languages and cultures" (2012: 4). Steven Salaita (2012) observes that while there have been many positive images and discourses with positive connotations related to the Arab Spring, particularly regarding Tahrir Square early on in Cairo, dominant media messages have nonetheless focused heavily on "Culture Talk, a way of translating foreign populations in the United States based on cultural determinism," the idea that that our cultures define our possible behaviors and beliefs, in line with the "clash of civilizations" view:

- The Arabs are finally awakening to democracy
- That Arabs appreciate (and often seek) the guidance of a fundamentally benevolent United States
- That Arabs constantly have to guard against their inherent barbarity (i.e., their natural impulse toward political Islam)
- That Arabs in control of their destiny are necessarily threatening
- That Arabs have been dormant throughout their history
- That Arabs attempt to enter into a modernity decontextualized from its invention and exportation by the West . . . and the United States in particular

(143–144)

As Salaita observes here, reducing diverse events across a substantial world region to the activities of "the Arabs" encourages a simplistic view of Arab culture as monolithic, though the facts across contexts are highly complex. His analysis also reflects how Arab Muslims have usually been represented as in contrast with, or opposed to, democracy, autonomy and personal liberty, and modernity. Similarly, Marion Dixon (2011) highlights media efforts to explain how democracy is not "at home," or naturally coexistent, with Islam, yet is seen to be gaining traction in the Middle East. These analyses highlight the way that diverse cultural and religious orientations are framed as monolithic and contrasted with a U.S. political culture, continually echoing the message of difference. Such homogenization and essentializing is akin to suggesting, for instance, that all English speakers in North America oppose (or have historically opposed) preserving tradition – a gross generalization that does not particularly aid understanding. Though it is not the primary responsibility of the news media to celebrate or raise attention toward diversity across the world, such messages bolster assimilationist views that Muslims cannot be at home in the West or the United States, precluding more optimistic views of Muslim integration and flourishing in these contexts.

Indeed, internal debates about representation within U.S. entertainment media can be seen to suggest that positive recognition or tolerance of Islam and Muslims of the sort pluralists or critical multiculturalists would defend is inappropriate, in place of references to terrorism, violence, and/or antagonism. As we saw in the last chapter, Muslims are framed (paradoxically) as insufficiently tolerant to be tolerated, in line with assimilationist "clash of civilizations" framings of Muslim-American relations. Muslims are rearticulated as bad guys within U.S. society in this context, as "normal" Americans are pitted against Muslim Americans, when the latter protest their stereotypical mainstream media representation.

There are various media domains one could explore here, from news editorial cartoons (Jackson 2010; Palmer, 1997), to talk radio (Kellner 2002; Steuter & Wills 2008), to television, print media (books), and film. Here I will focus primarily on recent events related to television, as it has been cited as the primary source of people's information about Muslims and Islam in opinion polls (Council on American-Islamic Relations 2006). My first example of this sort of representation deals with the treatment of Muslims in the popular Fox television series *24*. The series, which started broadcasting in the weeks after 9/11 and focuses on terrorism in the United States, has featured various ethnic-national individuals as threatening figures. However, the way that Muslims have been represented as terrorists has concerned representatives of different Muslim groups and communities in the United States, leading the main actor Kiefer Sutherland to offer a disclaimer before a particularly polarizing episode in 2005, acknowledging that U.S. Muslims are aligned with other U.S. citizens for peace and stability and against terrorism. In the broadcast at issue, Muslim terrorists are cast as responsible for large-scale deaths (some 12,000 people) in the Los Angeles area, leading to wide-scale internment (in the series) of all U.S. Muslims.

In dialogue with Fox News commentator and talk show host Bill O'Reilly, Arsalan Iftikhar, the legal director for the Council on American-Islamic Relations (CAIR), criticized the show for blurring the line between fiction and reality to paint "terrorism as a monolith," making unjust internment based on religious faith, equivalent to that against Japanese Americans during the Second World War, palatable, or possibly acceptable, to a mass U.S. audience (Fox 2007). His concern was with *24* encouraging its audience to consider it as possible or even reasonable for the United States to intern its entire Muslim population, regarding all Muslims officially as suspect – that the episode desensitized audiences to the idea that all Muslims could be held as suspect, as Japanese Americans (wrongly) were, during the Second World War.

Iftikhar and other Muslims concerned with *24*'s reflection of social norms around representing Muslims have been treated unsympathetically. O'Reilly defended the episode, claiming that to "combine fiction with reality" in this case is unproblematic given that "you have in this world Muslim villains. They are on the other side of the war on terror from us. There are Muslims who want to kill Americans, you know that" (Fox 2007). While O'Reilly is not known for his impartiality as a commentator, similar criticality toward offended

Muslims – not the stereotypes, or their producers – was also provided by NBC coverage. Titled "Muslims *Rip* '24' for Renewed Terror Role," Muslims are cast as aggressors in the article. Muslims are portrayed as attacking *24*, while the term "renewed terror role" obscures rather than supplies information, implying that Muslims are "ripping" something that is not new, or not really important to know about (such as that, for instance, Muslims perceive that they themselves are being "ripped"). While the text of the article cites specific Muslims and representatives of various groups in a more objective manner, this initial framing implies – ironically, given the nature of the concerns expressed by Iftikhar (Fox 2007) and the others (that terrorism and Islam are being painted as monoliths) – Muslims as a cohesive, violent social entity. The headline does not even articulate clearly that Muslims have been cast as terrorists, against their reasonable interests in fair representation. Instead, they are represented as aggressors – and *24* as their victim.

The title thus betrays a partial interpretation: Muslims *rip*, despite the vast majority of interviewees in the text suggesting their sense, rather, of *fear* since popular, harmful stereotypes are being propagated by a major, popular television series. Why not "Muslims fear stereotyping on *24*"? Or, "Muslims cite stereotyping..."? Muslims "fearing" or "citing" stereotypes may not be so newsworthy, perhaps; however, the provocative wording and oppositional framing of the situation in the title to the article reveals mass media journalists' lack of sympathy with Muslims' concerns and struggles for fair representation and balanced portrayals. That norms that can be seen to harm Muslims should be critically scrutinized is not emphasized, appreciated, or really even suggested, by such framings of the situation.

A second example regards controversies related to the "reality" television shows, *All-American Muslim* and *Shahs of Sunset,* both of which represent Muslims in the United States in different ways, to differing audience responses. *All-American Muslim* was released in 2011, and aimed to show regular Muslim families in Michigan, but was met with much negative publicity for sending a message of tolerance rather than intolerance toward Islam. The hardware retailer Lowe's pulled funding from the program after a backlash in its consumer base, while *The Washington Post* published a Family Florida Association criticism (Esposito 2011): "The show profiles only Muslims that appear to be ordinary folk while excluding many Muslim believers whose agenda pose a clear and present danger to the liberties and traditional values that the majority of Americans cherish." Such arguments echo Ravitch (2004) and Finn's (2002) views that one should focus on the *minority* of Muslims who are violent and threatening over the majority who are peace loving. *The Hollywood Reporter* review of the program held that it was moving, educational, and fascinating (Knowles 2011), but it was dropped after its first season, apparently due to low ratings (which, if true, was likely related to *All-American Muslims* being ordinary rather than extreme members of U.S. society).

On the other hand, a reality television show about Persian Americans in Los Angeles called *Shahs of Sunset* debuted in 2012 and is in its third season, despite protests from Persian American groups that it celebrates negative stereotypes – albeit different ones than are normally highlighted in media – by focusing on the "reality" actors' character defects and entertaining qualities, as is common in reality television programming. *Shahs* provides a mixed rather than negative representation of Muslim Iranian Americans, overall. As an Iranian American reflects on the question of "Does the show . . . accurately reveal what Iranian-Americans are *really* like?":

> Iranian-American interfaith relationships will make you question what you think you know about the Middle East. The show's inclusion of Jewish and Muslim Iranian Angelinos sets it apart from nearly every other depiction of Middle Eastern life on TV. In fact, religious identity is at the forefront of season one: Mike Shouhed, an Iranian Jew, dates non-Jewish women against his mother's wishes . . . Reza's anguish as the child of interfaith divorce (his Iranian-Muslim mother and Iranian-Jewish father "never had a shot" due to disapproving families) . . . Like Reza, I know about interfaith love first-hand: My Iranian-Muslim mom and Iranian-Jewish dad remained married in the rain-soaked Tehangeles outpost of Portland, Oregon. . . .
>
> There's much to dislike about "Shahs": Its celebration of consumerism, the cast's delusions of ethnic superiority and their nostalgia for a mythic "Persia" contracts truths I know as a sociologist.
>
> (Maghbouleh 2012)

Here we see one television series with negative stereotypes (albeit different ones than those normally evident) surviving despite protest, while one *without* negative stereotypes fails to succeed, in a context where a *lack* of negative stereotypes is identified as controversial (or, alternatively, as just not entertaining). It seems clear here that "what sells" as entertaining is a decisive factor in these cases, with negative stereotypes reigning.

My final example here deals not only with representations of Muslims, but also elaborates a privileging of non-Muslim voices over Muslim voices in U.S. society and popular culture. In 2013, media controversy swirled around the publication of a history of Jesus by a scholar who happens to be Muslim, Reza Aslan. On Fox News, he was asked why he would write a book about Jesus, as a Muslim. Since the initial interview, many commentators criticized Fox News for asking such a question (the host Lauren Green has stated that she did not write this question, but merely asked it). Muslims understand Jesus as a prophet and important religious figure within Islam, so the question first betrays ignorance about the Islam. However, the question also seems strange in a context where Christians discuss Islam and Muslims as experts regularly, including many journalists and guests to Fox News. As Omid Safi notes (2013),

> Bernard Lewis, of British Jewish background, has certainly had a career (and a half) of speaking on Islam and Middle East.

Fox itself certainly has no issue putting on the uber-polemicist Robert Spencer (who is of Christian background, though we should not project his hatred on Christianity or all Christians) as an "expert" on Islam. And no one questioned him about his degrees in Islamic studies (he has none) or his command of Islamic languages (he has none) . . .

. . . But to have Muslims . . . come on air and discuss Jesus gets to the very heart of the privilege that the host at Fox tried to preserve for the Christian tradition . . .

Incidentally, someone should remind Lauren Green, the host at Fox, that she herself had no issues offering comments on a tradition other than her own. Which, by the way, was when she (a committed Christian from the African Methodist tradition) opined on Islam in a negative fashion: "Is there something in Islam itself that makes believers more susceptible to radicalization? . . . I believe essentially there are three things that may make Islam more prone to radicalization. One is the Koran itself."

Fox News responded to negative coverage of the story with an interview with the founder of the conservative Media Research Center, who claimed it was "the right question to ask" and that Green was a "good, good woman," while the host similarly commented on Green's caring character, in defense of the episode (quoted in Kludt 2013). The event was, again, reframed as one of Muslims (and/or Muslim sympathizers) attacking non-Muslims, even when the specific issue at hand involved Muslims' right to respect and toleration in society.

These examples demonstrate that in recent news media of internal issues related to Islam and Muslims, it has been held as normal for Christians and anyone else to say negative things about Muslims in storytelling or nonfictional accounts, and as abnormal and threatening when Muslims defend themselves in such situations or offer alternative, ordinary self-representation. The examples illustrate a media climate that tolerates negative messages about Muslims and Islam but challenges alternative views as somehow inappropriate in society. Negative views and clashes are foregrounded, and peaceful and ordinary Muslims in the United States or elsewhere are obscured. As negative media coverage has been seen to increase generally over time in this context (Abrahamian 2003; Amiri 2012; Salaita 2012), it is unsurprising that favorable opinions of Americans toward Islam and Muslims have decreased in the years since 9/11 (Pew 2010).

Negative views are also more prevalent than positive views in fictional accounts representing Islam and Muslims. Many films dealing with Muslims with sensitivity or in balanced ways have been produced since 9/11, but they have largely gone unwatched, like *All-American Muslim*. In some cases, these have been scrutinized as not morally acceptable forms of entertainment. For instance, *United 93* (2006), which portrays the terrorists on-board the title flight in a relatively humane and realistic light, was criticized for "cashing in" on 9/11 and not paying due respect for the victims of the attacks, in line with President Bush's view that it was wrong to portray 9/11 instigators as in any way reasonable or relatable (Thomas 2006). Other films portraying Muslims with more sensitivity were not mass-marketed or mass-released, signally their producers' understanding that their message would not be palatable to the public at large, such as documentaries dealing with the post-9/11 events in Iraq (for example, 2004's *Control Room* and 2007's *Taxi to the Dark Side* and *No End in Sight*).

Before 9/11 Muslims (and Arabs) were consistently shown in popular culture sources as terrorists and villains. The most infamous case is that of *True Lies* (1994). Defended by producer and lead actress Jamie Lee Curtis as "good fun," *True Lies* centers on a fictitious Muslim terrorist group called "Crimson Jihad," dedicated to the destruction of the United States. The film is clearly over-the-top, showing its hero (Arnold Schwarzenegger) riding horse-back through malls, while Curtis's character, a meek housewife-turned-freedom-fighter, kills several "Jihad" members by accidentally setting off a machine gun and dropping it down a flight of stairs. While it is possible that critical viewers understood the film satirically, mocking the action-adventure genre as a whole, for young audience members, it is doubtful that these unrealistic portrayals of Muslims were critically received. Perhaps due to its overall lack of realism, those involved with the film dismissed criticisms of its representations of Muslims and Islam in public, though they did add at the end of the film a disclaimer regarding its "entirely fictive" basis, after many Islamic/Muslim groups charged the film with perpetuating hate (Shaheen 2001).

Since 9/11, pop culture representations of Muslims have been produced more self-consciously. More recent popular films representing Islam and Muslims include *Crash* (2005), *Babel* (2006), and *Iron Man* (2008). These films provide mixed messages and occasionally critical ones, toward the dominant political discourse of Islamic terrorism. Nonetheless, negative stereotypes can also be seen to linger in these relatively popular and mainstream films, as the focus remains steadily on Muslims in association with terrorism.

Crash (which won three Oscars in 2005 for Best Picture, Best Original Screenplay, and Best Editing), aims chiefly to consider relational aspects of diversity, exploring interactions of poor whites, African Americans, Asians, and others in Los Angeles during a thirty-six-hour period of time. Among the several major characters is the Iranian American store-owning family: Farhad, Shereen, and Dorri. The movie challenges stereotypes of Muslims and Middle Easterners as Arabs, with Farhad remarking, "They think we're Arab. When did Persian become Arab?" and shows the characters as individuals in complex situations, facing mixed emotions and debates with each other and others in the film. Additionally, Farhad buys a gun to protect his family against the clear danger the family faces by white anti-Middle Eastern xenophobes in the film, which undermines the stereotype of Muslim terrorism, framing the issue instead as one caused by white ethnocentrism.

Yet as one of few Muslims in the film (and the leading one), Farhad's character also seems to support representations of Muslims as irrational and violent. Farhad is paranoid about protecting himself and his family, and has a tendency toward violence in the film, wrongly (by audience reception) suspecting discrimination by a locksmith, whose innocent (white) daughter he haphazardly shoots at – fortunately with blanks. The representation, while not lacking in complexity, is nonetheless mixed, overall, leaving one commentator to state that despite the film's challenge to many popular stereotypes of minorities,

> Western media images of the Middle East as being full of deranged and fanatical peoples are not really challenged by this portrait and the contemporary threat to the Western City remains at the door of this other in the overall affect of the film.
>
> (Gormley 2007: 26)

In a film about the challenges and complexities involved in collaborating with others in settings marked by diversity, Muslims are still represented as violent, reactionary, and threatening.

Like *Crash*, *Babel* (2006) ties together various ethnically and nationally diverse characters, this time located around the world, and with regard to international terrorism. When a young Moroccan boy tests out his aim with a new rifle, accidentally shooting a white U.S. woman on a tour bus (played by Cate Blanchett), the Moroccan government hunts the boy as a terrorist, and the incident is portrayed as a terrorist plot against U.S. citizens by news broadcasters in the United States, Japan, and elsewhere. While sympathetically portraying the young, unintentional terrorist, the message remains that U.S. citizens are victimized by Muslims recklessly wielding and distributing deadly weapons.

Furthermore, in most sympathetically dramatizing the events in the lives of the characters played by Blanchett and costar Brad Pitt, one is more easily led to sympathize with their exasperation at the extraordinary problems they face getting medical help in Morocco, as roads are closed due to terrorist searches, and the town they find themselves in is without a medical doctor (though Pitt's character's outrageous behavior toward benevolent, helpful Muslims in the film is also sometimes painful to watch). While difficult (for the audience) sexual taboos, poverty, and ultimately pain and imprisonment are observed in the life of the Moroccan boy, creating a critical distance between him and the audience, Pitt emerges triumphantly and heroically in the film, fighting poor odds to save his wife in a place cast as pre-modern and less civilized (even toward its own citizens). In this film, one learns of how Muslims can be seen as terrorists and as backward, but not of how many Muslims are modern, fit in with U.S. norms, or can themselves be as heroic protagonists.

Iron Man (2008) also reveals a complex understanding of Muslims that nonetheless remains focused on the Muslim-as-terrorist framework, if significantly less so than previous popular film portrayals. The Iron Man (played by Robert Downey, Jr.) comes to understand that the Muslim world (in the film, Afghanistan) is victimized by the organization of international terrorism and Muslim terrorists, as is the United States; and against the terrorists, ordinary Afghani citizens are portrayed sympathetically. Additionally, there is a clear and present danger from the Iron Man's boss, a powerful American white man who is represented in the end of the film as just as fearful and cruel as the worst Muslim terrorists (though as significantly more modern, effective, and sophisticated). However, much of the plot centers on the Iron Man versus Muslim terrorists, and their plot to harm Americans, rather than their harm to innocent, peaceful Muslim citizens of Afghanistan. So while *Iron Man* offers the most complex rendering of Muslims out of these mainstream films that feature major representations of Islam, the associating of Muslims with terrorism remains ever-present, even if it is more critically addressed in this film. On the other hand, no popular film in the United States prominently represents Muslims as ordinary members of society; the narrowest margin of Muslim experiences is predominant, even when films play with, or express criticality toward, the stereotype. As one optimistic critic of *Iron Man* thus wrote:

> Being a Muslim myself, I'm very sensitive to Hollywood's demonizing of Muslims. I understand that United States is at war with some Muslims, and that Hollywood happens to be in the US, but it still irks me when I see Americans being portrayed as the heroes of the world and Muslims as their heathen counter-parts.
>
> To be fair, the movie did only demonize some "bad Muslims" that were actually oppressing innocent Muslim. This, in itself, is admirable. Also, one Muslim is even shown siding with and befriending Iron Man. And last but not least, the movie did touch upon the topic of American corporations selling arms to its own nation's enemies. The actual enemy ended up being an American as well so it wasn't as bad as with most movies out there that use Muslims as the new Nazis unapologetically.
>
> All in all, the movie really was great and extremely entertaining. Its handling of Muslims as enemies rubbed me the wrong way, *but was still handled better than most movies out there*.
>
> (Osama 2008; emphasis added)

The most critically reflective mainstream representations of Islam and Muslims in film are in Michael Moore's *Fahrenheit 911* and *Team America: World Police*, both released in 2004. Frequently, these two films provide critical commentaries on the representation of Muslims as terrorists. In *Fahrenheit 911* Moore explicitly argues that the media dramatizes Muslim terrorism while dismissing that perpetrated by non-Muslims, showing a peaceful, modern Iraq before the latest U.S. intervention. *Team America* satirically features a U.S. actor as the (animated) hero, whose role is to uncover terrorist plots by acting like a "Muslim terrorist," successfully entering terrorist cells by babbling incoherently about Allah and jihad (the actor initially professes to know little to nothing of Islam and Arabic, but is nonetheless encouraged to "act" his way into the cells, which he does to the audience's intended astonishment and laughter). Both films can be read as providing critical messages about U.S. institutions and mass media and popular culture, invoking and referencing in mocking ways movies and journalism that represent Muslims chiefly as terrorists.

Yet as with *True Lies*, and the other films discussed here, a more mixed, and thus less critical, message can be received by audiences to these films, as well. Particularly for young people (who are, again, among the target audience), who are likely unfamiliar with or uninterested in political commentary, the focus remains on Muslims seen as terrorists – not as ordinary citizens, or good people, or as victims of biased mainstream media representation. In fact, many reviewers and audiences find *Team America*'s treatment of Muslims neither satirical nor critical:

> The most offensive part of the film for me is the scene in which the protagonist, disguised as an Islamist (in a hilarious fashion playing on the American stereotype of the Middle Eastern terrorist – this does not offend me), wins his way into the terrorists' hearts and minds with a story about his own suffering at American hands. He tells a story about the "infidels" coming in Blackhawk helicopters to his village and killing his favourite *goats*. Everyone cries. This angers me for many reasons. First is the idea that Islamists are fighting for reasons as trivial as the killing of a goat – all the other terrorists start crying their eyes out at this story. The implication of close bonds between Muslim people and goats is pretty racist too, and it would be hilarious that this American is so off-target but for the fact that all the Islamists around him are so moved. . . . I don't think too many people in Fallujah would find that gag funny.
>
> Of course, this movie is not for the people of Fallujah. It's for the people of America. But to the latter, this movie just represents a propaganda piece that says, hey, everything's fine, hilarious even.
>
> (Kelly 2005; emphasis in the original)

For children and youth, it is hard to imagine that any critical message regarding the representation of Muslims as terrorists would be found in *Team America*. In addition, there are no ordinary, non-terrorist Muslims in *Team America*. In *Fahrenheit 911* stereotypical images are shown far more than are any other sorts of images of Muslims, echoing mainstream norms while also arguing against them.

In television too, more critical mainstream messages are beginning to emerge. Alongside *Shahs of Sunset* is today's *Homeland,* which continually played in its first and second seasons (in 2011 and 2012) with the notion that Muslims are dangerous. Its first season focuses on whether (fictional) recently returned U.S. prisoner-of-war Nicholas Brody is a war hero, or a "turned" enemy spy and terrorist. Through gradually revealing information about the mysterious Brody – such as that he became a Muslim during his imprisonment – the show encourages its viewers to think about whether being Muslim is suspicious, and possibly feel guilty as information is also revealed that makes Brody appear less and less as a villain. In the second season, something similar happens (on a smaller scale) with the treatment of a Muslim American CIA agent, who is also revealed over time to be falsely accused, rather than guilty, of participating in a terrorist plot.

Though provocative and critical, the story so far has framed every Muslim character as a potential or actual terrorist. Ultimately, there are no non-suspicious Muslims in the world of *Homeland*.

In summary, Muslim "bad guys" are not difficult to find in mainstream media in the United States, including news media since 9/11, about the event and its aftermath; in discussions of the "Arab Spring" today, and in domestic news stories. Even in stories that are focused on the harms of negative media stereotyping of Muslims, or the potential value of positive representation, Muslims appear framed as if they are overstepping bounds. Negative messages are boldly defended, and alternative discourses subject to scrutiny. In this context, the message emerges that negative discourses are more appropriate than positive ones. This message no doubt reflects a public understanding increasingly unfavorable toward Muslims and Islam over the course of the last decade (Pew 2010). In film and television fictional accounts, we have more reason to be hopeful. Muslims *are* being portrayed as both good and bad, and not merely as terrorists, although the terrorist script of danger and violence is always readily apparent, even in more mixed and critical framings. One must still *search* for the diversity within Islam, to find more than terrorists and crazed gunslingers, and learn about the vast majority of ordinary Muslims in the United States and worldwide.

Conclusion

To be clear, adults and young people do not view popular movies, or even news coverage of political or social events, as valid, transparent truth. As discussed here, researchers understand that people respond to media in a variety of passive and active or critical ways, comparing the data presented with their prior experience and knowledge of a situation or a group. However, when exposure to negative viewpoints about Muslims is sanctioned, while positive representations are subject to criticism, protest, and arguments for censorship (as in the case of *All-American Muslim,* and in Fox News' coverage of Reza Aslan), the field of experience of the public is limited, precluding the development of the kind of comparative framework one might hope to be able to develop in flipping the channel or web browser between Fox and CNN. People may consider what they watch and hear about Muslims and Islam critically, but they need alternative sources of evidence to do so. Mainstream, easily accessible news and popular culture media thus restrict what can be known about Muslims and Islam, when it emphasizes violence and culture clashes, even with regard to Muslims' desires to not experience discrimination and prejudice in society.

As of 2010, more Americans stated their opinion of Islam was unfavorable than favorable (38% and 30%, respectively); 38% agreed with the statement that Islam was more likely to encourage violence than other religions (Pew 2010). These findings are well aligned with what the media covers and fails to cover, as media stories about Muslims and Islam inside and outside the United States became more negative over time, since 2002. As I have discussed here, representations in U.S. media and popular culture of Muslims hardly scratch the surface when it comes to the diversity of the group of believers, worldwide. Out of heterogeneous images and narratives, realistic and fantastic, ultimately emerges a common, normalized associating of Muslims with terrorism and/or conflict, violence, irrationality, and overreaction.

While the attacks of 9/11, in the context of the mainstream media's tendency to feature the extraordinary – the ordinary just is not seen as "news" – informs, inevitably perhaps, such an association, in later events involving Muslims mainstream media sources also *normally* frame them as unnecessarily antagonistic or combative, even when the subject's expressed goal is to *diminish* negative and harmful prejudice and stereotyping. And while mixed messages are perhaps most popular today in film and television portrayals, the association of Muslims with terrorism nonetheless lingers on, as few (if any) mass-marketed sources represent Muslims without major, prevalent references to terrorism. The result is that even if media do not intend to *teach* audiences and the public to associate Muslims with terrorism, their audiences will nonetheless learn that it is *normal* to do so – that it is recognized in the mainstream media as reasonable or acceptable, rather than significant in harmfulness to Muslims, who face discrimination, prejudice, and hatefulness when the breadth of their realities goes unknown, lacking an education that critically responds to the predominant stereotype.

Education in a democratic society can play an important role here. It can inspire people to seek out alternative information sources and attempt to understand information in an independent way. It can thus enable people to participate more effectively within a liberal democratic society, by voicing critical and skeptical alternative perspectives, questioning slanted stories, and otherwise taking part in public life, actively deliberating about important issues rather than passively accepting dominant discourses. In the next section, I consider the state of public education about Islam and Muslims today, before discussing how education can do more to decrease the influence of biased perspectives and empower young people as citizens to see the social and political world more clearly, while the media will no doubt continue to tell ghost stories that haunt rather than inspire us, when it comes to the United States, Muslims, and Islam.

References

Abrahamian, Ervand. "The US Media, Huntington, and September 11." *Third World Quarterly* 24 (2003): 529–544.

Aladdin. Movie. Directed by Ron Clements and John Musker. Burbank: Walt Disney Studios, 1992.

Amiri, Mohammad Abid. "Muslim Americans and the Media After 9/11." *Islam and Muslim Societies: A Social Sciences Journal* 5 (2012): 1–13.

Babel. Movie. Directed by Alejandro González Iñárritu. Hollywood: Paramount, 2006.

Borradori, Giovanna. "Dialogue with Jürgen Habermas." In *Philosophy in a Time of Terror: Dialogues with Jürgen Habermas and Jacques Derrida*. Chicago: University of Chicago Press, 2003.

Bush, George W. "Statement by the President in His Address to the Nation," speech delivered, Washington, DC, September 11, 2001.

Bush, George W. "Americans Will Not Be Intimidated," speech delivered, Annapolis, Maryland, November 30, 2005.
Carey, James A. "American Journalism On, Before, and After September 11." In *Journalism After September 11,* edited by Barbie Zelizer and Stuart Allan, 71–90. London: Routledge, 2002.
CNN. "Attacks Draw Mixed Response in the Mideast." *CNNWorld,* September 12, 2001. archives.cnn.com/2001/WORLD/europe/09/12/mideast.reaction/ (accessed October 18, 2013).
Common Core. "English Language Arts Standards: Speaking and Listening, Grade 9–10." 2012. www.corestandards.org/ELA-Literacy/SL/9–10 (accessed October 18, 2013).
Control Room. Movie. Directed by Jehane Noujaim. New York: Magnolia, 2004.
Cortés, Carlos E. "How the Media Teach." In *Media Literacy: Transforming Curriculum and Teaching,* edited by Gretchen Schwarz and Pamela U. Brown, 55–73. Malden: Blackwell, 2005.
Council on American-Islamic Relations. *American Public Opinion About Muslims and Islam, 2006.* Washington, DC: Council on American-Islamic Relations, 2006.
Crash. Movie. Directed by Paul Haggis. Los Angeles: Bob Yari, 2005.
Dixon, Marion. "An Arab Spring." *Review of African Political Economy* 38 (2011): 309–316.
Editorial. "It's Racist, But Hey, It's Disney." *New York Times,* July 14, 1993.
Esposito, John. "The Madness Over All-American Muslim." *Washington Post,* December 16, 2011. www.washingtonpost.com/blogs/on-faith/post/the-madness-over-all-american-muslim/2011/12/16/gIQAquwtyO_blog.html (accessed October 18, 2013).
Fahrenheit 911. Movie. Directed by Michael Moore. Burbank: Lions Gate, 2004.
Fallows, James. "Nothing to Celebrate in Saddam's Hanging: This Act Makes Neither America Nor Iraq Look Good." *The Atlantic,* January 1, 2007. www.theatlantic.com/magazine/archive/2007/01/nothing-to-celebrate-in-saddams-hanging/305577/ (accessed January 8, 2014).
Finn, Jr., Chester E. Introduction to *September 11: What Our Children Need to Know,* edited by the Fordham Foundation, 4–11. Washington, DC: Thomas B. Fordham Foundation, 2002. www.edexcellence.net/publications/sept11.html (accessed January 8, 2014).
Fox News. "Is '24' Hurting Muslims? Bill O'Reilly, the O'Reilly Factor." *Fox News,* January 22, 2007. www.foxnews.com/story/2007/01/22/is-24-hurting-muslims/ (accessed January 8, 2014).
Galal, Ehab, and Riem Spielhaus. "Covering the Arab Spring: Middle East in the Media – the Media in the Middle East." *Global Media Journal* 2 (2012): 1–6.
Gormley, Paul. "Crash and the City: Race and Rage on the Streets of L.A." *Intellect Quarterly* 5 (2007): 24–26.
Hall, Stuart. "Encoding/Decoding." In *Culture, Media, Language: Working Papers in Cultural Studies.* London: Hutchinson, 1973.
Iron Man. Movie. Directed by Jon Favreau. Hollywood: Paramount, 2008.
Jackson, Liz. "Images of Islam in U.S. Media and Their Educational Implications." *Educational Studies* 46 (2010): 3–24.
Kamalipour, Yahya R., ed. *U.S. Media and the Middle East: Image and Perception.* Westport: Praeger, 1997.
Karim, Karim A. *Islamic Peril: Media and Global Violence.* London: Black Rose, 2003.

Kellner, Douglas. "September 11, the Media, and War Fever." *Television and News Media* 3 (2002): 143–151.

Kellner, Douglas. "September 11, Terror War, and Blowback." In *Miseducation of the West: How Schools and the Media Distort Our Understanding of the Islamic World*, edited by Joe Kincheloe and Shirley R. Steinberg, 25–42. Westport: Praeger, 2004.

Kelly, Mark G. E. "Only in America: On *Team America: World Police*." *Bright Lights Film Journal*, May 2005. www.brightlightsfilm.com/48/teamamerica.htm (accessed January 8, 2014).

Kludt, Tom. "Fox News Defends Anchor Who Grilled Reza Aslan Over Being Muslim." *Talking Points Memo*, July 31, 2013. http://livewire.talkingpointsmemo.com/entry/fox-news-defends-anchor-who-grilled-aslan-video (accessed January 8, 2014).

Knowles, David. "All-American Muslim: A Review." *Hollywood Reporter*, November 8, 2011. www.hollywoodreporter.com/review/all-american-muslim-tv-review-258770 (accessed January 8, 2014).

Levine, Peter. "Educating Voters in a Time of Political Polarization." *Democracy Fund*, June 13, 2013. www.democracyfund.org/blog/entry/educating-voters-in-a-time-of-political-polarization (accessed January 8, 2014).

Maghbouleh, Neda. "'Shahs of Sunset': The Real Iranians of Los Angeles?" *Salon*, December 1, 2012. www.salon.com/2012/12/01/shahs_of_sunset_the_real_iranians_of_los_angeles/ (accessed January 8, 2014).

Morley, David. *The "Nationwide" Audience: Structure and Decoding*. London: BFI, 1980.

Mousa, Issam Suleiman. *The Arab Image in the U.S. Press*. New York: Peter Lang, 1984.

Mulan. Movie. Directed by Tony Bancroft and Barry Cook. Burbank: Walt Disney Studios, 1998.

NBC. "Muslims Rip '24' for Renewed Terror Role: Islam Groups Fear Backlash; Show Says It Portrays Wide Range of Wrongdoers." *Today*, January 18, 2007. www.today.com/id/16691306#.Ugs4nGQpZcQ (accessed January 8, 2014).

No End in Sight. Movie. Directed by Charles Ferguson. New York: Magnolia, 2007.

Osama. "The Iron Man Movie: A Muslim Point of View." *Towards Mecca*, May 12, 2008. http://towardsmecca.com/2008/05/12/the-iron-man-movie-a-muslim-point-of-view/ (accessed January 8, 2014).

Palmer, Allen W. "The Arab Image in Newspaper Political Cartoons." in Kamalipour, ed., *U.S. Media and the Middle East*. In *U.S. Media and the Middle East: Image and Perception*, edited by Yahya R. Kamalipour. Westport: Praeger, 1997.

Palmer, Monte, and Princess Palmer. *Islamic Extremism: Causes, Diversity, and Challenges*. New York: Rowman & Littlefield, 2008.

Pew Research Center for the People and the Press. "Public Remains Conflicted Over Islam: NYC Mosque Opposed, Muslims' Right to Build Mosques Favored." *The Pew Forum on Religion and Public Life*, August 2010.

Ravitch, Diane. *The Language Police: How Pressure Groups Restrict What Students Learn*. New York: Vintage, 2004.

Safi, Omid. "What Fox News vs. Reza Aslan Is Really About (Hint: Not Just Fox News' Idiocy." *Religious News Service*, July 29, 2013. http://omidsafi.religionnews.com/2013/07/29/reza/ (accessed January 8, 2014).

Said, Edward W. *Orientalism*. New York: Vintage, 1979.

Said, Edward W. *Covering Islam: How the Media and the Experts Determine How We See the Rest of the World*. New York: Vintage, 1997.

Salaita, Steven. "Corporate American Media Coverage of Arab Revolutions: The Contradictory Message of Modernity." *Interface: A Journal for and About Social Movements* 4 (2012): 131–145. www.interfacejournal.net/wordpress/wp-content/uploads/2012/05/Interface-4-1-Salaita.pdf (accessed October 18, 2013).

Schrag, Robert L., and Manoocher N. Javidi. "Through a Glass Darkly: American Media Images of Middle Eastern Cultures and Their Potential Impact on Young People." In *U.S. Media and the Middle East: Image and Perception*, edited by Yahya R. Kamalipour, 212–221. Westport: Praeger, 1997.

Shaheen, Jack G. *The TV Arab*. Bowling Green: Bowling Green University Press, 1984.

Shaheen, Jack G. *Reel Bad Arabs*. Brooklyn: Olive Branch Press, 2001.

Smith, Aaron, and Lee Rainie. *The Internet and the 2008 Election*. Washington, DC: Pew Internet and American Life Project, 2008.

Steinberg, Shirley R. "Desert Minstrels: Hollywood's Curriculum of Arabs and Muslims." In *Miseducation of the West: How Schools and the Media Distort Our Understanding of the Islamic World*, edited by Joe Kincheloe and Shirley R. Steinberg, 171–180. Westport: Praeger, 2004.

Steuter, Erin, & Deborah Wills. *At War with Metaphor: Media, Propaganda, and Racism in the War on Terror*. Lanham: Lexington, 2008.

Taxi to the Dark Side. Movie. Directed by Alex Gibney. New York: THINKFilm, 2007.

Team America. Movie. Directed by Trey Parker. Hollywood: Paramount, 2004.

Thomas, June, Agger, Michael, Lithwick, Dahlia, and Meghan O'Rourke. "*United 93*: A Brief *Slate* Debate About the Controversial New Movie." *Slate*, April 6, 2006. www.slate.com/articles/arts/culturebox/2006/04/united_93.html (accessed January 8, 2014).

True Lies. Movie. Directed by James Cameron. Hollywood: Twentieth Century Fox, 1994.

United 93. Movie. Directed by Paul Greengrass. Universal City: Universal, 2006.

4 Islam and Muslims in public schools

Introduction

As we saw in the last chapter, discourses in the mass media that focus on Muslims and Islam often connect them with conflict, violence, and terrorism, normalizing the association in mainstream society today. Though more mixed, good and bad, representations are also emerging, particularly in fictional film and television media, they remain difficult to find in nonfictional media, as Muslim experts or "all-American" Muslims can face challenges today when they resist and (more unwittingly) embody challenges to the patriotic-assimilationist discourse of "clash of civilizations."

However, media is not the sole source of education about different groups and religions in society and worldwide. This chapter explores how Islam and Muslims are being represented in U.S. public schools today, with special attention to changes in representation since 9/11. I focus on state educational standards for social studies and textbooks in world history and geography, examining how Islam and Muslims are discussed in these resources. More substantive and factual than those provided in the mass media, representations of Islam and Muslims in standards and textbooks are clearly less biased and partial than media representations, and are also a major improvement on past educational treatments. However, typical educational representations are minimal, usually historical, and identify Islam and Muslims in contemporary settings with conflicts in the Middle East and Western Asia and terrorism, given the focus, as in the media, on the narrowest minority of Muslim experiences seen as exceptional and socially significant from a U.S. foreign policy perspective. After reviewing these sources, I also consider other important elements of formal (school) education: evidence about teachers' pedagogy and beliefs, and their use of supplementary resources, which is quite common in social studies subjects today.

Such coverage mirrors more than it provides a counterbalance to predominant views in media, and it overall fails to meet the educational need to debunk stereotypes and add nuance to generalizations, or enable a balanced and more comprehensive understanding of Muslims and Islam in U.S. society and worldwide today. Additionally, it is worrisome to note the impact of assimilationist, "clash of civilizations" thinking on textbook approval processes today. As in the media, there is not just a possibility of slanted information being provided. Instead, there is an active campaign to censor educators from providing alternative viewpoints, as assimilationists argue for no educational tolerance of difference in the case of Islam, as we saw in the second chapter. Textbooks, produced by private publishers who aim to profit, are no different from mainstream media in the sense of being shaped, in an indirect but nonetheless meaningful way, by a cross-section of the public that may not be particularly well-informed, and as a result, may not act in its own best interest, but instead protests views contrary to the most simplistic, "patriotic" understanding of events like 9/11 and Islam and Muslims. Educators are also individually scrutinized for toleration, accused of "choosing the wrong side" when they teach toward pluralistic or critical multicultural goals. These are troubling developments when it comes to ensuring that education meets students' needs to learn about the world they live in and the people they live there with, in a relatively non-ideological, evidence-based information environment.

Islam and Muslims in educational standards

Standards are one of today's basic means for guiding teaching practices and evaluating public school teachers' success in teaching content knowledge in reading, math, science, and social studies. Standards normally discuss what content knowledge students should know, and related skills: learning outcomes at various educational levels within different subjects. No official standards currently exist for social studies at the national level, though the Common Core State Standards Initiative (2012) is one organization pushing for national standards today. Nearly all states set lengthy standards to ensure that students graduate from public high schools with knowledge of world history and geography, U.S. history, and contemporary political and social affairs (in courses such as civics, world affairs, U.S. society, etc.). Regularly revised, typically in public view (most states make standards documents available to the public on government websites), the standards are developed to indicate what information and topics teachers should emphasize, to ensure college preparation, and possibly also to provide civic values, local socialization, and related knowledge.

Standards for social studies education may not be as helpful for informing the most appropriate pedagogy and approach to the subject, in comparison with other subjects, like English or math, and I will discuss some different perspectives on this issue in the sixth chapter of this text. One limitation critical multiculturalists point out is that the time normally allotted to the subject overall is insufficient for enabling the broad or deep exploration of many significant social issues (Kincheloe 2001). The potential for exploring any topic in history or geography is seemingly endless, but with a small amount of time allocated to these subjects, there is a risk of trying to teach too much content knowledge, which can result in a focus on facts over development of skills. In relation, teaching facts is often seen as easier and possibly more important than teaching skills, particularly as high-stakes testing becomes increasingly popular and significant to student progression and teacher performance evaluation; thus, "fragmented, content-driven history programs often run students through a series of memorizations, barring them from a deeper exploration into an event or a period of history" (Kincheloe 2001: 596).

For instance, teachers in Illinois are held accountable for teaching students in eighth grade to "identify causes and effects of turning points in world political history," including "the rise of the Islamic empire" (Illinois State Board of Education 2008: 36). While another standard involves students identifying the relationship between fact and interpretation, this (sole) reference to Islam or Muslims in the Illinois state standards suggests a preferred interpretation of the causes and effects of the rise of Islam across a vast physical region, which students are expected merely to identify, rather than weigh and evaluate amongst other possible factors. Diverse perspectives exist on the causes and effects of the rise of the "Islamic empire," in different geographical, cultural, and historical contexts; this becomes clear when one considers textbook discussions of this topic, in the next sections of this chapter. From a historical perspective, there is no single, correct, one-sentence position on such a topic, or any ideal way to choose one answer over another as official school knowledge, on this or other complex social questions. And given the quantity of standards, time does not allow for a critical classroom examination of different perspectives, or for students to develop nuanced points of view on this or other standards topics.

As in Illinois, in most state standards, there is no significant emphasis on students learning very much about Muslims, particularly in modern history. Islam and Muslims are only included in standards for world history and world geography courses, of which most states require at least one course at the middle-school level, and one to two years in high school. Though frameworks also require high school U.S. history and government and/or civics, and home state history and geography, Islam is not a subject requiring coverage in these courses. Islam's representation within these frameworks is fairly homogenous. At the very least, states require in world history and/or geography the following:

1 A comparison of the basic beliefs and practices of Muslims with those of other large-scale or world religions
2 Identification of the five pillars, the prophet Muhammad's vision, the Koran as the perceived word of Allah (God), and some reasons for Islam's early growth
3 Some basic appreciation for the cultural and scientific, mathematical, and technological achievements/heritage of Islamic civilization

Such standards position Muslims' significance in the world within the medieval era rather than within contemporary life. Muslims' relegation to the historical and geographical domain in educational standards (rather than in U.S. Geography and/or Civics) surely attributes to this emphasis on the basic cultural information and pre-modern history of Islam. Yet where Muslims do appear in more modern or contemporary standards, they hardly fare better in terms of the nature of their representation. The one common standard referencing Muslims beyond ancient or medieval history regards conflicts in the Middle East and Western Asia, in relation to the United States' interests in the region. For instance, the State of Georgia mandates in seventh-grade social studies' second unit titled "The Modern Middle East" (2008, emphases in original):

> Students will examine how *conflict and change* have shaped and continue to shape the political boundaries of this region. When examining the specific elements of *culture,* students will work towards a deeper understanding of the prominent religions in the area. Students will examine the *governance* of the region including the role religion plays in governance and international relations of this area . . .

One notices immediately in this introductory text to the standard guidelines that "conflict and change" and "culture" are highlighted, with religion emphasized in relation to both culture and governance. Such a focus on conflict and change is not present in state standards for other world regions, such as Africa or Southeast Asia.

The Georgia standards also include the following:

a Explain the historical reasons for the establishment of the modern State of Israel in 1948; include the Jewish religious connection to the land, the Holocaust, anti-Semitism, and Zionism in Europe.
b Describe how land and religion are reasons for continuing conflicts in Southwest Asia (Middle East).
c Explain U.S. presence and interest in Southwest Asia; include the Persian Gulf conflict and invasions of Afghanistan and Iraq.
(Georgia Department of Education 2008)

As regularly revised documents, these standards have changed slightly in the last few years. Before 2008, these standards read as the following (Jackson 2011):

a Explain the historical reason for the establishment of the modern state of Israel in 1948; include anti-Semitism in Europe, Zionism, and the Holocaust.
b Describe the continuing conflicts between Israel and the Arab world.
c Explain the economic impact of oil on the region.
d Explain U.S. involvement and interest in North Africa/Southwest Asia; include the Persian Gulf War, invasion of Afghanistan, and Operation Iraqi Freedom.

One can see that changes made to these standards reflect a focus on religion as the source of conflicts, as in the contemporary media discussions of the Middle East; additionally the "Jewish connection" to the land has been emphasized in the new standard text, while Zionism has been linked through phrasing to Europe, and anti-Semitism detached from it. As I will discuss in relationship to textbook approval, documents such as these standards are scrutinized not only at the level of fact, but also for what they emphasize and how they frame issues: for what they include, and what they do not include. Teachers might think they should explain anti-Semitism in Europe in the earlier standards, but in the later standards, they are encouraged to teach of anti-Semitism generally but of Zionism in Europe, although in either case, both phenomena require consideration within and outside Europe. It is not that one way of teaching the issues is absolutely correct or incorrect, but one frames Europeans more positively, which is a desire of many assimilationist educators, in relation to discussing Islam and Europe, Western civilization, or the United States, as discussed in the second chapter.

Another standard for the unit is

a   Compare the parliamentary democracy of the State of Israel, the monarchy of the Kingdom of Saudi Arabia, and theocracy of the Islamic Republic of Iran, distinguishing the form of leadership and the role of the citizen in terms of voting rights and personal freedoms.
(Georgia Department of Education 2008)

Again, this standard is not asking teachers to give misinformation or an inappropriate framework for understanding Middle Eastern politics. However its choice of countries results in an interpretation of the Middle East, apart from Israel, as extremely restrictive and oppressive. According to Freedom House's (2012) survey of worldwide political rights and civil liberties, Saudi Arabia and Iran are two of the most restrictive and oppressive countries in the region. Labeled as "not free," Saudi Arabia has particularly been featured by Freedom House (among other organizations) as one of the most restrictive and oppressive countries worldwide (2012), while several Middle Eastern countries are listed in the middle of category, of "partly free," such as Lebanon, Jordan, Kuwait, and Bahrain in 2007, contemporary with the standards document (Freedom House 2007). Saudi Arabia and Iran are also exceptional (even within the Middle East) for gender oppression; both are in the top ten worst countries for women worldwide, according to the Global Gender Gap Index of the World Economic Forum (Hausmann, Tyson, & Zahidi 2011). (For reference, the United Arab Emirates, Kuwait, and Bahrain, are in the 25th percentile). Indeed, none of these countries are exemplars of political liberty or gender equality. However, by focusing on Iran and Saudi Arabia in contrast with Israel one of the bleakest possible pictures is provided.

Georgia's standards are much more substantial than that of others, when it comes to Islam and Muslims. Many standards hardly mention Islam, though they are lengthy and specific with regard to what content should be covered. In Oregon social sciences standards (Oregon State Board of Education 2011: 12), there is one reference to Islam: "Describe and compare the beliefs, the spread, and the influence of religions throughout Europe, Asia, and Africa, Islam, Crusades, Holy Roman Empire." Californian standards (2000–2009; California State Board of Education 2000) require roughly equal coverage of the birth and development of Islamic/Muslim civilizations in the Middle Ages (treated as one subject) and each of the following: (2) ancient Egyptian civilization, (3) Judaism, (4) Ancient Greece, (5) early India and China, and (6) early Rome; civilizations of the Middle Ages in (7) Rome, (8) China, (9) Japan, (10) sub-Saharan Africa, (11) Europe, and (12) Meso-America; and (13) the European Renaissance, (14) the Reformation, and (15) the Scientific Revolution. Given Islam's place as the second largest practiced religion (making up about 23% of the world's population), it seems strange that Muslims and Islam should be given less total space than Chinese or Roman civilizations, and less than one-tenth of curricular space dealing with world history and geography. The Middle East, Western Asia, and Southeast Asia (where Muslims are in the majority) are also absent as regions of significance in California, as they are in Oregon, only referenced in pre-modern history and with regard to American interests and interventions.

Islam's minor representation in standards is no doubt related to its being a religion, as coverage of Islam in the standards generally mirrors that afforded to other world religions such as Christianity, Judaism, Hinduism, and Buddhism, which tends to be quite insubstantial, owing to the tense relationship between church and state, within and outside public schools (Kincheloe 2001; Noddings 1993; Nord 1995). Teachers can be afraid to discuss religion in public schools for fears of being accused of proselytizing. This is a likely possibility today for educators in more conservative communities, as I will discuss in more detail later in this chapter, who risk being accused of indoctrination when aiming to portray religious diversity (and Islam) sympathetically. Though it has always been the case that public schoolteachers are legally permitted to teach about one or more religions, many people see a gray area in practice, between proselytization and education. As religion can be politically divisive, teachers can also be nervous about being seen to impact student's political beliefs and attitudes. In the more subjective realm of religious belief, people fear that it is impossible to teach with a neutral and pluralist orientation, which expresses toleration toward a variety of traditions, without endorsing secularism, as an anti-religious stance, or moral relativism, the idea (incoherent in its practical implications) that all beliefs are equally valid or true (Nord 2010).

Nonetheless, students must learn to understand Islam and other religions in a more substantive, balanced way, to be prepared for democratic citizenship responsibilities of decision making and civic participation within a diverse liberal society. As I argued in the second chapter, it is possible to express a minimal toleration to discourage prejudice or ethnocentrism, while at the same time not endorsing or denigrating one or more religions. This may be challenging, as I will discuss in more detail in later chapters, but the alternative to the teaching of a diversity of beliefs (and unbelief) is a kind of de facto secular, anti-religious education, which is also inappropriate in the *religious* United States today, as Nord argues:

> *Public* institutions have a particular responsibility to take the public seriously. When our culture is deeply divided in matters of great importance – as is the case in regard to religion – then, in order to sustain social peace and community, it is imperative that we take each other seriously and not align our public institutions with any particular faction. To exclude some voices from the conversation is to disenfranchise people, much as if they were not allowed to vote. Public education has, in effect, disenfranchised religious folk.
>
> (1995: 377–378; emphasis in the original)

As Nord suggests, to avoid discussing religions because they are controversial is to misrepresent religious communities as unimportant or unreasonable within the public sphere, despite their prominence and place in human social life. It results in an incomplete education about U.S. society and the world today. The situation is particularly grave with regard to Islam, given the nature of information about the religion and community available elsewhere in society, from the media to the textbooks. Indeed, as the next sections show, teachers increasingly face an upward challenge in discussing Islam and Muslims since 9/11 without focusing more or less exclusively on terrorism and violence.

Islam and Muslims in the textbooks: Historical and political perspectives

From a historical perspective, things have greatly improved in terms of the nature of the representation of Muslims and Islam in U.S. school textbooks. William Griswold (1975) has documented how in the early-twentieth century, textbook discourse was heavily biased and ethnocentric, depicting a world in which all people were striving to catch up with European or Western civilization, and highlighting bizarre and unusual practices that hardly characterize any past or present Muslim group, such as drinking pen ink. A text called *Natural Advanced Geography* from 1898 states of people in the Middle East that "these people have gradually become somewhat civilized, though their civilization is as rude and imperfect as that of Europe was a thousand years ago"; none "have become civilized enough to know how to organize governments for the benefit of the mass of people" (Redway & Hinman 1898: 135, 136; quoted in Morgan 2008: 327). Muslims are called "Mohammedans," a term offensive to Muslims in its suggesting of Muslim allegiance to the prophet Muhammad rather than Allah (God), and while

> the majority of the authors don't directly state that Islam is a violent or backward religion . . . because they say that the people of this faith are

backward, strange, hateful, and violent, a reader can easily come to the conclusion that it is the religion of those people which is the cause of their behavior.

(Morgan 2002: 162)

The picture does not improve a great deal from 1920–1940:

> *The World and Its People* has about fifteen pictures, which . . . portray an almost primitive way of life; almost all of them have people on camels. They, the people, are dressed in robes. There is only one picture of a city (Cairo), but this is a poor picture . . . because there is only one person in it, and he is wearing a robe near a donkey. This suggests that most people in Cairo wear robes and use animals for transportation. The authors could have featured a more typical scene showing a busy city street full of cars, and some people wearing more modern clothing.
>
> (Morgan 2002: 89)

Other texts note that "making raids is carried out by so many of the Arabs" and that "Mohammedans . . . attempted to make people accept their faith by the sword," emphasizing Muslims as uncivilized and violent (Branom & Ganey 1928: 117; Brigham & McFarlane 1933: 295; quoted in Morgan 2002: 99, 117). Similar biases have been found in analyses of popular world history and geography textbooks of the 1980s and early 1990s (Abukhattala 2004; Barlow 1995; Morgan 2002; 2008).

Textbooks of the late-1990s and before 9/11 are, as a whole, less negative in the way they represent Islam and Muslims in world history and today, but highly minimal overall, owing in part to the unique textbook production and adoption process that has developed over the last few decades. As Frances Fitzgerald noted (1979: 22–24),

> Texts are not "written" anymore; they are, as the people in the industry say, "developed," and this process involves large numbers of people and many compromises . . . In the matter of prose style, the editors invariably impose constraints on the writer. The public schools require that all textbooks be adjusted to standard reading level . . . The text houses must therefore see to it that all manuscripts follow standard "readability" formulas, which measure the frequently with which difficult words occur and the complexity of the sentence structure . . . Since few historians can contrive to write by these rules, the editors usually have to rewrite the final draft. In the process, they may or may not change the essential meaning of the original, but, almost necessarily, they remove all individuality from the writing, homogenizing it so that it is in fact nearly unreadable.
>
> In respect to political content, too, the editors have a fairly good idea what will and what will not sell. . . .

Today's textbook approval processes, which consider the needs and interests of various private groups, make the task of presenting adequately and substantively the complexity and breadth of the social domain highly challenging. As Texas, Florida, and California account for one-third of total textbook sales (Finn & Ravitch 2004), their approval processes are consequential for the whole country, ultimately deciding which texts will be produced. Those participating in Texas's process thus engage in "an exertion of power that attempts to control the contents of the U.S. history book" (de Leon Mendiola 2007: 60):

> The theory behind the practice . . . is that some educational authority should stand between the world of commerce and the hard-pressed teachers to insure that the books meet educational standards. The standards are not, however, entirely academic. . . .
>
> The whole system is less than democratic, because it is biased toward the large adoption units . . . toward the ones that make a narrow selection of books. For example, the recommendation of a social-studies book by the Texas State Textbook Committee can make a difference of hundreds of thousands of dollars to a publisher. Consequently, that committee has traditionally had a strong influence on the context of texts. . . .
>
> Because of the Texas State Textbook Committee, New England children, whose ancestors heartily disapproved of the Mexican War, have grown up with heroic tales of Davy Crockett and Sam Houston. . . .
>
> The school establishment is not the only group that shapes American history in the textbooks. It is often private-interest groups or citizens' organizations that bring about the most important political changes to the texts. . . .
>
> (Fitzgerald 1979: 33–35)

As is the case in producing educational standards, what goes on in the Texas textbook approval debates is less about what knowledge is correct or incorrect, than about whose views or orientation should be represented, as well as the ends of social studies education in terms of the development of attitudes about the world. Pluralist demands for recognition of the plight of sociopolitical minorities in society versus assimilationists' interests in a particular form of patriotic education collide here, as can be seen in a transcript from a recent approval process:

> At the August hearing, Penny Venerable said, and I quote, "Multiculturalism conflicts with patriotism" I used to be like Ms. Venerable frightened of change. I no longer am. You see, I love my son-in-law, Dr. Jose Geordi Cortez. . . .
>
> Our grandson, Geordi Cortez Neavel, assures me he is proud to live in a nation that cherishes justice and freedom. Unlike Ms. Venerable, I don't believe his multicultural origin will conflict with his patriotism. . . .

Critical thinking. That is not what this textbook approval charade is about, is it? The textbook battle is a clash of belief systems. It's about a single issue people trying to make everyone's grandchildren venerate stereotypes like a Judeo-Christian God, an infallible nation, uncontrolled capitalism and rigid Calvinist morality.

Many of the speakers have criticized not errors of fact in the textbook, but humanist ideas. Some brag that they have pressured textbook publishers to substitute ideas they like for the ones they dislike. Who gave them the right to do that? We did not elect those people. They have ignored the Board's formal approval system. Therefore, we will never know the mischief that they have created.

(de Leon Mendiola 2007: 134–135)

Since 9/11, Christian and conservative groups have put textbook publishers on the defensive when it comes to Islam and Muslims, publishing damning reviews of their "pro-Islamic propaganda" (e.g., Radu 2004; Sewall 2003; Stillwell 2008). In 2010, the Texas Board of Education formally resolved to ban the use of textbooks that they claimed were biased toward Islam and against Christianity. Charging that "pro-Islamic/anti-Christian bias has tainted some past Texas Social Studies textbooks," the resolution gives three instances of textbooks providing less lines of text (in some cases, half as many lines) "to Christian beliefs, practices, and holy writings [than to] those of Islam" (Texas State Board of Education 2010). Additionally, they found that "half-truths, selective disinformation, and false editorial stereotypes still roil some Social Studies textbooks nationwide." At length, these are given as

- Patterns of pejoratives towards Christians and superlatives toward Muslims, calling Crusaders aggressors, "violent attackers," or "invaders" while euphemizing Muslim conquest of Christian lands as "migrations" by "empire builders";
- "Politically-correct" white-washes of Islamic culture and stigmas on Christian civilization, indicting Christianity for the same practices (e.g., sexism, slavery, persecution of out-groups) that they treat non-judgmentally, minimize, sugarcoat, or censor in Islam;
- Sanitized definitions of "jihad" that exclude religious intolerance or military aggression against non-Muslims – even though Islamic sources often include these among proper meanings of the term – which undergirds worldwide Muslim terrorism.

(Texas State Board of Education 2010)

At first glance, the comparative nature of the analysis seems to suggest a *pluralist* approach to curriculum, as does the conclusion of the resolution:

chronic partiality to one of the world's great religions, and animus against another, flout democratic values . . . the SBOE will look to reject future prejudicial Social Studies submissions that continue to offend Texas law with respect to the treatment of the world's major religious groups by significant inequalities of coverage space-wise and/or by demonizing or lionizing one or more of them over others.

(Texas State Board of Education 2010)

However, the references that the Texas Board cites in interpreting the overall content of the textbooks as "demonizing" and "lionizing" are works with a more assimilationist, "clash of civilizations" viewpoint, than a pluralist stance on curriculum. The first major reference, an analysis of several world history and geography textbooks by Gilbert Sewall, emphasizes that popular understanding in the United States of jihad as "holy war" should trump that of other sources, such as the views of many Muslims themselves (Sewall 2008: 13):

> Defining *jihad* is admittedly difficult, as definitions in circulation vary radically. The common assertion now is that translating jihad as "holy war" is entirely wrong and that old translations are incorrect. But in fact, authorities and scholarship of varying perspectives conceive jihad to be a sacred obligation to extend Islam's power – religious and territorial – by persuasion or force. . . .
> Jihad is constructed as "holy war" in much Muslim scripture . . . Today, in government circles, in the foreign policy establishment, in the international community, among newswriters and editorialists and academics, that is how the word jihad is used. It is how Middle Eastern terrorists and Al Qaeda use the term . . .
> Islamic scripture is inconsistent toward infidels, but a harsh, punitive, and aggressive voice, not a charitable or kindly one, prevails . . .
> Yet the Islamic organizations that act as academic reviewers for textbook publishers assure editors that jihad is something entirely different. It is a struggle against evil impulses, they say, misunderstood by the rest of us and in no way bellicose. To characterize jihad as holy war, they insist, would be a grave textbook error, yet a 2007 Pentagon-based study shows almost conclusively that Islamic law sanctions violence and that the Islamist threat to world security has a doctrinal basis.

To summarize Sewall's argument, nearly everyone except for non-violent Muslims and related sympathizers interested in peaceful Muslim-American relations (Sewall cites the Council on Islamic Education, or CIE), define jihad as "holy war": *some* specific academics, *some* specific government reports, Saddam Hussein (who is directly quoted in the text), and al-Qaeda. Although *other people*, many of whom happen to be Muslims, see it as something other than "holy war," it is better to teach what is thought by certain experts on this manner. It is difficult to know here *who* argues for a non-violent understanding of jihad apart from CIE and unnamed textbook reviewers, which would make it a "common assertion" or cause "variations in circulation [to] vary radically." Yet most Muslim leaders would promote a nonviolent understanding of jihad, within and outside the United States (Council on American-Islamic Relations 2006); in one well-known hadith, Muhammad defines jihad as "speaking a word of truth to an oppressive leader" (Awad 2013). These perspectives are dismissed in favor of those of some religious, anti-American extremists and American non-Muslims, however.

Likewise, Sewall argues that a passage in a textbook on the variety of hijab and its meanings in different times and places "is a total instructional failure [which] contains vast misinformation [and] makes no sense." There is no direct response from him on *how* such discussions are incorrect, or *what* should replace the writings, other than that they "fuss the widespread gender-based subjugation that marks Islamic societies," as "Women in some Muslim countries who do not conform to strict social norms of gender separation and homebound seclusion may be shunned, oppressed, or punished" (2008: 22). Here we see one framing of hijab preferred over others, to the exclusion of other sources of evidence or points of view (see Gereluk 2008; Ruitenberg 2006).

Sewall additionally argues that terrorism should be explained in textbooks only as "Islamic terrorism," as a nearly exclusive domain of Muslims, and states that discussions about the vast majority of Muslims against terrorism and violence "demand qualification," as there is "unremitting," "wide and vocal support for extremist groups" in Saudi Arabia, Iran, and Pakistan. He concludes that political parties have caused a "white-washing" of textbook content dealing with Islam, although no evidence is provided for this claim, and that texts should explain that Islam is "aggressive in the postcolonial world" and its "ability to embrace modernity and secular society remains an open question" (2008: 36–38). This is hardly an unbiased understanding of the religion and its diverse followers. Of interest here is not just what Sewall defends, but what he challenges; he not only wants negative things about Muslims to be emphasized in textbooks, but he also wants positive things to be limited, qualified, restricted, or eliminated, as if some instances of anti-Americanism in a few Muslim-majority countries should characterize all Muslim Americans, Muslim Indians, Muslim Indonesians, and so on.

The second and final review cited in the Texas Board resolution (Bennetta 2005) finds similar faults with one textbook, *World History: A Global Mosaic*, though it uses less scholarly language in claiming, for instance, that the textbook "disguised Muslim myths and woo-woo as history." It argues chiefly that

- "Muslims are badly deluded" if they believe, as the textbook claims, that Jews and Christians worship the same god as Muslims;
- that Muhammad could not have "'accepted' all" Jewish and Christian scriptures, because the latter "were so diverse and contradictory" that no one could have;
- Associating Muhammad with tolerance in the textbook is "laughable"; and

- The text fails to dwell on Saudi Arabia today, and therefore "can appeal only to the most ignorant and incompetent teachers . . . who will swallow any woo-woo that comes their way."

(Bennnetta 2005)

Both reviews take fault primarily with the lack of bold negative generalizations about Islam and Muslim societies and the presence of positive generalizations and claims of compatibility of Islam with Christianity and/or Judaism, and liberal Western civilization. Both argue that any positive generalizations should be precluded by a specific counterpoint, and dismiss *any* such qualifications to negative viewpoints that might be presented in the texts. Their main point is that students need to know more negative things about Islam and Muslim societies (and not necessarily anything about Muslims as a group, inside and outside Muslim societies), including general negative viewpoints and specific negative examples. As in the examination of assimilationist views on educating about Islam in the second chapter, any positive portrayals seem to preclude their ideal account, as it is seen as overly pluralistic to not consistently compare Islam negatively to American or Western culture, as in Huntington's (1993) "clash of civilizations" view of mutually exclusive, conflicting social realms.

When one returns to the Texas resolution with this background in mind, one is led to consider a possible contradiction between two points the resolution gives:

Definitions of "jihad" . . . exclude religious intolerance or military aggression against non-Muslims – even though Islamic sources often include these among proper meanings of the term – which undergirds worldwide Muslim terrorism. . . .

Chronic partiality to one of the world's great religions, and animus against another, flout democratic values.

On the one hand, it may reasonably be seen as a problem if the view of jihad connected to terrorism by "Islamic sources" and Muslim terrorists is entirely excluded from textbooks, as it is one well-known definition in U.S. society. To not mention it at all in this case, in favor of other definitions, may make the textbook information ineffective and unhelpful to students, who may critically receive or resist such knowledge claims that they may see to contradict what they "know" from other sources. Yet on the other hand, textbooks should not show chronic hostility toward any of "the world's great religions." Presumably this indicates that students should not learn to *dislike* any religions, based upon textbook content.

These statements about jihad as holy war and pluralism toward world religions are not incompatible. That students should learn more balanced information, including critical points about all major faith traditions in our world, as well as positive views, is not an unreasonable position. However, when one considers the sources cited in the Texas Board view (they also cite a third source: a newspaper article stating that an Emirati bought shares in the Education Media and

Publishing Group, which owns Houghton Mifflin and Harcourt – neither this article nor any other reports indicate this should have any impact on the content of U.S. textbooks), it seems their perspective might be tilted to a different view of what constitutes "fair and balanced" from that of most Muslims, about Islam. In fact, Sewall claims that ordinary Muslims in Western society are not a significant part of the Muslim world to consider in the textbooks, as they should focus only on terrorism and problems, which sounds more like "chronic partiality" (2008: 25).

In sum, Texas demands that textbooks, in its state and by practical implication across all others, give approximately equal coverage of Islam and Christianity both in terms of total space as well as the types of negative and positive coverage of the traditions and their roles in historical and contemporary world affairs. However, the implication of the resolution, if it has any impact, is to bolster an anti-Muslim, assimilationist view, as voices invoked promote a dramatically negative view of Islam and Muslims in the world today, and protest more positive views, even citing popular "knowledge" in the United States as evidence about what negative things students should learn in schools. This contemporary context is helpful to bear in mind as we consider what the textbooks from before and after 9/11 relate, and fail to relate, about Islam and Muslims.

What the textbooks say

The first thing one is likely to notice in searching for references to Muslims and Islam in contemporary world history and geography textbooks (my review includes several editions of nationally popular titles from 1995 to 2012) is how small the total space considering the subjects is. Searching by index (under "Islam," "Islamic Civilization," "Muslims," and so on), but also browsing relevant sections for graphic and written representations, one finds that representations of Muslims are generally provided within sections on Islamic civilization or the birth of Islam (which, in the geographically rather than historically framed texts, is often considered along with that of the other monotheistic religions in sections on the Middle East). This content takes up 2% to 5% of textbook space. *World Adventures in Time and Place* (Banks et al. 1997) considers Muslims in two sections of a chapter, "Ancient Arabia," in about six pages of the 500-page text. *To See a World* (Armento et al. 1997), a more advanced text published at the same time, provides several chapters about Islam, Muslims, and Muslim-majority countries (Iran and Egypt), and discusses Islam in India. However these references still take up no more than 5% of the text.

New references to Islam and Muslims abound in all textbooks since 9/11, including negative additional portrayals and discussions of Islam and Muslims. In the 2004 text *World Cultures: A Global Mosaic* (Ahmad et al.), new references in the index include "literature of," pilgrimages, "Taliban and," "Islamic extremists," and "women and." Greenblatt and Lemmo's 1999 and 2001 *Human Heritage: A World History* textbooks include identical index references related to Muslims and Islam, while the 2004 edition adds references to "the Islamic group of al-Qaeda." Clearly, the expanded attention to Muslims and Islam in recent editions is the result of texts responding to 9/11, aiming to provide some background on people and current events related to it (including the war on terror, and consequent interventions in Afghanistan and Iraq). While such additional attention is a response to a reasonable need to know, as with the media's recent interest in bin Laden, it nonetheless can also be seen to result in an increase in negative representations of Muslims in the texts overall, as Muslim leaders condemning terrorism or living peacefully in Europe or the United States, for instance, are generally absent from these representations.

All textbooks minimally supply information required by state standards in a fairly neutral tone, with few or no additions, leading to minimal coverage of Islam that is mostly historically framed. They introduce Islam in broad terms, describing it as a set of basic beliefs and practices, and discuss its growth and development, and historical achievements of Muslims and Islamic societies. Though texts from before 9/11 generally did not mention Muslims as part of U.S. society or other societies, today geography texts are more forthcoming about the religious make-up of the United States and other countries, thus mentioning that Muslims make up one of the many religious communities in the United States, Canada, and so on.

The most minimal discussion is in Bednarz et al. (2003; 2005) middle school geography text, *World Cultures and Geographies,* which discusses Islam in a section titled "Birthplace of Three Religions." Muhammad being revealed God's word by the angel Gabriel, the Koran, and the Five Pillars are discussed (and graphically portrayed), as are Muslim caliphs, Muslim works of translation, and Muslim expansion into Europe. Basic structures of the Ottoman Empire are also briefly considered. The total space given to these topics is less than five pages (with graphics). In its 2007 version, this discussion is slightly enlarged, with an additional section titled "Muslim Empires," which elaborates these latter elements with a few more pages. In most texts, the Ottoman Empire is the focus of at least a subsection (taking up at least a page or two of text), if not a full section of the text, and other historically significant places and societies, such as Baghdad and Muslim Spain, are discussed at some length.

In addition, texts sometimes provide limited information about Muhammad's life and times and discuss medical, scientific, and philosophical contributions of Islamic civilizations, including the discovery of blood circulation, astronomical knowledge, the invention of algebra, and so on. Images accompanying the text represent artifacts of Islamic and Muslim civilizations, such as mosques (in particular Mecca during the hajj), copies of the Koran, paintings and drawings contemporary to the periods discussed, and jugs. Clearly these representations constitute an improvement upon negative stereotypical ones, showing good qualities of historical Muslims and a variety of Muslim things and places, rather than images of state enemies or more ordinary, but oppositional, characters, as is common in news media representation.

In line with many state standards, texts also include comparisons of Islam with Judaism and Christianity, as well as other religions, specifically Buddhism,

Hinduism, and Confucianism, in a comparative manner. *World History: Patterns of Interaction* (Beck et al. 2004) offers a global view of the distribution of these "world religions" and discusses the major sects, practices, symbols, and organizations of each, complementing each with attractive pictures of arts and practices, before graphically comparing them in terms of their followers worldwide, deities (which is "not applicable" for Buddhism), their founder, holy book, leadership, and basic beliefs. In other textbooks tables and charts comparatively consider religions' respective achievements, as well, and birthdates and key places, among other categories.

While this approach is clearly aiming to make belief systems that are foreign to many students more relatable, such comparisons are not entirely helpful, however, as the religions are not necessarily parallel phenomena within people's lives. The texts frame all religions as like phenomena, failing to address each substantively in its own context. For instance, many texts cast Confucianism as a religion, when few followers of the moral and ethical framework would describe it as such. *World Geography Today* states that

> Confucius had little to say about gods, the meaning of death, or the idea of life after death. For this reason some people do not consider Confucianism a religion, although the goal of Confucianism is to be in "good accord with the ways of heaven." Many followers of Confucianism practice his ideas as religion. *Why do some people not consider Confucianism a religion?*
> (Sager & Helgren 2003: 107; emphasis in the original)

This is a particularly ethnocentric way of framing Confucianism, as those "some people" who would not consider Confucianism as a religion include most "followers," who also would not agree they "practice his ideas as religion," to align themselves with "heaven," in the Christian orientation.

Some texts omit Confucianism, atheism, and agnosticism altogether, presenting pictures of the world as entirely religious. *World Cultures and Geography* (Bednarz et al. 2007) colors one world map with religions: Christianity, including Roman Catholic, Protestant, Eastern Churches, and "Other Christian"; Sunni and Shiite Muslim; and Hinduism; Buddhism; Judaism; "Traditional"; "Mixed/Traditional"; and "Sparsely inhabited." According to this map, China is entirely Buddhist, and it appears as if one "Traditional" religion is followed in central South America, Northern Canada, Northern Russia, Mozambique, and parts of Australia, Indonesia, and Southeast Asia. Similar maps can be found in nearly all of the texts, which might show religious diversity within larger countries (i.e., as half green and half orange) or depict them as homogenously religious. These maps depict a world of internally homogenous communities, in line with simplistic cultural understandings of religious diversity such as the "clash of civilizations" view, by drawing lines between diverse religious believers who often live side by side. Additionally, such representations suggest the norm of believing in only one religious tradition, as is the case for many Christians in the United States, while in many places in Asia and Africa, it is not considered problematic to believe in or practice different religious and ethical traditions and faiths at the same time.

Reasons or causes for Islam's expansion, or the emergence of Muslim-majority societies, during the Middle Ages is also discussed in nearly all texts. Typically they use neutral phrasing; however, partial evidence or viewpoints can easily be given in neutral tones in the textbooks. For instance, *Global Mosaic* (2004) references "the idea of jihad" as the belief that "Muslim warriors who died in the service of Islam would win a place in paradise," perpetuating the stereotypical idea of jihad as holy war, rather than as personal struggles to be good and holy, while *Patterns of Interaction*, one of the more advanced texts, states that

> [h]istorians have identified many reasons for the Muslims' military success in addition to the faith of the Muslim soldiers. The Muslim armies were well disciplined and expertly commanded. Their tactics enabled them to overwhelm forces unaccustomed to their style of warfare.
> (Beck et al. 2003: 238)

Here we see a contrast between *Global Mosaic* and *Patterns*'s treatment of the growth of Islam, with the former interpreting findings as facts, and the latter emphasizing historian findings, marking the text as interpretive and theoretical. Other factors cited in texts include the strength of faith of Muslims, and Muslim societies' more tolerant treatment of minorities (Jews and Christians).

The most common reference to Muslims not normally mentioned in standards deals with the treatment of Muslim women traditionally and/or contemporarily. Of particular interest is the way in which most (though not all) of the texts present positive or negative evaluations of the situation of particular Muslim women as facts, seldom encouraging students to consider the cases of diverse Muslim women more comprehensively (e.g., Ruitenberg 2006). *Connections to Today* (Ellis & Esler 2003) highlights variations in practices and lifestyles (dress, employment, and so on) across groups by location. In the text, hijab is considered from various perspectives. In a special subsection about women in the Muslim world, hijab is a vocabulary term, defined here well as "covering," and the text draws out where and how the practice of covering has gained popularity in recent history, noting that "changes have taken place at different rates in different places," and offering an insider's perspective: "'I think of Muslim dress as a kind of uniform,' one Egyptian student said. 'I can sit in class with men and there is no question of attraction and so on – we are all involved in the same business of learning.'" Muslim women interpreting hijab more negatively, who are, the texts claim, "against social and political forces that put severe limits on their lives," present a counterpoint, allowing students to recognize that there are two sides, at least, to this issue.

World History (Spielvogel 2008: 202) similarly shows images of women wearing hijab, chador, and burka, thus highlighting cultural and religious diversity, and states that, "In the Quran, *hijab* has different meanings. In some verses, it is a curtain or partition dividing rooms. In other verses, it is a sacred divide between two things, such as early and holy, god and humans, light and dark, and men and women." It additionally asks students at this point, "In what other religions or cultures do women cover their heads?" Such a question highlights commonality between religions while the images reveal internal variety of experiences as well. Another reference is made in this text to hijab in relation to the ban of religious clothing in France in 2004, showing connections between cultures, but also framing the issue as one of Muslim women versus the French state, echoing a clash view where internal diversity within both camps can also be found (Jackson 2005).

However, these two books are the exception to the rule; other text treatments and discussions of women in Muslim societies are either clearly positive, taking a pluralist orientation to the subject matter, or analyzing in a more negative, critical fashion Islam's impact on women's lives. Such portraits treat all Muslim women as if their experiences are the same: as if class, race, nationality, ethnicity, and other cultural aspects of their identities play no major role. *Human Heritage* highlights how Islam improved life for women initially, with regard to marriage (in the early context of the predominance of polygamist practices), education, and rights to property. The text states that "Islam was born in a society where men could have an unlimited number of wives and the killing of female children was common. Islam attempted to correct the situation. . . . Before Islam, women could not inherit property from their parents" (Greenblatt & Lemmo 2004: 293). This text presents Islam simply as a positive force in women's lives, despite more complex or negative views that are common today.

Global Mosaic, on the other hand, simple states – without making any reference to possible prior or surrounding social contexts – that "the Koran permits men to have as many as four wives, as long as he treats each of them equally" and that "among Muslims, tradition and customs made women subordinate to men," as "Muslims believed that women were more likely than men to bring dishonor on their family." After explaining that "Islam gave women protections they had not had in the past," including protection against female infanticide, the text goes on to state that "in early Islamic societies, women had enjoyed greater freedom than they sometimes did at a later time. Customs, such as wearing the veil, living in seclusion, and separating men and women in all activities came into practice gradually" (Ahmad et al. 2004: 273).

Similar to educational standards, the same text can change its perspective over time, likely in attempts to respond to any potential challenges publishers may face from critics of textbooks, or from deliberations of the Texas textbook approval process. In the 1999 version of *Patterns of Interaction* it is noted that

> Muslim women had more rights than European women of the same time period. The Qur'an provided for the care of widows and orphans, allowed divorce, and protected the women's share of inheritance . . . In the early

days of Islam, women could also participate in public life and gain an education.

(Beck et al. 1999: 243)

The section ends there. The 2012 version changes and adds the following (additions and changes have been emphasized):

Muslim women had more *economic and property* rights than European, Indian, *and Chinese* women of the same time period. *Nonetheless, Muslim women were still expected to submit to men. When a husband wanted to divorce his wife, all he had to do was repeat three times, "I dismiss thee." The divorce became final in three months.* . . . In the early days of Islam, women could also participate in public life and gain an education. *However, over time, Muslim women were forced to live increasingly isolated lives. When they did go out in public, they were expected to be veiled.*

(Beck et al. 2012: 274)

These texts portray the lives and possibilities of Muslim women historically in very different lights. In comparing the texts, one sees that the rights Muslim women had "more" of are specified (qualified?) in the later text, and the groups they are compared with are expanded not to paint the contemporary European society in a particularly negative way. The two texts are contradictory on the point of divorce, with the later text adding bold statements about women's submission to men, which is cryptic and difficult to clearly grasp in its exact meaning (what kind of "submission"?), and emphasizing "they were expected to be veiled," and isolated. Both excerpts are no doubt true, but where and when, exactly? And who expected them "to be veiled"? Their mothers, their husbands . . . the state? The "I dismiss thee" observation was never a universal feature of the Muslim world, yet it is presented as such in the later text edition. This comparison highlights the way the texts can paint broad pictures of highly complicated social and cultural history. It also suggests the authors facing pressure over time to add more negative descriptions of Muslims, in line with the Texas Board's recent resolution, even if the educational effectiveness or objectivity of such additions is questionable.

As in state standards documents, Muslims are not substantively discussed in relation to contemporary affairs in any of the textbooks produced prior to 9/11, if some Muslims are referred to (without mentioning religion) in sections dealing with the Middle East, particularly the Persian Gulf War, and the situation of Israel and Palestine. While these are not technically representations of Muslims per se, when these are the most common representations of modern Muslims, this can nonetheless lead to the perpetuation of stereotypical associations of Muslims with conflict and problems in the Middle East and Western Asia.

Images proliferate in place of discussions of Muslims today, in many cases. However, their captioning, as a way to guide students in interpreting what they see, repetitively orientate readers toward a binary, mutually exclusive, "clash of civilizations" view of modern/Islam, as Zagumny and Richey observe (2012a; 2012b):

> "A man wearing a *traditional* headdress chats on a cellular phone . . ."
>
> "Just as cultures mix in this part of the world, so tradition intermingles with the newest technology. Ancient customs persist even in the most modern cities . . ."
>
> "The modern home in Saudi Arabia is furnished with many items of Arab culture" . . . somehow indicating that items, once placed in the context of modernity, become relics of culture and imbibed with static tradition . . .
>
> In Cairo, "Only blocks away from modern department stores that display the latest Paris fashions are the traditional Arab open-air markets, or bazaars . . ."
>
> In a picture of a "Southwest Asian Market" (no city or country is given) . . . : "In many cities of the region, the traditional *suq* provides a marked contrast to modern department stores". . . Focusing on this constructed paradox takes away the organic normalcy of city life – what would be taken for granted in a discussion of a European or American city. . . .
>
> (2012b: 203–205)

Similar to analyses of the "Arab Spring" in news media that emphasize modern democracy as separate from the Muslim world (discussed in Chapter 3), Lisa Zagumny and Amanda Richey's analysis highlights how the historical nature of modern Muslim societies is continually emphasized and presented to the reader, framing contemporary non-Western cultural elements as traditional and historical – not modern, though existent today. This discursive splitting of simultaneous phenomena as historical and modern, non-Western and Western, reinforces the "clash of civilizations" view, in emphasizing different artifacts or features of the landscape as if they are unnaturally placed together. It would be akin to imagery showing contemporary people trading at a several-hundred-year-old historical produce market in Europe or the United States, with a caption asking the reader to observe how historical and cultural elements mix with the modern. Such elements are ordinarily together in life, in U.S. society and elsewhere.

Since 2001, all of the texts and revised text editions mention or discuss 9/11 and the war on terrorism, in Afghanistan and Iraq. The 2004 edition of *Global Mosaic* offers the most minimal coverage, discussing neither Islam nor Muslims. The text merely replaces a paragraph from its 2001 edition discussing 1998 terrorist bombings in Kenya and Tanzania and over Scotland with the following:

> After terrorists killed about 3,000 people in attacks on New York City and Washington, D.C., on September 11, 2001, the United States launched a global campaign against terrorist groups based in Afghanistan. Many nations joined the United States effort against the terrorist attacks.
>
> (Ahmad et al. 2004: 474)

Islam is not even mentioned here. Similarly, in Richard Boehm's 2012 *World Geography and Cultures*, it is simply stated, in one section on Afghanistan, that "International terrorist Osama bin Laden was believed to be hiding in Afghanistan," and he is identified as responsible for 9/11. He is mentioned once more in a sentence explaining the invasion of Afghanistan in 2001, in the chapter on the United States today.

Other textbooks offer slightly greater coverage that also manages to minimize connecting Muslims to terrorism. In the *Human Heritage* 2004 version, two pages are added explaining 9/11. Bin Laden's views are discussed as warranting "any action – such as the killing of American citizens" to remove U.S. influence in the Middle East, and the text states that his view "does not follow the beliefs of the religion of Islam." It is noted that "the Taliban strictly controlled the Afghan people, especially women and children," while the Taliban is not described here as Muslim or Islamic (Greenblatt & Lemmo 2004: 513). Also fairly brief, *Connections to Today* associates terrorism rather vaguely with Muslims. It describes the Taliban as a "fundamentalist Muslim group" that "imposed an extreme form of Islam on Afghanistan," suggesting falsely that the Taliban is fundamentally committed to Islamic principles. The text goes on: "The Taliban also supported al-Qaida, an international terrorist group led by a Saudi named Osama bin Laden. Bin Laden and al-Qaida . . . planned and carried out the attacks . . . on September 11, 2001. . . . Thousands of people died" (Ellis & Esler 2003: 887). Though this does not relate Muslims closely to terrorism, it does connect the Taliban to Islam. However, in none of these slight representations of 9/11 are Muslims directly linked to terrorism, as they are in the mass media.

Yet in texts providing more substantial coverage, Islam is typically associated with terrorism. For instance, in *USA Today*-sponsored supplements in the 2003 McDougall Littell textbooks, the Taliban is described as a "strict Islamic government," suggesting that their restrictive and oppressive laws are in line with Islamic beliefs ("Muslim" would be a more appropriate adjective here), and "extremist Muslim Taliban," "Muslim terrorists," and "Muslim extremists" are all referenced, repetitiously associating Islam and Muslims exclusively with terrorism, lacking discussions of any moderate or peaceful Muslims.

The text supplements give somewhat sympathetic treatment to terrorism in one place – stating that there are "traditional motives, such as gaining independence, expelling foreigners, or changing society," in discussing "anti-government extremist Timothy McVeigh," who they claim was "motivated by the belief that the government has too much power to regulate people's lives." Yet they identify Muslim "religious" terrorism as isolated and distinct from other kinds of terrorism with no reason other than religious belief, effectively associating Islam with the most severe, or significant terrorism, as no other religions are discussed in connection to terrorism. By identifying McVeigh as in some sense reasonable while portraying Muslim terrorists as fueled simply by a dangerous religious fervor, the text supplements perpetuate associations of Muslims with terrorism, fear, and unreasonableness, to the detriment of ordinary Muslims, and despite more critical interpretations of the causes of terrorism perpetuated by Muslims and others around the world.

The *USA Today* supplement does include a small disclaimer toward the end, however, which is one of very few attempts in any of the texts that cover 9/11 to distinguish between Muslims cited as terrorists and Muslims generally:

> The United States tried to make it clear to Muslim nations that the antiterrorism campaign was *not* anti-Islamic and that Americans respected the religion of Islam. For the United States, maintaining the support of modern Muslim leaders was important to the long-term success of the war against terrorism.
> (Bednarz et al. 2003: US11; emphasis in the original).

While the attempt to differentiate between Muslims generally and Muslim terrorists is made, referring to a particular *kind* of religious terrorism that seems to have no rationale outside of "radical Islam" makes it less than obvious to the reader that there is nothing particularly Islamic (just as there is nothing particularly Christian or atheistic) about terrorism. Additionally, as this discussion is near the end of the text, it appears not as primary to the discussion, while representations of Muslims as terrorists, and as particularly unreasonable terrorists, are. Furthermore, in tying respect for Muslims bluntly to American interests, the need to tolerate different traditions and Muslims as individuals *regardless* of particular national interests is not emphasized as important. Rather, it is suggested that one should respect Muslims and Islam because it accords with national foreign policy; it is not framed as important per se, but as important to the United States' interests.

The latest texts have expanded their discussion of politics in Iraq and Afghanistan in order to stay up to date, and generally in this context, discussions of bin Laden and 9/11 have been minimalized from mid-decade editions, with a greater focus in some cases on the actions of U.S. political leaders and New Yorkers. Though patriotic responses in support of the activities in Iraq and Afghanistan seemed simplistic in the earlier texts – merely putting forward the official government position (Jackson 2011) – more recently, debates over these activities and national security issues at home have been highlighted, in place of facts-based, neutrally worded explanations. This is a positive trend from the perspective that texts should not mask complexity with cryptic, partial views. However this trend appears difficult to sustain in discussing issues more closely related to Islam and Muslims. For instance, in Spielvogel's (2008) *World History* an attempt is made at considering roots of terrorism with reference to different theories and viewpoints. In a section following the explanation of 9/11 and its immediate aftermath titled "Islamic Militants," the text states:

> The causes of recent world terrorism are complex. Some analysts say this terrorism is rooted in the clash of Western and Islamic cultures. They argue

that the Christians and Muslims have viewed each other with hostility since at least the time of the Crusades. Others suggest that poverty and ignorance lie at the root of the problem. Extremists find it easy to stir up resentment against wealthy Western societies. Finally, some say terrorism would be rare if the Israel-Palestinian conflict could be solved.

One reason Middle Eastern terrorists have targeted Westerners can be traced to Western investment in the Middle East oil industry, which began in the 1920s. This industry brought wealth to ruling families in some Middle Eastern kingdoms, but most citizens remained very poor. They often blamed the West, especially the United States, for supporting the ruling families.

(1047)

The text goes on to explain Muslims' fear of cultural contact weakening Islamic faith as a final explanation for Muslims "targeting" Westerners.

Such a discussion in the text is interesting for the way it frames a consideration of different viewpoints as a critical thinking exercise for students, but does not give enough information in order for students to really be able to consider the different knowledge claims independently. The first idea, of a culture clash, does not require much supporting evidence as laid out simply by Huntington, other than the Crusades and 9/11 (though to challenge this view, one could draw upon examples countering the idea that "Christians and Muslims have viewed each other with hostility since at least the time of the Crusades" – for instance, historical and modern Turkey's east-meets-west location, religious integration, and norms; or the peaceful coexistence of Muslims and Christians in various countries such as Jordan, Lebanon, Spain, and so on). The other explanations mentioned are insufficiently elaborated to make sense of, however. For instance, who states that "terrorism would be rare if the Israeli-Palestinian conflict could be solved"? This seems an extreme oversimplification of a more nuanced view. The second paragraph here suggests that terrorists target the United States because it has invested money in these countries, which is a highly reductive consideration of the situation; additionally this statement is written as neutral fact: "One reason . . . can be traced."

Such writing suggests that this latter information is verified, resulting in a very simplistic discussion overall, which can be summarized as: "Some people think there is a culture clash, while some others think we should resolve Israel and Palestine; Middle Easterners terrorize the United States because of its investment in the region; and some Muslims do not like the Western way of life." The textbook extract does go on to state that, "Most Muslims around the world do not share this vision, nor do they agree with the use of terrorism," but the political relations between the Middle East and the United States nonetheless seem oversimplified to the point of being invisible in such text discussions of terrorism. It is likely given the aforementioned political climate of textbook publishing that, as in mass media, publishers fear mentioning political issues that might paint the United States in less than glowing light, precluding any overtly political discussions that could gain the ire of Texas.

As with news coverage of Muslims, while some efforts are made to distance terrorists from Muslims, as a whole most accounts fail to discuss Muslims leaders condemning terrorism or provide information about any normal, ordinary Muslims in the Western or Eastern world, or the case of American Muslims who faced discrimination and prejudice before or after 9/11. And while the historical treatments of Muslims and Islam in the textbooks before and since 9/11 are generally fair-minded and seem to earnestly attempt to not put forward harmful stereotypes about present-day Muslims (when compared with past portrayals), nor promote their beliefs or practices, coverage is incredibly brief and broad, and phrased neutrally to present often cryptic and complex issues as matters of clear-cut fact, such as in the case of Islam being good or bad for women in a particular past or present place. Finally, though there are some exceptions, texts discourage student critical thinking or distance from the text, by failing to offer substantial alternative viewpoints on a subject, instead treating the complex and diverse phenomena related to Muslims as objective facts, thereby likely enabling young people's uncritical association of Muslims with terrorism in the contemporary world, rather than their development of more nuanced, accurate views.

Similar problems related to texts avoiding controversy have been observed by many social studies educators, with regard to religious education generally, and in relation to education about other minority groups. For instance, Kincheloe notes that

> As fundamentalist Christians and right-wing pressure groups continue to challenge textbooks that approach controversial issues . . . publishers often skip over the vital role that religion has played in the development of human history and institutions. . . . They compromise: Print as little as possible . . . and maybe no one will be offended. Choosing safety over conceptual understanding textbook publishers strive to keep their markets happy or at least unruffled.
>
> (2001: 60)

Banks similarly notes with regard to minority treatment in texts that

> although textbooks had largely eliminated sexist language and had incorporated images of ethnic minorities into them, they failed to help students to develop an understanding of the complex cultures of ethnic groups, and an understanding of racism, sexism, and classism in American society.
>
> (1996: 20)

Such limitations to the texts, which reflect in part textbook publishers' general reluctance to deal extensively with controversial topics (lest they insult key groups in the market) are not necessarily lost on classroom teachers. Many teachers thus also incorporate other, supplementary sources today, as I discuss in the next section.

Teaching about Islam: Supplementary resources and educator practices

Though I have examined textbook coverage of issues related to Muslims and Islam at length here, in everyday practice, teachers often use resources beyond the textbook to broaden student horizons, or teach more substantial lessons, particularly when it comes to contemporary or controversial subjects in social studies. While research suggests that on average 75% to 90% of class time is spent using textbooks in public secondary schools, most predictably among younger or less subject matter-experienced teachers (Barker 1992), case studies that focus on social studies and current events curriculum challenge this statistic (Kaviani 2007). As Rod Barker observes,

> as a result of state and district social studies mandates, textbooks are generally defining the scope and sequence of instruction for most [but] even when this is the case, teachers are making use of a wide variety of other supplementary materials in conjunction with supplied textbook packages.
>
> (1992: 110)

Some teachers he observed use textbooks rarely, while "those who relied most heavily on their textbook were using many outside resources" (Barker 1992). Khodadad Kaviani's study of world history and geography teachers exploring the Middle East and Islam found that many of them actually used textbooks infrequently, with the exception of one teacher, who used four different textbooks in class.

Using outside resources is particularly important when teaching about contemporary events. After 9/11, educators experienced a need for resources in the context of the new need to know about Islam and Muslims, generally lacking formal training or preparation for discussing this and related controversial issues and topics more substantively in the classroom. In some cases immediately after the attacks, teachers were asked by administrators and school counselors to not dwell on any subjects related to 9/11, to get "back to business," and avoid any controversy or distracting displays of emotion on the part of teachers and students (Noppe et al. 2006). However, in many cases teachers were freer to do what they saw as most appropriate for their specific classroom context or were even encouraged to discuss the issues with students by administrators and school counselors. There were also instances where teachers felt the strong need to learn more about Muslims in global politics themselves, lacking much (or any) background in religion or international affairs, as prejudicial views of Muslims were brought into their classrooms by students. As one teacher recalls in the months following 9/11:

> They said, ". . . we need to take some military action." I said, "Against whom?" And they said "Muslims . . . the Middle East." Then I pulled

down the map. . . . "Oh, why don't we just bomb any country out there?" And I was like, "Whoa, you know it's like there are people there." [Some kids were like,] "Yeah yeah, they killed 5,000 of ours let's kill 10,000 of theirs." And I said, "Okay, so what if they retaliate and they kill 20,000 – what are you going to do? Wipe out the whole Middle East?" And they're like, "Yeah, we could do that. We got the bombs."

(Lowenstein 2006: 167)

To gain the necessary background information to guide or instruct students in the emotional context of 9/11, some teachers engaged in independent study, to provide for more substantial classroom coverage than that mandated, owing to this newly recognized need for students to know more about Muslims and Islam. As one teacher recalls in early 2002:

I extended the 3 days in February that the curriculum called for teaching about Islam to 3 weeks, choosing specific aspects of Islam that I thought were particularly relevant. . . .

In those cold winter days, I remember the intensity and focus that I brought to my task; in a way, creating meaningful, well-informed lessons on Islam was my own personal method of healing after the events of the fall. I would often spend my weekends in the cozy bookstores of New York City, devouring books about Islam, and then at the end of the Sunday (and several cappuccinos later), carefully returning the unbought books to their shelves, satisfied that I had gleaned just enough information for the next morning.

(Hochman 2006: 92)

Teachers such as the two quoted above found it personally and professionally fulfilling to learn more and focus class time on teaching about Islam and Muslims, to meet their own and their students' need to know, given the minimal coverage of Muslims in their textbooks. Many teachers after 9/11 reported using a variety of additional resources in the classroom as well, including newly published specialized text supplements, books about the Middle East (such as those by Lewis, Huntington, and Said), excerpts from national and international news sources, passages from religious texts, and/or political cartoons (Kaviani 2007). The most commonly used form of educational supplement is sources from the media, particularly news articles. Given the typically greater readability (when compared with textbooks) and "freshness," articles from contemporary daily news are most often used, as content knowledge and for critical thinking purposes. Teachers commonly discuss articles with students, or ask students to analyze editorials, to create greater interest, make things "more real," educate, and provide for a wider variety of more contemporary and original perspectives.

However, it is not clear that teachers commonly use a critical lens when using media sources as educational supplements. Those who relied on media for content knowledge in one recent study by Kaviani (2007) seemed aware of the limitations of perspective of CNN or other mainstream U.S. news sources for adequately representing Muslims and Muslim perspectives. Most referred to multiple international sources, including Muslim, Arab, and/or other non-Western sources, thereby modeling a critical use of media, rather than simply treating the media as valid evidence in the classroom. A cohort of particularly well-educated (and well-traveled) teachers – many with graduate degrees in social science disciplines and/or with work experience abroad – these teachers approached the subject and their use of resources with more of a critical multicultural perspective on difference than an a priori assimilationist or pluralist point of view:

> Brandon viewed balanced instruction to be a dichotomous binary where two dominant sides were presented. He said, "Balanced means if there are at least two viewpoints, two opinions that you should try to balance . . ." He emphasized that his school was a "public agency" and it was his role to provide both sides of an issue to his "18, 19 year old students" so that they could "think critically." . . .
>
> For Sherry, balanced instruction meant "there's often more than one side. There are often more than two sides." She gave the example of the presidency in Egypt where the Egyptian presidents have stayed in power beyond their nine-year limits and have behaved more like kings. For her, balanced instruction meant examining an issue like the presidency in Egypt from multiple perspective [sic] of the Egyptian society and asking questions about the power structure and who was benefiting from those arrangements.
>
> For Rose, balanced instruction meant providing a space for a variety of opinions to be expressed.
>
> (Kaviani 2007: 80)

While many in Kaviani's cohort emphasize the importance of providing for multiple and/or balanced perspectives in the classroom, it is likely that many educators use in a more matter-of-fact way various outside resources and educational supplements, however, providing less balanced perspectives in their classrooms (I will discuss this issue more in the next chapter).

Another supplementary resource educators can use is the specialized school text supplement. To increase educator knowledge and supply additional classroom resources to explore topics related to Muslims and Islam, a handful of educational supplements have been made readily available online, which can be used by teachers who lack previous experience with the subject themselves, and the time and/or ability to self-educate themselves systematically. These supplements typically take on the subject matter using an assimilationist, pluralist, or critical multicultural orientation, however. The Fordham Foundation's (2002) *September 11: What Our Children Need to Know,* revised and republished in 2011, and *Terrorists, Despots, and Democracy: What Our Children Need to Know* (2003); and *Rethinking Schools*'s (2001) special report on "War, Terrorism, and

Our Classrooms," are some of the most well-known teachers' guides, echoing these multicultural discourses toward the end of providing teachers and students alike with additional information, attitudes, and orientations, about Muslims and Islam.

Mentioned earlier in the second chapter, *September 11* and related Fordham Institute publications puts forward an assimilationist view regarding Islam and Muslims, usually framing Muslims as threatening rather than as tolerable in Western civilization. The president of the Fordham Institute, Finn, describes the collections as aiming toward a relatively more accurate view of Islam, which he explains by reference to Sewall's writings (discussed at length here in relation to the Texas resolution) that U.S. social studies textbooks fail to explore sufficiently "*jihad* and the advocacy of violence among militant Islamists to attain worldly ends, the imposition of *sharia* law, the record of Muslim enslavement, and the brutal subjection of women" (Sewall 2003: 77; quoted in Finn 2003: 12–13). Many articles in the related (often overlapping) collections discuss Muslims in a predominantly negative light, identifying, for instance, "Islamic fundamentalism and fascism" as "a great plague upon the world that would destroy the rights of women, the very notion of religious tolerance, and all the gifts of the Enlightenment" (Hanson 2003: 23).

In some of the essays included in the *September 11* collections, a kind of balance is attempted. In Schwartz's contribution, "Two Faces of Islam," it is noted that Islam is not a monolith and is a "religion of peace" (2003: 89), while another essay identifies Islam's "tradition of tolerance and its historic championship of the arts and learning," along with its "potential for jihad and violence – a potential that has been as significant a part of its history as tolerance and learning" (Klee 2002: 35; 2003: 59). However, the more mixed discussions still emphasize there being significantly negative aspects of the religious community today, while in most essays, a predominantly negative representation of Muslims and Islam is put forward. Using such guides as resources would be not only be insufficient for educating students about the religion today, but could result in harms to Muslims, as prejudicial, discriminatory attitudes are likely developed and maintained when such negative, imbalanced representations prevail.

In 2011 the Fordham Institute republished ten articles with an updated introduction by Finn on what has happened in politics and U.S. education over the last ten years. The new introduction is flattering to educators but harsh on scholars and others with views differing from Finn's own, on the "key lessons" of 9/11. Finn's two main foci here are the National Association of School Psychologists (NASP) and the National Education Association (NEA), both of which he depicts as powerful and influential organizations which the Fordham Institute cannot compete with on financial and political terms: "A small outfit like Fordham cannot counteract the malign influence of large national organizations like NCSS and NEA" (2011: 8).

Finn goes on to note that it has become widespread to "simply disregard . . . patriotism and democratic institutions [in place of] non-judgmentalism toward those who would destroy them, and failure to teach about the heroism of those who defend them" (2011: 7). He cites a statement of NASP promoting teaching of tolerance and compassion after 9/11, responding that "some of that is needed, to be sure, but rarely did the promulgators suggest that teachers should also read books with their pupils that address patriotism [and] deal realistically with the presence of evil, danger, and anti-Americanism" (2011: 7). We see again here this pitting of toleration against teaching negative information about Islam and Muslims, with the suggestion that one can never do enough when it comes to the latter. Of course, NASP is an organization of psychologists clearly focused on student emotional and mental wellbeing – not demands of nationalism. As for NEA's faults, he cites documents he claims are no longer available (online) as evidence of political agendas replacing good pedagogy, before noting parenthetically that "searching that website for September 11 material still yields some lulus" (2011: 8). As with Bennetta's (2005) aforementioned discussion of social science "woo-woo," it is not clear what is meant here specifically, other than to mock perspectives that differ from the author's own.

Like Sewall, Finn makes an interesting case for the existence of imbalanced interpretations and representations of events and people by pluralist educators in his writing: "Nothing there about accurate history of the U.S., the Middle East, Islam, or the world. Nothing there about democratic values and their protection. Certainly nothing about patriotism. Everything was about either tolerance or mental health" (Finn 2011: 8).

Finn argues that others are wrong not for what they *include*, but for what they *exclude*, approaching his view as one primarily of seeking a better *balance* of information and viewpoints. Yet he implies here that 20 or 50 "bad guys" worldwide are more important to study than 1 billion more ordinary, good and bad, Muslim people. As in the Texas statement, fair and balanced coverage entails saying a few good things about Muslims, possibly, but certainly *many more negative things,* in line with a privileging of certain voices over others who have very one-sided understandings of Islam, terrorism, jihad, etc.

On the other hand, *Rethinking Schools*'s (2001) special report, "War, Terrorism, and Our Classrooms," provides almost entirely positive perspectives and representations of Muslims, and few critical perspectives, in line with a pluralist or critical multiculturalist orientation toward difference. While a helpful primer is offered in the collection for teachers seeking basic information about Muslims, such as the major sects of Islam, alternative meanings of jihad, and where the largest populations of believers live (mostly in Indonesia, Pakistan, and Bangladesh), most of the essays in the collection, created (as Finn's is) for students and teachers alike, respond to critiques of Muslims and Islam primarily with counter-critiques of U.S. society, and defend Muslims and Islam, while minimally attending to the substance of critiques and negative views. As a result few of the essays effectively provide particularly critical alternatives to assimilationist perspectives, as they merely show the other side of the coin, rather than guide students to come to their own informed conclusions about pressing real world issues, by engaging the "other side" in dialogue.

An interview with Said among the essays is one case in point: When asked about the roots of Muslim terrorism, Said responds that Muslims differentiate the United States they are attracted to for education, business, vacations, and training, and the "United States of armies and interventions"; he then discusses Islam as a point around which U.S. politicians rallied during the Cold War who, he notes, called Muslims fighting the Soviets "freedom fighters" (Said 2001: 25). While providing an alternative to assimilationist points of view, Said presents Muslims, which he discusses in the interview in terms of "all of the Muslims I know," as a monolithic entity, if a *reasonable* one, failing to articulate or discuss that many differences of opinion prevail in the Muslim world, as in any community or cultural (or religious) group. (For instance, it is doubtful that Muslim Americans view "the United States they are attracted to for education, business," and so on in one single, critical way). In addition, conflicts are highlighted between groups rather than peaceful coexistence as a common norm, obscuring once again Muslims as diverse and ordinary citizens of U.S. society or of others worldwide.

Such is the case throughout the collection of essays, which also discuss U.S. interventions in the Middle East and Western Asia as terrorist acts, without engaging genuinely with mainstream or assimilationist arguments on U.S. foreign policy. While providing an alternative to popular stereotypical views, these essays fail to deal substantively with the more difficult issues related to Islam, such as the development of extremist groups, and complicated situations involving women's rights and equality. They also lack many Muslim perspectives, effectively painting a few knowledgeable and critical voices as a monolithic voice of Islam. As a whole, the supplement lacks relevance to what students (and teachers) learn and see elsewhere, such as in the news media, and appears disconnected from real-world problems related to religious difference.

Following a critical multicultural orientation, the mainstream view is discounted as disingenuous, deceptive, or simply wrong-headed; there is a presumed lack of humanity among U.S. political leaders today which educators and students are likely to find unpalatable. For instance, in an article discussing U.S. sanctions against Iraq titled "How Many Must Die?" the following learning activity is suggested: "former Sec. of State Madeleine Albright acknowledged the enormous suffering and death of children in Iraq but said it was 'worth it.' Find out why Albright and other U.S. government officials believe this" (Capaccio 2001: 21). Albright is clearly framed in a particularly negative way here, precluding a more comprehensive viewpoint (though perhaps, in finding the answer to this question, students may develop a more nuanced perspective, themselves). Like the Fordham Foundation guides, the *Rethinking Schools* report promotes an imbalanced perspective that is not entirely helpful or productive for developing clear understanding of complex, contradictory views of Islam and Muslims, and U.S. interactions with the Middle East.

Thus, while textbooks say little, pressing teachers to use alternative resources in the classroom, the representations in text supplements or news clippings teachers choose can vary widely, from approaches emphasizing assimilationist perspectives, to those defending and promoting Islam and/or Muslim societies, and criticizing U.S. foreign policy in relation. And given claims regarding both anti-Muslim bias *and* pro-Islamic propaganda in U.S. public school classrooms in recent years, it is likely that supplements putting forward such imbalanced, positive and negative, orientations are being commonly used in a less than critical manner by many teachers.

While the teachers discussed previously expressed feeling startled and upset by students' prejudicial views of Muslims, aiming to correct for them by providing alternative, positive views, in other cases teachers appear to be no less prejudiced than the most ignorant and biased of their students, as Muslims in public schools have attested since 9/11. We know from Muslim student protests that some teachers have mocked or misrecognized the religious beliefs of their students, tying Muslims to violence and terror, or ridiculing customs such as hijab:

> A teacher pulled back the religiously-mandated head scarf from a 17-year-old female student . . . in Harvey, Louisiana, during a world history class on January 30, 2004. After pulling on the student's scarf, the teacher allegedly said: "I hope God punishes you. No, I'm sorry, I hope Allah punishes you. I didn't know you had hair under there."
>
> (Elnatour 2005)

Although this teacher was removed shortly after this incident, it is difficult to know how often similar sorts of formal (that is, in front of the classroom) and/or informal discrimination go unchallenged, in a social context that makes simply being a Muslim a challenging or defiant act. Fazal Rizvi (2005) recalls being contacted four weeks after 9/11 by "a man I had never met before," concerned about claims of constant mockery and stereotyping from his daughters – devout Muslims, and loyal American citizens – in a U.S. public school. According to the father, despite being called "terrorists," and facing (with little to no protection) rather serious daily harassment and bullying, the girls did not want their father to say or do anything, lest he exacerbate their situation by expressing antagonism toward unconcerned and/or oblivious teachers and administrators. (Again, we see here how Muslims face being seen as aggressors even when defending themselves from unjust harassment). The girls simply wanted to be invisible or normal, like most schoolchildren do, given the predominantly anti-Muslim status quo (Rizvi 2005). In such contexts where discrimination and bullying is prevalent and likely goes unchallenged, teachers can easily make use of supplements such as those put out by the Fordham Institute in order to inform and frame their own and their students' views of the religion and its followers.

On the other hand, we also know there are teachers who use supplements such as that put out by *Rethinking Schools,* which provide an alternative to popular stereotypical views (if they are also limited in perspective in different ways). Kaviani observed a pluralist approach among many of the teachers he observed, who aimed to positively portray Islam and Muslims first and foremost, if also enable students to take on more balanced views (2007). However, in many cases such teachers express facing pressure by parents, administrators, and other parties concerned with teachers promoting the religion substantively in schools today. The Fordham Institute, the Textbook League, and the American Textbook Council all publish studies scrutinizing textbooks and supplements, and the schools and educators who use them, for representing Muslims and Islam positively rather than negatively. They also encourage parents to take a firm, intolerant stand. For instance, the educator discussed previously, who spent her winter of 2001–2002 studying Islam in her own time, recalls as a result of her efforts receiving a letter from a parent after her lesson on Muslims and Islam, who feared that the educator's attempt to "'understand where they are coming from' would blur the lines between right and wrong, important boundaries in a child's development" (Hochman 2006: 93). Here we see "basic" information contrasted with the value of tolerance in the parent's letter, reflecting the present climate as one in which assimilationist views, and related ideas about education's role in patriotic nation building, often prevail.

In sum, given the brevity of state standards and textbook discussions of Islam and Muslims, educator practices are hardly standardized, when it comes to teaching substantively about these subjects. Generally lacking formal education on the topics or substantive information about Muslims in the commonly used textbooks, teachers seeking to meet students' need to know about Muslims and Islam since 9/11 are often compelled to seek out supplementary resources for their own and for student learning. As I have illustrated here, they have a rich variety from which to choose, which can be seen to support assimilationist or pluralist orientations toward difference. Without any training or many formal resources, it is likely that many teachers simply teach the information in supplements such as those produced by the Fordham Institute and *Rethinking Schools,* teaching as valid a priori negative or positive orientations toward the religion and its followers in their classrooms. Yet this hardly meets students' need to develop critical autonomy about controversial subjects and groups through social studies education. In the next chapter, I propose a multicultural orientation and pedagogy that is more strongly oriented toward preparing students as democratic citizens in relation to teaching and learning about Muslims and Islam today.

Conclusion

While representations of Muslims in standards and textbooks are more balanced and neutral than those in the mass media or in textbooks used in earlier periods in U.S. history, it is likely that students will learn little, overall, about Muslims or Islam from these sources. While information that is very basic and historically related to Islam and Muslims is provided, discussions about complicated and controversial issues, such as gender relations in Muslim societies, and Islam's association with terrorism, are expressed neutrally in textbooks, despite often lacking real balance, and the texts rarely encourage students to take a critical, independent perspective on the topics, thereby frequently portraying controversial groups and subjects as simple (bland, cryptic) matters of fact.

Such presentations hardly enable students to develop clear or balanced views of Islam and Muslims, particularly as discussions of the subjects in modern history largely mirror those in mainstream media, connecting the religion and the community to terrorism, rather than referencing alternative discourses more relevant to the experiences of the vast majority of Muslims, that challenge media stereotypes. Students are likely to see Muslims as terroristic, Middle Eastern, and West Asian within the modern world from these sources, as Muslims in the United States, Europe, and elsewhere in the world, condemning terrorism and living peacefully in diverse communities, are nowhere to be found in the formal curriculum, perpetuating rather than challenging mainstream media representations. Additionally, there is a backlash against pluralist and critical multicultural understanding today, as textbook publishers are admonished with threats of being banned, by private and public institutions, for not saying enough bad things (and qualifying any good things) about Muslims and Islam.

Given the inadequate portrayals of controversial topics and groups in the texts, it is not uncommon for social studies teachers to rely on outside resources in their classrooms. Since 9/11, it is likely that the majority of teachers today make use of one or more of the wide variety of outside resources, from media representations and researched accounts, to curricular supplements provided by private groups, to supply additional information on the subject, often lacking much prior training, education, or experience with Islam or Muslims, themselves. Yet when one examines the classroom resources available for use and individual teacher practices since 9/11, one sees a smorgasbord of attitudes being put forward on Islam and Muslims, from those promotional toward Muslims and Islam, to those providing biased and imbalanced, stereotypical "clash of civilizations" conceptions of the worldwide religion and group. Lacking background knowledge or formal preparation for exploring such complex and controversial subjects and groups effectively in the classroom, teachers are ultimately "left on their own," when able to discuss the subject more substantively in their classrooms. Worse, they may be blocked by administrators, parents, or other organizations, in attempts to teach an alternative view to that of Muslim "bad guys."

Teachers can thus face many different challenges in teaching effectively about Islam and Muslims today in public schools. The common approaches to social difference, assimilationism, pluralism, and critical multiculturalism are unhelpful for this task. Media messages tend to show Muslims in a negative light. In this context, it can be increasingly difficult to teach across the grain about Muslims and Islam in public schools; textbooks are scrutinized for "Islamic propaganda," while teachers' loyalties can be questioned for seeking to teach lessons about world peace and justice (Apple 2003). Small and weak though they may paint themselves, the Chester Finns of society are not doing badly for themselves today.

The next two chapters focus on an alternative path forward. In Chapter 5, I propose another orientation toward difference, in contrast with the multicultural approaches discussed thus far, which I find more apt in considering the case of Islam and Muslims in U.S. education: *interculturalism*. I spell out what this alternative orientation indicates for classroom teaching. I consider further implications, such as additional educational requirements for teachers, for implementing such an approach today, in the sixth chapter.

References

Abukhattala, Ibrahim. "New Bogeyman Under the Bed." In *Miseducation of the West: How Schools and the Media Distort Our Understanding of the Islamic World*, edited by Joe L. Kincheloe and Shirley R. Steinberg. Westport: Praeger, 2004.

Ahmad, Iftikhar, Herbert Brodsky, Marylee S. Crofts, and Elisabeth Gaynor Ellis. *World Cultures: A Global Mosaic*. Pearson Prentice Hall, 1996/2001/2004.

Apple, Michael. "Politics of Compulsory Patriotism." In *Education as Enforcement: The Militarization and Corporatization of Schools*, edited by Kenneth J. Saltman and David A. Gabbard, 291–300. London: RoutledgeFalmer, 2003.

Armento, Beverly J., Gary B. Nash, Christopher L. Salter, Louis E. Wilson, and Karen K. Wixson. *To See a World: World Cultures and Geography*. Boston: Houghton Mifflin, 1997.

Awad, Nihad. "A Word of Truth on Jihad and Islam." *Islam-OpEd*. Council on American-Islamic Relations, 21 August 2013. https://cair.com/press-center/op-eds/11877-a-word-of-truth-on-jihad-and-islam.html (accessed October 18, 2013).

Banks, James A. "The African American Roots of Multicultural Education." In *Transformative Knowledge, and Action: Historical and Contemporary Perspectives*, edited by James A. Banks, 30–45. New York: Teachers College Press, 1996.

Banks, James A., Barry K. Beyer, and Gloria Contreras. *World History: Adventures in Time and Place*. Columbus: MacMillan McGraw-Hill, 1997.

Barker, Rod Philip. *The Frequency and Extent of Textbook Usage Among Arizona High School Social Studies Teachers*. Flagstaff: Northern Arizona University, 1992.

Barlow, Elizabeth. "Middle East Facts and Fictions." *The Journal of the International Institute* 2 (1995): 1–5.

Beck, Roger B., Linda Black, Larry S. Krieger, Phillip C. Naylor, and Dahia Ibo Shabaka. *World History: Patterns of Interaction*. Boston: Houghton Mifflin, 1999/2003/2004/2012.

Bednarz, Sarah Witham, Ines Miyares, and Mark C. Schug. *World Cultures and Geography*. Boston: McDougall Littell, 2003.

Bednarz, Sarah Witham, Charles S. White, Mark C. Schug, and Inez M. Miyares. *World Cultures and Geography*. Boston: McDougall Littell/Houghton Mifflin, 2005.

Bednarz, Sarah Witham, et al., *World Cultures and Geography*. Boston: McDougall Littell, 2007.

Bennetta, William J. "How a Public School in Scottsdale, Arizona, Subjected Students to Islamic Indoctrination." *The Textbook League*. 2005. www.textbookleague.org/tci-az.htm (accessed January 8, 2014).

Boehm, Richard G. *World Geography*. Columbus: Glencoe McGraw-Hill, 2012.

Branom, Frederick K., and Helen M. Ganey. *Eastern Hemispheres: Geography of Europe, Asia, Africa, Australia, and the Polar Regions*. New York: William H. Sadler, 1928.

Brigham, Albert P., and Charles T. McFarlane. *Our Continental Neighbors*. New York: American Book Company, 1933.

California State Board of Education. *History-Social Science Standards for California Public Schools, Kindergarten Through Grade Twelve.* Sacramento: California Department of Education, 2000.

de Leon Mendiola, Annalisa. *Traditionalists Versus Multiculturalists: Discourses From the 2003 U.S. History Textbook Adoption in Texas.* San Antonio: University of Texas at San Antonio, 2007.

Capaccio, George. "How Many Must Die?" In "War, Terrorism, and Our Classrooms: Teaching in the Aftermath of the September 11th Tragedy," edited by *Rethinking Schools,* 21. Milwaukee: Rethinking Schools, 2001.

Common Core. "English Language Arts Standards: Speaking and Listening, Grade 9–10." 2012. www.corestandards.org/ELA-Literacy/SL/9–10 (accessed October 18, 2013).

Council on American-Islamic Relations. *American Public Opinion About Muslims and Islam, 2006.* Washington, DC: Council on American-Islamic Relations, 2006.

Ellis, Elisabeth Gaynor, and Anthony Esler. *World History: Connections to Today.* Upper Saddle River, NJ: Pearson Prentice Hall, 2003.

Elnatour, Mohamed. *Perceptions of Muslim Students' Needs and Challenges in a Public High School in the Midwest.* Aurora, IL: Aurora University, 2005.

Finn, Jr., Chester E. Introduction to *September 11: What Our Children Need to Know,* edited by the Fordham Foundation, 4–11. Washington, DC: Thomas B. Fordham Foundation, 2002. www.edexcellence.net/publications/sept11.html (accessed January 8, 2014).

Finn, Jr., Chester E. Introduction to *Terrorists, Despots, and Democracy: What Our Children Need to Know,* edited by the Fordham Foundation, 5–16. Washington, DC: Thomas B. Fordham Foundation, 2003. www.edexcellence.net/publications/terrorists.html (accessed January 8, 2014).

Finn, Jr., Chester E. Introduction to *Teaching About 9/11 in 2011: What Our Children Need to Know,* edited by the Fordham Foundation, 5–9. Washington, DC: Thomas B. Fordham Foundation, 2011. www.edexcellence.net/publications/teaching-about-911-in-2011.html (accessed January 8, 2014).

Finn, Jr., Chester E., and Diane Ravitch. *The Mad, Mad World of Textbook Adoption.* Washington, DC: Thomas B. Fordham Foundation, 2004.

Fitzgerald, Frances. *America Revised: History Schoolbooks in the Twentieth Century.* New York: Atlantic Monthly Press, 1979.

Fordham Foundation, ed. *September 11: What Our Children Need to Know.* Washington, DC: Thomas B. Fordham Foundation, 2002. www.edexcellence.net/publications/sept11.html (accessed January 8, 2014).

Fordham Foundation, ed. *Terrorists, Despots, and Democracy: What Our Children Need to Know.* Washington, DC: Thomas B. Fordham Foundation, 2003. www.edexcellence.net/publications/terrorists.html (accessed January 8, 2014).

Freedom House. *Freedom in the World 2007.* New York: Freedom House, 2007.

Freedom House. *The Worst of the Worst 2012: The World's Most Repressive Societies.* New York: Freedom House, 2012.

Georgia Department of Education. "Social Studies Grade Seven Standards." In *Georgia Standards.* Atlanta: Georgia Department of Education, 2008.

Gereluk, Diane. *Symbolic Clothing in Schools.* London: Continuum, 2008.

Greenblatt, Miriam, and Peter S. Lemmo. *Human Heritage: A World History.* Columbus: Glencoe McGraw-Hill, 1999/2001/2004.

Griswold, William J. *The Image of the Middle East in Secondary School Textbooks.* New York: Middle East Studies Association of North America, 1975.

Hanson, Victor Davis "Preserving America, Man's Greatest Hope." In *Terrorists, Despots, and Democracy: What Our Children Need to Know*, edited by the Fordham Foundation, 23–24. Washington, DC: Thomas B. Fordham Foundation, 2003. www.edexcellence.net/publications/terrorists.html (accessed January 8, 2014).

Hausmann, Ricardo, Laura D. Tyson, and Saadia Zahidi. *The Global Gender Gap Report 2011*. Geneva: World Economic Forum, 2011. www3.weforum.org/docs/WEF_GenderGap_Report_2011.pdf (accessed January 8, 2014).

Hochman, Dalia. "Hominid Development: On Being a Social Studies Teacher During September 11." In *Forever After: New York City Teachers on 9/11*, edited by Teachers College Press with Maureen Grolnick, 85–96. New York: Teachers College Press, 2006.

Huntington, Samuel P. "The Clash of Civilizations?" *Foreign Affairs*, Summer 1993.

Illinois State Board of Education. *Social Science Performance Descriptors*. Springfield: Illinois State Board of Education, 2008.

Jackson, Liz. "Choice Versus Equal Opportunity: What Toleration Requires in the Case of the *Hijab* in French Schools." In *Philosophy of Education 2005*, edited by Kenneth R. Howe, 272–275. Urbana, IL: Philosophy of Education Society, 2005.

Jackson, Liz. "Islam and Muslims in U.S. Public Schools Since September 11, 2001." *Religious Education* 106 (2011): 162–180.

Kaviani, Khodadad. *Teachers' Gatekeeping of the Middle East Curriculum*. Seattle: University of Washington, 2007.

Kincheloe, Joe L. *Getting Beyond the Facts: Teaching Social Studies/Social Sciences in the Twenty-First Century*. New York: Peter Lang, 2001.

Klee, Mary Beth. "Civics, Schools and September 11." In *September 11: What Our Children Need to Know*, edited by the Fordham Foundation, 34–35. Washington, DC: Thomas B. Fordham Foundation, 2002. www.edexcellence.net/publications/sept11.html (accessed January 8, 2014).

Klee, Mary Beth. "What Schools Should Do on September 11." In *Terrorists, Despots, and Democracy: What Our Children Need to Know*, edited by the Fordham Foundation, 56–57. Washington, DC: Thomas B. Fordham Foundation, 2003. www.edexcellence.net/publications/terrorists.html (accessed January 8, 2014).

Lowenstein, Ethan. "Voices From the Crossroads." In *Forever After: New York City Teachers on 9/11*, edited by Teachers College Press with Maureen Grolnick, 159–176. New York: Teachers College Press, 2006.

Morgan, Hani. *The Portrayal of the Middle East in School Textbooks from 1880 to the Present*. New Brunswick: Rutgers, the State University of New Jersey, 2002.

Morgan, Hani. "American School Textbooks: How They Portrayed the Middle East from 1989 to 1994." *American History Educational Journal* 35 (2008): 315–330.

Noddings, Nel. *Educating for Intelligent Belief or Unbelief*. New York: Teachers College, 1993.

Noppe, Illene C., Lloyd D. Noppe, and Denise Bartell. "Terrorism and Resilience: Adolescents' and Teachers' Responses to September 11, 2001." *Death Studies* 30 (1006): 41–60.

Nord, Warren A. *Religion and American Education: Rethinking a National Dilemma*. Chapel Hill: University of North Carolina Press, 1995.

Nord, Warren A. *Does God Make a Difference? Taking Religion Seriously in Our Schools and Universities*. Oxford: Oxford University Press, 2010.

Oregon State Board of Education. *Oregon Social Sciences Academic Content Standards*. Salem: Oregon Department of Education, 2011.

Radu, Michael. "*The Challenge of Terrorism: A Historical Reader:* This Book Doesn't Teach What Students Need to Know." *The Textbook Letter* 12 (2004). www.textbookleague.org/122terr.htm (accessed January 8, 2014).

Redway, Jacques Wardlaw, and Russell Hinman. *Natural Advanced Geography*. New York City: American Book Company, 1898.

Rizvi, Fazal. "Representations of Islam and Education for Social Justice." In *Race, Identity, and Representation in Education*, edited by Cameron McCarthy and Warren Crichlow, 167–178. New York: Routledge, 2005.

Ruitenberg, Claudia W. "How to Do Things with Headscarves: A Discursive and Meta-Discursive Analysis." In *Philosophy of Education 2006*, edited by Daniel Vokey. Urbana, IL: Philosophy of Education Society, 2006.

Sager, Robert J., and David M. Helgren. *Holt World Geography Today*. Austin: Holt, Rinehart and Winston, 2003.

Said, Edward. "Root Causes of Terrorism." In "War, Terrorism, and Our Classrooms: Teaching in the Aftermath of the September 11th Tragedy," edited by *Rethinking Schools*, 25. Milwaukee: Rethinking Schools, 2001.

Schwartz, Stephen. "America and the Crisis of Islam. In *Terrorists, Despots, and Democracy: What Our Children Need to Know*, edited by the Fordham Foundation, 88–90. Washington, DC: Thomas B. Fordham Foundation, 2003. www.edexcellence.net/publications/terrorists.html (accessed January 8, 2014).

Sewall, Gilbert T. *Islam and the Textbooks: A Report of the American Textbook Council*. New York: American Textbook Council, 2003.

Sewall, Gilbert T. *Islam in the Classroom: What the Textbooks Tell Us*. New York: American Textbook Council, 2008.

Stillwell, Cinnamon, "Islam in America's Public Schools: Education or Indoctrination?" *SFGate*, June 11, 2008. www.sfgate.com/politics/article/Islam-in-America-s-public-schools-Education-or-2482820.php (accessed January 8, 2014).

Spielvogel, Jackson J. *World History*. Columbus: Glencoe McGraw-Hill, 2008.

Texas State Board of Education. Resolution. September 24, 2010.

Zagumny, Lisa, and Amanda B. Richey. "Orientalism(s), World Geography Textbooks, and Temporal Paradox: Questioning Representations of Southwest Asia and North Africa." *International Journal of Qualitative Studies in Education* 2012a: 1–19.

Zagumny, Lisa, and Amanda B. Richey. "Textbook Orientalism: Critical Visuality and Representations of Southwest Asia and North Africa." In *The New Politics of the Textbook: Problematizing the Portrayal of Marginalized Groups in Textbooks*, edited by Heather Hickman and Brad J. Porfilio, 195–214. Rotterdam: Sense Publishers, 2012b.

5 A path forward
Interculturalism

Introduction

As discussed in the last few chapters, young people in the United States face many challenges to learning substantial and accurate information about Muslims and Islam today. They face the prevalent discourses of a mass media that is oriented more toward exploring tragedies and negative exceptionalities over ordinary, everyday life, which is not newsworthy. In addition the media privileges non-Muslim voices critical toward the faith and community over more unexceptional, internal Muslim perspectives. This trend echoes in educational debates in Texas and elsewhere in the country, where teachers can face scrutiny and challenges to teaching information that is not negatively biased, by parents and private organizations. In this context, is it likely students are not learning a great deal about Islam or Muslims, or about a *great deal of* Muslims and Islam, over a few select "bad guys," who hardly represent this large cross-section of humanity today. While alternative information sources are available, such as the *Rethinking Schools* special report on 9/11 and terrorism discussed in the last chapter, this information is also partial and extremely critical toward U.S. leaders, avoiding opportunities to really focus on potential challenges in integrating Muslims in the United States. Its perspective may be useful to compare alongside other sources in the course of a high-level classroom discussion; but it does not teach enough information about Islam and Muslims on its own.

In this chapter, I turn to some solutions. I introduce more fully a framework toward difference I mentioned briefly in the second chapter, as one phase or category of traditional pluralism, which is worth revisiting today: *interculturalism*. As I discussed, interculturalism was a strategy replaced by pluralism in U.S. educational history during the mid-twentieth century. At that time, it meant cross-cultural engagement of different groups in U.S. society, across race, religious, culture, and class, to learn about each other's issues and challenges at the interpersonal level, and work together to constructively focus on solutions. Today this concept has been expanded upon and is beginning to be employed to consider issues related to social diversity in various Western societies, such as Canada, Germany, the United Kingdom, and France, through education as well as other social institutions. I reconsider this method of thinking about and grappling with difference in this chapter, comparing it favorably to the traditional multicultural approaches, and I discuss teaching practices that align with the intercultural lens.

As I mentioned in the second chapter, that there are limitations to traditional methods of understanding and navigating difference in U.S. society, such as assimilationism, pluralism, and critical multiculturalism, does not imply that these are useless or inappropriate solutions for all cases. However, I compare interculturalism favorably to these approaches particularly when we consider social difference and Islam in U.S. education today. In its focus on setting the stage for dialogue and democratic communication across lines of social difference, it is preferable in relation to learning and teaching about Islam and Muslims, in contrast to the multicultural frameworks, which authorize teacher-centered practices of knowledge construction about diversity in society.

Interculturalism reintroduced

Interculturalism is not well known today in the United States but is becoming commonly understood and popular in countries in Western Europe, Canada, Australia, and New Zealand. As mentioned in the second chapter, this approach to social difference focuses on laying the groundwork for dialogue across difference to take place. At the heart of the earlier U.S. intercultural education project, different groups came together formally to discuss common challenges from diverse perspectives (Banks 2012). Against assimilationist views, intercultural educators hold that diversity is a good in a (political) liberal democratic society. To benefit from a diversity of views, strengths, and experiences in a society, public institutions must encourage creativity, openness, and innovation, as well as virtues of toleration, empathy, and compassion. However, it remains inescapable that diversity can also create challenges for treating everyone in society equally, as different groups and individuals can be seen to have different conceptions of the common good and personal wellbeing. This is one of the reasons, perhaps, for assimilationist educators' reluctance or intolerance toward positively recognizing Muslims as a part of U.S. society.

Though pluralism of beliefs is seen as a good thing in a society in an intercultural perspective, it also requires difficult decision making to arrive at policies that treat diverse people fairly and equitably. While assimilationists will hold that the status quo should triumph over sociopolitical minority concerns, pluralists aim to enable each community to flourish: However, as discussed in the second chapter, this can create a challenge related to individual rights of exit versus community rights, in public education. Additionally there are some people with more individualistic and more communitarian orientations in both majority and minority groups in society. It seems in this context that one cannot please all concerned parties in relation to public cross-cultural issues, such as the ban of hijab (women's head-covering) in French public schools. A line is not only drawn between Muslims and non-Muslims or secularists here, but lines can also be drawn within these camps, as the meaning of hijab can be seen as controversial in French (including French Muslim) society today (Jackson 2005).

Given these sorts of emerging challenges, in recent years, many Western European leaders have commented on the "death of multiculturalism," in relation to Muslim integration in nation-states such as Germany, the United Kingdom, and France. As in the United States, there is public concern about terrorism, radical Islamists, and a challenge for Muslim assimilation due to the prevalence of Christian and/or secular norms in schools and other public institutions. At the same time, there has also been a conceptual shift in thinking, from likening of Muslims in Europe to temporary visitors, to realizing that Muslims are at home in Europe (Emerson 2011). As temporary visitors, there would be no need for comprehensive integration, conceptually and practically; however, as permanent residents and citizens Muslims must be enabled to participate meaningfully in all aspects of society within democratic political systems. In order for such integration to take place, common understanding across groups must be attained to ensure that steps toward integration and harmonious living together are viewed as reasonable and practical across groups. This requires laying groundwork for dialogue across individuals and groups.

Interculturalism is seen as a solution toward integration in these contexts that in some respects compromises between assimilationism and pluralism (Emerson 2011), which has sympathy toward the plight of disadvantaged members of society in social and political terms, but does not assume they must assimilate or be respected or accommodated a priori. Society is not recognized as sufficiently just to all its members, but in need of active solutions that are mutually agreed upon in order to increase equality and opportunity across different segments. Crucially, where to draw the line between pluralist recognition and toleration and assimilationist integration cannot be decided outside of a social context, without the democratic participation of those involved, as no two situations are alike, as we know from the various cases of European countries' efforts to integrate increasing, diverse Muslim communities.

> There is a mass of policy variables that can determine how the stance of policy may be assessed as tending towards the multicultural or assimilationist end of the spectrum, or toward the middle ground of interculturalism . . . At the same time it would be excessive and artificial to try and fit each possible setting of each variable into this straitjacket of categories. The reality is too complex. . . .
>
> [An] example concerns religious symbols in public buildings or public spaces, especially regarding elements of clothing like the headscarf or full face cover (burka). The multicultural policy will tend to be supportive of such symbols, while the assimilationist policy will be restrictive of exclusionary. The intercultural compromise may be tolerant toward the headscarf but exclude the burka, for example, with many finer gradations of policy possible over the visual importance of the symbol or the borderline between the public and private space . . .
>
> (Emerson 2011: 4, 6)

116 *A path forward: Interculturalism*

Like pluralists and critical multiculturalists, intercultural theorists understand so-called cultural difference as inevitably tied to political differences between social groups, and inequality of capability to practice or engage in dialogue across lines of social difference. Interculturalists are additionally aligned with critical multiculturalists (and liberal assimilationists) in being suspicious of what is meant by culture, and how it is constructed in social contexts in ways that favor some groups over others. However, as Peters (2012: 36) writes with regard to the binary cultural thinking I attribute here to critical multiculturalism, culture is not reframed helpfully as oppressed/oppressor, but should be understood rather as more dynamic with regard to issues of power and equality within, and across groups.

> This oppositional logic tends to obscure relational processes [and] underestimate both the importance of subcultures and contemporary movements that have the power to redefine cultures and also fails to conceptualize the relationship between cultures and individuals in order to take account of dissent and disagreement within cultures.

Defining what culture is and the difference it makes in people's lives has nonetheless been a challenge for intercultural theorists, as they do not regard it simply as a tool or set of items, but as the ongoing development of different ways of social being. This obscure conception of culture is no great aid to interculturalism, as it makes it difficult to ascertain the most appropriate educational solutions for dealing with "cultural" difference, as Richter (2001: 100) reflects on intercultural education in Germany historically:

> In the beginnings of the development of the concept something like resignation reigned with regard to clarification of what might be understood . . .
> Correspondingly, we find in the context of the argument supporting an early practical experiment by Unal Akpinar a rather naive, merely pragmatic handling of this unsolved problem, such that the mere coming together and acting together of German and foreign children/pupils is supposed to constitute intercultural practice (in the desired sense): "When children are given the opportunity to interact with each other and to do something in common, one no longer need to talk of culture, because they are practicing. This is intellectual praxis."

In this context, intercultural educators in Europe such as Richter (2001: 99) have favored discussing "migrant culture," as a fluid concept that denies both easy assimilation of diverse members of society, as well as some traditional, static, monolithic cultural past: "intercultural education would not need to have recourse to statically fixed sets of national cultural characteristics, but, as a flexible model of 'living' change, would place the fluid, processual nature of events at the center of its thinking." Culture is understood for its everyday, pragmatic implications rather than in an anthropological sense of identifying contrastable items between communities, as communities are interdependent and interrelated, and do not develop in isolation from one another, as in the "clash of civilizations" view. This does not mean that culture can be dismissed outright, as liberal assimilationism implies, but that it must be understood in a functional, but not binary majority/minority or oppressor/oppressed way.

To return again to the example of hijab in France, arguments that focus on binary power relations more exclusively will tend to suggest that Muslims face cultural oppression through a French ban on hijab; that Muslims are generally against the ban, while the non-Muslim French generally support it (e.g., Corngold 2005). Yet if we complicate the analysis, seeing it not as a general abstract case, but in its distinct entirety, it becomes obvious that the discussion in France is about more than just Islam in France; it impact on other religious communities as well. Additionally, no evidence is provided in most accounts in supporting the common presupposition that the majority of French citizens or residents supported the ban while, on the other hand, a significant percentage of Muslim women opposed it. Hijab does not symbolize or have the same meaning across the "Muslim world," despite the binary understanding of cross-cultural relations (Jackson 2005; Ruitenberg 2006). Thus, no theory can guide us before we enter this situation, or can help frame the social makeup of French society most accurately without examining the particularities. In this sense, traditional multicultural approaches to difference in society cannot be effectively applied to future cases, but each future case involves its own ethical learning in a unique, particular political and cultural context.

Emerging European interculturalism has its roots in a United Nations theme from 1998, "Dialogue of Civilizations," which borrows from a theory of former Iranian president Seyed Mohammad Khatami, and is no doubt a direct response to Huntington's (1993) "clash of civilizations" view (Besley & Peters 2012: 9). The United Nations Educational, Scientific and Cultural Organization (UNESCO) further took up this call to dialogue with the aim of working to secure peace and democracy worldwide, through laying foundations for dialogue "based on universally shared values and to undertake concrete activities" (Besley & Peters 2012: 10), in a spirit of mutual respect and reconciliation. Tina Besley distinguishes the "intercultural" from the "cross-cultural" by noting that the latter is inherently comparative, while "intercultural implies interaction and more of a relationship between people" (2012: 88). Besley suggests the Fulbright Program and related exchange programs as exemplars of interculturalism in the United States. Such programs require work to be successfully implemented, however, and so intercultural education focuses on developing these preconditions in terms of skills and attitudes development.

Dialogue is defined in this context as "an interaction that goes back and forth to ascertain another person's viewpoint without necessarily agreeing with them and is not so much a specific communicative form of question and answer" (Besley & Peters 2012: 16). For intercultural dialogue with the aim of ascertaining others' views gradually, Besley and Peters (2012) cite Nicholas Burbules's (1993) requirements for dialogue within a particular kind of interpersonal or social relation. These are prerequisite feelings or stances on other persons or the possibility of engaging productively in dialogue: concern, trust, respect, appreciation, affection, and hope. Respect, as Burbules elaborates, requires "the idea that everyone is equal in some basic way and entails a commitment to being fair-minded, opposing degradation and rejecting exploitation" (1993: 19). This is an initial pluralism and attempt at neutrality: an early optimistic attitude toward others' viewpoints, in trust that their view is rational from their perspective and not put forward with the aim of giving offense. The sense of equality it implies cannot be taken for granted, in education or in society generally, however. As Waddington and colleagues note, new immigrant groups' beliefs, views, and attitudes are *not* equal to "those of the dominant cultural space into which they have moved" in a society (2012: 318). Mutual understanding among diverse members of society can be difficult to achieve in practice, as media and assimilationist politics and institutions can threaten some members of society, while reinforcing prejudices and stereotypes that may be held by mainstream members of society. As discussed here, in the United States being Muslim makes it difficult to be heard as reasonable in society, despite many American Muslim leaders' efforts.

For such dialogue to be possible in these contexts, there must be a public shared language for discourse and efforts made to ensure that dialogue does not cause an undue burden to any members of society, from the privileged to the disadvantaged. Additionally, from this perspective, demands for pluralist recognition relate not to the technical, demographic makeup of the society, but to the more particular needs of different groups for fair and nondiscriminatory public representation. Similar to pluralism, intercultural educators aim to respond to social injustice via positive recognition, but they aim to do so with a broader view of how systemic or structural injustice challenges communication itself. In the case of Islam, these structural elements are neglected by pluralist educators who would merely advocate positive classroom recognition of Islam and Muslims, though it is unlikely to make the difference sought, within a political climate where mediated discourse is often quite negative about Islam and Muslims. In such contexts, students may easily ignore such lessons or even frame them critically in relation to what they have "learned" elsewhere.

As Waddington et al. (2012: 327) discuss the view of Quebec on the issue of religious diversity and intercultural education today, they argue,

> Religious diversity is not educationally significant in and of itself. Thus, the point is not simply whether the majority of citizens practice one or the other religion, or whether they identify with this or that ethnic or national heritage. From an intercultural viewpoint, the relevant criterion is how important the consequences of students' interaction with religious diversity are with respect to the goal of increasing social cohesion. In other words, if our goal is favoring tolerance, mutual respect and dialogue among the members of this particular citizenry, then we should not look at the percentage of people who practice a particularly religious in their everyday life . . . rather,

look at what is the most important source of intolerance and conflict within a particular society in order to adapt civic education to the obstacles to social integration of particular societies.

Waddington et al. (2012) emphasize that the weighting of the needs of different groups for recognition and understanding, for others around them to actively work toward understanding, is not something that can be assumed a priori, but must also be considered within a concrete, political context. Thus, if the orientation of the Texas Board of Education in developing its resolution on textbooks and Islam (discussed in the last chapter) was *intercultural* rather than *pluralist* (or *assimilationist,* given the Board's reference points), there would be no need to reduce positive claims about Islam and Muslims in the text, as Muslims can be identified as victims of scapegoating, negative stereotyping, discrimination, and prejudice in society, in comparison with other religious groups in the United States. If pluralist recognition of all religions was the goal, it would be necessary to increase positive representations of Christianity in the curriculum (as the Texas resolution recommends); however, from an intercultural perspective that takes stock of the current social context of Texas and/or the United States today, this would not be necessary, since Christianity does not face social intolerance or negative public representation relative to Islam.

Tolerance is not emphasized in the Texas document, or in assimilationist educational arguments, however, though "democratic values" are. Yet arguably tolerance is needed for democracy, when the latter is understood in a thick sense, as a rigorous form of earnest dialogue across lines of social difference. One must tolerate others' right to be and express themselves in good faith in order to listen to them with an open mind, as discussed in Burbules's requirements for dialogue. Robert Shaw (2012: 378) thus argues that interculturalism that focuses on the preconditions for a thick sense of participatory democracy, such as tolerance, mutual recognition, and understanding, challenges democracy as a thin prescriptive or directional tool, which allows for decision making without mutual understanding and recognition. As a case, Shaw focuses on Afghanistan, where democracy has been pushed by Western powers despite the incapacity of most citizens, who are largely illiterate, uniformed, and uneducated, to practically participate in democratic decision making without prior substantive educational development. They can make a choice or vote, but how meaningful are such "rights," when one does not have access to diverse sources of information, or the capacity to comprehend and analyze diverse internal (domestic) texts and discourses? Democracy in a procedural sense can be seen to block fuller, richer enactments of democracy in this case, as people make decisions, but do so without the skills and knowledge required to be genuine authors of their decisions. Democracy itself is thus seen as a disingenuous demand of some Western countries toward some Muslim-majority countries, which lack preconditions for democracy to meaningfully flourish at the level of individual autonomous decision making. Intercultural education therefore starts with what is required for *meaningful,* not just *procedural,* dialogue and democracy to take place.

Intercultural education, then, prepares students to make decisions in society, with adequate information about sources of controversial difference and different perspectives on the various ways to respond to them. *Method* is emphasized over *content*, requiring a student-centered approach to education. As discussed in the second chapter, assimilationists typically regard expressions of cultural difference from mainstream society as barriers to social success, while pluralists view differences from majority norms that are common in minority communities more positively, as a priori legitimate and worthy of recognition and inclusion. One promotes ethnocentrism, as the majority culture is held as superior (pragmatically if not essentially), while the other supports a kind of apolitical pluralism of groups in society. Neither approach encourages students to understand social differences as context based, however, precluding students being able to make up their own minds about what differences matter and the situations of minority groups in society. Instead, they obscure the process of framing social difference from students, expecting or desiring that students take their perspective on minorities and difference in society, regardless of the availability of, or student intuitions regarding, alternative plausible views. In the case of Muslims, assimilationists expect students to view Muslims with a critical eye, while pluralists require their toleration or appreciation – neither presents the other perspective as worthy of serious consideration.

Similar to critical multiculturalists, intercultural educators have as their goal students developing a critical distance from others' views. Seeing their students as future independent meaning makers rather, intercultural educators encourage in students a critical distance toward majority views and values that privilege ethnocentrism over mutual understanding. However, among critical multiculturalists, there is a further tendency to dismiss mainstream or assimilationist viewpoints, and treat their proponents in an accusatory way, which is not educationally productive in public schools. Unlike critical multiculturalists, intercultural educators do not see themselves as necessarily experts on what is right and wrong, and what is and is not truth, useful knowledge, or critical consciousness, as they understand that no two situations are exactly the same, and that what makes sense in one case need not be presumed as the answer in the next. As Peters (2012: 44) writes of intercultural dialogue, a somewhat agnostic, never-finished understanding of the world can enable more open, productive, continual conversation on the vital issues in society.

> There is no final vocabulary and therefore no foolproof way of capturing the meaning of existence besides continuing the conversation . . . There is only conversation that rests on our preparedness to listen and to learn from others, and in this conversation, so long as we can manage to keep it going, we may come to understand what it means to be a citizen of the *polis* and how the relationship between the citizen and policy might be enhanced through education.

In comparison with the traditional multicultural approaches to difference in society, interculturalism relies upon a selective type of "moderate cultural relativism," derived from the initial "presumption of equal worth" (Taylor 1992) implied in the prerequisites for dialogue such as trust, respect, and so on. Intercultural educators thus do not take a firm stance on social issues and the right way to think about or resolve them a priori. Rather, teachers guide students to develop reasonable views in light of ethical principles, such as the need to avoid undue harm to others in society, a plausible universal value in the abstract (although what it implies in practice is typically less straightforward in diverse societies). Richter (2001:103) follows Heller (1984) in arguing that when one is engaged with and concerned with issues of social justice in their practical implications, in terms of violence and oppression, neither ethnocentric nor pluralist or culturally relativistic knowledge can prevail. Yet a kind of moderate cultural relativism enables continual reexamination of the most relevant criteria to consider across cultures.

> Heller states that the postulate made by the sense of justice under the obligatory premise of humanity demands the reduction of domination, force, and violence. Accordingly cultures that display a smaller total quantity of violence and domination than others are superior to these others. In relation to her overriding question as to the problem of relativism v. universalism, Heller plumps for a *moderate* cultural relativism: not comparing the non-comparable, but relating to the actions relevant to "domination, coercion, and violence." An extreme cultural relativism, by contrast, would contradict our sense of justice, because it does not permit us to protest against cases of application of "dual morality."

One should not simply view other cultures as deficient from one's personal viewpoint, nor should one view all cultures as equal and only verifiable according to internal criteria. In reality, cultures are constantly changing and interacting with each other, and neither lens aids people in understanding cultures in such a way that can help promote social justice given cultural and social diversity.

As discussed in the second chapter, pluralists can be seen to promote moral relativism in recognizing diverse cultures in a substantive way; yet this can impinge upon students' right of exit, which is essential within public schools. Teachers should not be partial toward the cultural orientations of one of more of their students' backgrounds in public schools. However they should also not insist that society is perfectly just, as assimilationists can be seen to often do in their defenses of mainstream society against pluralists and critical multiculturalists. As for the latter, they too can be seen to have an absolute stance toward morality, seeing groups in society as good/bad in line with advantage and disadvantage in an unhelpful way when it comes to learning about diversity and freedom and mechanisms of equality, and oppression. Intercultural education aims to orientate students toward believing that there *is* right and wrong, but asks students to take responsibility for developing a reasoned stance with regard to ethical issues, holding a position of pluralistic generosity toward positions a priori, but ultimately encouraging moral judgment by students when it comes

Table 5.1 Differences across multicultural perspectives (as in Chapter 2) and interculturalism

	Assimilationist Conservative	Assimilationist Liberal	Pluralist	Critical Multiculturalist	Interculturalist
"Society is just."	*	*			
"Society is neutral."		*			
"Minority 'culture' is misconstructed."		*		*	*
"Teachers are sources of ethical truth."	*	*	*	*	

to analyzing evidence about social events and situations. Table 5.1 summarizes distinctions between these positions, adding interculturalism to the four kinds of multiculturalism discussed in the second chapter.

Teaching for such lofty goals as democracy and interpersonal understanding, mutual recognition, and dialogue, is no easy matter in practice, however. The rest of this chapter discusses some best practices in teaching about Muslims and Islam within an intercultural approach, to articulate the more abstract points made here in their educational implications. As discussed previously, it is valuable for teachers to use multiple angles in discussing social issues and groups in class. In the last chapter, some model educators were discussed, who attempted to gain balance or pursue multiple perspectives in class with the use of a variety of resources to engage student critical thinking skills. Within an intercultural approach, I argue that while a variety of perspectives is necessarily incorporated in discussions to provide students with balanced and accurate understandings, teachers must also (1) enable students to practice democratic dialogue about diversity and controversy in the classroom and (2) critically model and teach students critical media literacy skills.

Intercultural education as embodied in the examples I give here differs from multicultural educational approaches to difference in society by focusing on the conditions for a substantive, thick sense of democracy and how to understand difference in society broadly: the development of students' capacity to engage with others earnestly, critically, and independently. This requires understanding their right to free speech in society for its practical implications, as people cannot be heard if they are treated with prejudice and intolerance. Thus, the emphasis is on the development of skills rather than knowledge or content. Some might prefer then to call intercultural education merely a more student-centered variant of critical multiculturalism or pluralism, although unlike critical multiculturalism, intercultural education does not have key student outcomes in terms of ethical conclusions related to critical consciousness in mind. Indeed, the multicultural approaches to differences I have discussed here all have outcomes with regard to content knowledge – attitudes and beliefs about society and diversity within it – but do not emphasize skills, unless skills such as "critical thinking" are conflated here with outcomes, as particular attitudes, beliefs, and understandings (i.e., you think *critically*, because you think *x*).

Some may find generally that my pedagogical recommendations are not different from normal classroom practices within highly effective schools, as many educational theorists across ideological lines agree that quality education should develop students' skills to function as members of a dynamic and continually flourishing political liberal democratic society. I nonetheless find it useful here to identify interculturalism as a new orientation, because it focuses on dialogue and skills rather than presuming any given understanding of diversity in society and the most appropriate ethical response toward difference. The emphasis on democratic deliberation in the classroom and media literacy is more apt than the educational orientations of the other multicultural frameworks discussed here when it comes to teaching and learning about Islam and Muslims in U.S. society, as a focus on discussion, debate, and pursuing information is crucial in place of prescriptive rules about the best way for students to think, or the best things (i.e., content) to teach. This case of social difference and its implications in society cannot be resolved for the future, today; tools rather than answers should be provided. As such, intercultural education is a kind of substantive civic education, as well as a pedagogy for social studies education, in aiming to develop skills for living in a democratic society, rather than simply learning the best or most important contemporary multicultural knowledge deemed important to learn by Texas or state standards. Of course, there are obstacles to my recommendations becoming common elements across the public school system. I will discuss some of them in the next chapter.

Interculturalism and democratic deliberation

Intercultural educators focus on developing students as active, independent thinkers, whose ability to explore and consider various points of view and sources of evidence through dialogue and democratic deliberation they aim to develop and enhance in the classroom. This is somewhat similar to the critical multicultural perspective as examined in the second chapter, except for critical multiculturalists' assumption about "power wielders," and that educators should strive primarily to identify and blame them with their students (Kincheloe & Steinberg 1997). As I discussed previously, seeing anyone in society based on privileged markers of difference such as race or class as intentionally wielding power within a network to harm others (in part, for their own gain) is highly ideological and hardly more productive than teaching that all Muslims are part of a violent terrorist network.

Anticipating the consideration of alternative perspectives on social difference, then, intercultural teachers share with students sources of information and ideas about what connects different people across borders, as well as the internal diversity of groups who are often treated as homogeneous in more basic accounts. This helps to lay groundwork for an analysis of various claims and perspectives. Next, intercultural educators prepare students to evaluate knowledge claims about difference independently and develop informed views about social groups and issues, by critically exploring with them different points of view in the classroom, and asking them to develop their own stance through reflective analysis and comparison of their views to those of others. They do not teach particular perspectives, such as their own, as the truth of the situation.

When it comes to teaching about Muslims and Islam, providing for alternative orientations toward what difference means entails (1) considering the diversity of Muslims today, as well as (2) comparing and contrasting Islam with other religions (such as the mainstream ones in the United States, Christianity and Judaism), which is commonly provided for in textbooks and standards, if in a rather general, broad, and ethnocentric way (as discussed in the last chapter). Both of these practices are facilitated not to simply argue against mainstream conceptions, or discover and disseminate the "real truth" of the matter, but rather to ensure that students develop independent points of views on these topics, informed by critical and reflective analyses of others knowledge sources and perspectives, rather than from their more blind acceptance of their earlier intuitions or what their texts, or their teachers claim.

In Kaviani's (2007) study of teachers, one in particular, "John," makes considering the diversity of Muslims the goal of one lesson. In his class,

> he pointed out that Islam was not a uniform religion that could be understood without the proper "cultural" context in which it was practiced around the world. He made this point by saying "What do I know about Islam in Bangladesh? Nothing!"
>
> (Kaviani 2007: 133)

John then asks his students about what they can find out. His students conduct research and find information about different historical and present-day Muslim communities to increase diverse representations of Muslims in the classroom. Discussing where Muslims live across the globe can additionally help students to recognize that the Middle East is not Muslims' sole, or even primary domain, as is likely assumed by young people today, given how they are usually represented in the mass media and in standards, textbooks, and common text supplements. Students are active rather than passive in this lesson, and the educator models the insight that no one person can know everything or possess the ultimate truth about a social or cultural group, but that it is each person's responsibility to develop and refine their own orientation and gain experience analyzing sources.

Teachers can additionally discuss the differences and similarities among Islam, Judaism, and Christianity in their classrooms, highlighting what they all share, as well as the things that are seen to divide them, which is something that is highlighted in many state educational standards, but dealt with in an ethnocentric way in textbooks (as discussed in Chapter 4). While some assimilationist educators, as previously mentioned, suggest it is inappropriate since 9/11 to identify Islam and Christianity as similar religions, given their association of Muslims with terrorism or threats to mainstream U.S. society (e.g. Bennetta 2005), one need not communicate that it is a "fact," for instance, that these monotheistic religions have more in common than not, particularly if one perceives that this is a contentious perspective, which may be regarded as inappropriately political to put forward in their classroom. Rather, in cases where claims may cause upset or be contrary to widely held views (such as the "clash" view), an educator can teach *about* this view of the religions' similarities, and consider with students its merit, without putting forward the claim as the truth.

Indeed, teaching about religious truths is a commonly endorsed approach when considering religious matters in schools, as a focus on others' perspectives rather than a so-called objective or ultimate viewpoint can protect teachers from accusations of proselytization or otherwise overstepping their authority in this contentious field (Kunzman 2006; Nord 1995). The point here is not necessarily to change a point of view or steer it one way or another, as an educator aligned with any of the traditional multicultural approach might aim to do, but instead to ensure that students' understanding has been systematically developed rather than more unconsciously intuited from that of the teacher, the society, or popular culture. An educator need not frame his or her own personal beliefs or perspectives as relevant or correct (or as their own viewpoints) here, in discussing these or other controversial topics, in order to be effective in exposing students to a variety of points of view from which they can better make up their own minds. Indeed, teachers can be highly effective in discussing controversial contemporary events while leaving their personal beliefs at the door, and it is in line with an intercultural perspective for the educator to not have the right answer, as there is no essential truth about what social difference indicates in intercultural education – just different points of view that may make more or less sense depending upon one's perspective, background knowledge and experience, and the particular social context or situation under investigation.

For instance, there are some Christians, Muslims, and Jews who would challenge the view that their beliefs and practices are similar to those of the other monotheistic traditions (Bennetta 2005). Indeed, it is not implausible to think of each faith as encompassing as many different orientations toward belief, and the nature of other religions, as there are individual believers. Thus, it is not a matter of truth, but of perspective, to argue that the belief systems are more similar than they are different, for example. Any a priori view on such a complex issue is less helpful to students as future participants in democratic decision making in society than is their engaging in practice considering varying views for themselves.

An intercultural approach to difference thus practices a kind of moderate cultural relativism as mentioned previously, not choosing sides on issues, but aiming for students to arrive at individual preferred positions though analysis of alternatives and through interpersonal dialogue. This is different from the binary right/wrong some people may desire in public education (Hochman 2006), but crucially, it is not the place of public school educators in the religiously plural, liberal democratic society of the United States – where individuals are free to have diverse views – to give or formally assess students' moral principles.

Relatedly, when one remains focused on developing students' critical thinking skills rather than teaching them certain interpretations of difference, it makes little sense to privilege one perspective in the classroom above others, unless, of course, that perspective is more informed by the critical examination of multiple factors and points of views. This indicates that teachers should discourage students from aligning themselves with their educators in such conversations, which may be a natural student response in some situations (or for some students). As one educator puts it:

> I don't necessarily want my kids to have the same views as me. I want them to come to their own decisions in a valid way, and what I mean by "valid" I mean understanding the issue, learning about it, figuring it out, and then coming to an educated decision. Because if you reflect the way your parents think and it's because it's the way your parents think, it's not educated.
>
> (Kaviani 2007: 79)

A quality student perspective here is thus defined in relation to its engagement with others in rigorous analysis, rather than for the similarity or difference of its content to that of other points of view. As the educator quoted above expresses, if the students think as you do, because it is how you do, you are not teaching them to think for themselves. One need not obscure his or her own perspective from the classroom – by deliberately hiding it, or simply not mentioning it in class discussions – to teach students in line with this approach, but one should at least emphasize in discussing their view how it has been informed by personal experiences and independent reasoning, and should *not* be taken as the truth on a subject matter, as in this teacher's practice of modeling ethical decision making in front of her class:

> Sherry revealed her opinions on selective issues. . . . "Whatever I have to say, I can tell them my opinion, if I can back it up." If students disagreed with what she was saying, then she gave them "newspaper articles" to read that supported her views and encouraged them to find evidence to back up their views too. She also told her students that she was "still learning. There are things that are difficult for me. I might be leaning one direction – and I don't want to say that I'm wishy-washy." She recalled that at some point in the past she was "100 percent pro-Israeli." However, she no longer felt that way.
>
> (Kaviani 2007: 167)

There are different ways one can share or obscure his or her own view point to enable democratic discussions in his or her classroom. Yet marking one perspective as the correct one should not be the teacher's aim, as much as illustrating how intelligent decision making involves independently weighing different options, engaging in democratic interpersonal deliberation, and scrutinizing one's sources of evidence in relation to a particular issue. That it is wrong, for instance, to view Islam as more terroristic or threatening than Christianity, or to regard Islam and Christianity as completely unrelated belief systems, can be expressed as a point of view requiring student exploration and reasonable engagement, without identifying agreement with it as the objective of a lesson: as a knowledge claim students must concur with in order to academically succeed.

Furthermore, as the truth or the best response to a situation should not be determined beforehand with regard to controversial issues, students should also be exposed to the idea that one can, and in some cases should, change their mind over time, as "Sherry" does, above, as they gain more information and a more conscious and reflective understanding of what constitutes sound and unsound reasoning. Teachers should explore with students the difference between being "wishy-washy" (as "Sherry" puts it), and being willing and brave to stand corrected, and reevaluate their view, if further information makes it suddenly appear as untenable or too limited, naïve, or idealistic, etc. Autonomy and independence of mind and voice should also be contrasted with stubbornness and/or a refusal to engage meaningfully and effectively with others, and this line should be traced in real life situations, asking students to share, for example, a time when their view did not stand up to comprehensive investigation of a situation. The teacher thus begins to share the moderate kind of cultural relativism to democratic dialogue here, which requires that one stand up for what they believe in, but also be willing to revise their view as they develop a broader and more inclusive, dialogical perspective.

Intercultural education is also concerned, as I mentioned, with the universal capacity for all members of society to engage in free and equal public speech. Similarly, critical multiculturalists question the possibility of enabling equal democratic classroom deliberation, out of a concern that classroom perspectives expressed in line with normalized conceptions in the public sphere – such as, in this case, the "clash of civilizations" view, associating Islam with threats to U.S. society (Huntington 1993) – will "win" out in the classroom, lacking the counter perspective offered by a strong voice, or the influence of a more critically informed instructor. Indeed, such negative views related to Muslims and Islam can be successful in public school classrooms today, as educators and textbooks are often policed to not say too many positive things about Islam and Muslims (Hochman 2006), within a media context where non-Muslims' voices are regularly privileged over those of Muslims, even about Muslim issues (Safi 2013). Thus, as Megan Boler writes:

> All speech is not free. Power inequities institutionalized through economies, gender roles, social class, and corporate-owned media ensure that all voices

do not carry the same weight. . . . Similarly not all expressions of hostility are equal. Some hostile voices are penalized while others are tolerated. Hostility that targets marginalized people . . . carries more weight that hostility expressed by a marginalized person toward a member of the dominant class.

(2004: 3)

Boler and others who understand that dominant and harmful social messages often become dominant and harmful classroom messages sometimes promote and practice "affirmative action pedagogies" in their classrooms. This involves critical responses and in-depth interrogations of majority perspectives on controversial issues in the classroom, such as the "clash of civilizations" view, and the privileging (or positive recognition) of non-dominant perspectives when and where they come to surface. Because it is harder for non-dominant points of view to be expressed in the classroom, as in society at large, Boler and others conscientious toward an unequal discursive context promote these, over other views that are more in line with the status quo.

Yet this strategy risks privileging dominant discourse in another sense, by focusing on it as more worthy of in-depth classroom exploration, given the implication that dominant views require more scrutiny than less dominant views, no matter which ones are put forward more critically. For instance, one might express a well-read understanding of Huntington's "clash" theory, after seeing an interview with him on television, for example, while another student might put forward a more opaque and unclear statement on Muslim positive recognition. Affirmative action pedagogy seems to imply in this case that the former student's views are given more classroom space, to become more refined and better defended, than the latter student's non-dominant perspective. Thus, a privileging of those expressing dominant viewpoints (and the viewpoints themselves) can be perpetuated in affirmative-action pedagogy, despite teachers' more critical and reactive aims.

Some wary about this predicament, and its effects on classroom power dynamics more generally, advocate alternatively a *silencing* of student expressions of dominant discourses in the classroom. Barbara Applebaum describes as another form of affirmative-action pedagogy silencing speech she regards at hateful, harmful, and supportive of a status quo biased against disadvantaged members of society – for example, the association of Muslims with terrorism – to deal with students expressing them in a different place and time, in such a way that the harmful perspective is not the focus of the classroom conversation, as she sees such as "an instrument of subordination as much as . . . an expression of [a] viewpoint" (2003: 157). Applebaum's stance seems to imply that there are right and wrong viewpoints in her classroom, that are a priori given, in order to protect the least advantaged members of society and of the classroom community. As in critical multiculturalists' orientation towards inequality in society, it is assumed that some views are better than others in the classroom, in their relation to outside forces they are associated with, which may be more or less powerful and powerless (Jackson 2008a).

However, as touched on in the second chapter discussion of critical multiculturalism, while this educational approach is well-intentioned, this firmer reaction to prevailing discourses on controversial subjects and groups is ultimately too moralistic to be either appropriate or effective, from a pedagogical point of view. Students in U.S. public schools do not normally view their teachers' role as a moral authority in their lives (particularly at higher levels), and students are likely to separate their teacher's behavior in such cases from their own ethical and social views. (It is also worth noting here that Applebaum and Boler write more often in the context of higher education rather than in that of secondary education and so may reasonably give students more responsibility for the views they hold than I do here.) As Martin Buber pragmatically observed:

> I try to explain to my pupils that envy is despicable, and at once I feel the secret resistance of those who are poorer than their comrades. I try to explain that it is wicked to bully the weak, and at once I see a suppressed smile on the lips of the strong. I try to explain that lying destroys life, and something frightful happens: the worst habitual liar in the class produces a brilliant essay on the destructive power of lying. I have made the fatal mistake of *given instruction* in ethics, and what I said is accepted as current coin of knowledge; nothing of it is transformed into character-building substance.
> (1955: 105; Gordon 2007: 346).

Classroom knowledge and ethics lessons need not be privileged by students over informally gained knowledge from elsewhere in society, which makes critical multicultural orientations that tackle discursive power structures head-on in the classroom ineffective. Furthermore, moral education can be received by students as classroom rules, when ideas are not subject to critical democratic investigation, but admonished by teachers who should be teaching *how to think* rather than *how to act* or *what to think* (Jackson 2008b). As Cris Mayo has observed in related discussions of anti-gay bias in schools, "by making discrimination . . . against the rules . . . schools do not need to engage in substantial discussion of" what makes a person a disadvantaged or stigmatized minority and why, leading to students learning not to use particular terms (in Mayo's research, "faggot"), but not of the social significance of their use, or of the meaning they imply, within students' lives (2004: 37–40).

Furthermore, admonishments or prohibitions of speech fail to encourage democratic deliberation by students, who may actually rely upon diverse backgrounds unbeknownst to their teacher in staking their claims, which can themselves be more or less accurately interpreted by the well-intentioned, facilitative educator. That is, it is presumptuous to decipher all expressions that appear to align with harmful, predominant points of view in society as representations of unequal power relations and injustice in the classroom, rather than as students' (inevitably) poorly informed and/or expressed initial hypotheses on complicated issues. Teachers' interpretive capacities are often imperfect, as the following example of educating about 9/11 illustrates:

> "Isaac, those people who live in the desert; the dudes who wear those rags on their heads, why did they do this to us?" . . . Gabriel has boldly gone and asked the question that most of his classmates were itching to ask. Here it was, and what was my response?
> "First of all, Gabriel, those rags are not rags. They are part of the dress of Arabic people. They are called keffiyehs. . . ." *Yeah, right,* I was thinking. Gabriel had shown bravery and asked a difficult question, and I responded with a lesson on semantics. By answering this way, was I sniffing out a "higher purpose"? . . . Here we have endured the most blatant hate crime against the American people in anyone's recent memory, and I am chiding Gabriel on his caricature on Arabs. Was I bypassing this "teachable moment" and choosing to address the issue of a breach in political correctness? (I realized half a year later that when he said "rags" he was shortening "do-rags" and drawing a parallel between the seemingly exotic dress of Arabs and the dress of his friends and neighbors in South Harlem. So, who was less understanding of cultural difference, him or me?)
>
> (Brooks 2006: 36)

In this narrative, one sees the educator struggling not to moralize and conceding difficulty with fully understanding the intent of his student's speech. The student, Gabriel, had not meant to perpetuate hate and harm others with his question; rather, he had relied on the (albeit biased and stereotypical) information he had, including his personal experience with "rags," to move the conversation into a field about which he earnestly (and as his teacher saw it, bravely) wanted to know more about. For the teacher to steer it instead into a moralistic discussion of words and the presumed implications of their use in the context of a larger social order of power and oppression, elites and victims, would be to miss the student's point entirely – as Gabriel goes on, "Right, whatever. Why did those dudes do this to us?" In this case, Gabriel's language is read more reflectively by his teacher, half a year later, not as an unjust act, but as an ignorantly worded question, which demanded a richer and more in-depth answer than "First of all, Gabriel, those rags are not rags . . .". Moralistic tones can thus stifle earnest attempts at dialogue, and teachers who use moralism liberally in the classroom can also fail to model respect and tolerance for others, an optimism about others' attempts to communicate, understood in intercultural education as one condition for democracy via dialogue.

Of course, controversial issues are issues that *matter* to individuals in different ways, and thus discussing controversial subjects democratically in the classroom is no easy, simple, or straightforward task. For one, these topics tend to be highly complex: not easy for informed adults to sum up accurately and broadly in the course of a public school class period, let alone effectively communicate interpersonally with their students about. In the case of education about Muslims, one is dealing with a highly complex "community," that is hard to make many blanket assertions about – or entirely *deny* such blanket assertions. In addition, social and political issues and topics tend to be emotional, and the teacher or students might risk acting rashly under pressure if they sense the importance of the subject in the real world and feel sensitive to the connections between classroom learning and life outside of school. Even the frustration of not having the appropriate knowledge or background, or of being unable to effectively express oneself about extraordinarily complex and sensitive topics, on the part of the educator or students, can create significant tension.

Furthermore, controversial topics inevitably encompass ethical and moral issues, and people (teachers and students) are likely to experience their sense of morality stretched and challenged as they grapple to interpret others' points of view (such as, for instance, one's student thinking of keffiyehs as "rags"). Many have difficulty seeing religious issues as something that should be discussed in the classroom, and fear overstepping their boundaries by discussing religious groups or practices that they see themselves as largely unrelated to. Thus, it is reasonable to want to decrease threatening or reactive speech in the classroom, and of course to thereby outlaw clearly threatening expressions and behavior, such as students referring to one another, or to disadvantaged groups in society, in ways that are readily identifiable as prejudiced and hateful (such as by calling Muslims "ragheads" or "terrorists," for instance).

However, it is not pedagogically effective or in the aim of students' development of critical thinking capacities to claim that contentious views put forward more abstractly about difference, such as those about the qualities or behaviors of different groups of people, are matters of black and white, or right and wrong, because these are often complex and controversial issues that do not readily lend themselves to objective matter-of-fact analyses. As thinkers publicly identified as experts, from Huntington (1993) to Said (1997), have very different beliefs about Islam and Muslims to put forward, to foreclose discussion on one of their points of view in the classroom demonstrates to students a lack of willingness to consider different perspectives – hardly a model practice in democratic deliberation.

Thus, helping students to understand why people think the way they do, scrutinizing their sources of evidence, and the orientation or perspective from which they see the world (for instance, for Huntington, a focus on international conflicts, and for Said, a focus on the nature of cultural difference) enables student engagement and critical thinking far more than does morally educating them to agree with certain perspectives. When it comes to Muslims, teaching students, for instance, that it is simply inappropriate or wrong to view Muslims in specific ways precludes richer and more effective grappling with why students think and feel as they do about Muslims, as well as students' experience with democratic deliberation across contrasting points of view. While some teachers may prefer to express their own perspectives while others do not in the classroom, one can be effective using an intercultural approach despite the complexities and emotionality of controversial issues, by emphasizing the importance of coming to one's own conclusions as a personal and interpersonal process of considering different evidence and exploring different perspectives, and being open-minded, questioning, and willing to make mistakes. And such is essential to aiding the development of one's students to do likewise, as Barbara Houston notes:

> There are numerous reasons why democratic dialogue among students has become suspect. . . . Nevertheless . . . it is hard to imagine how one might sustain democracy in its absence. . . . Central to democracy's enactment is a will to the common good, or "good will," and while there may be disagreement about exactly how we cultivate good will sufficient for democratic citizenship, it is recognized that there is a kind of relatedness integral to it. . . . [W]e cannot compel moral goodness; we can only nurture it. In this regard, adopting a certain generosity toward human frailty and mistakes is a more likely route to success. . . . [E]ducation is an arena where, nominally at least, we learn what our mistakes might be and how to correct them. If we discourage dialogue about these matters in schools, education risks losing even the possibility of transformative value.
>
> (Houston 2004: 106–107)

Houston's view is helpful to keep in mind in light of critical multiculturalists' arguments that there are privileged students who do resist alternative knowledge willfully, possibly wreaking havoc on a productive democratic classroom community (Applebaum 2007). There may be instances where this is true, but this does not imply that the educator can do better than model trust, respect, and optimism, to still connect with students who are interested in learning and practicing democratic discussion. Indeed, some of those "naughty" students may become difficult adults to work democratically with in the future, and teachers do their students no great service by sheltering them from reality or attempting to do so, in the name of social justice.

While constructively grappling with difference – that is, trying to understanding differences of opinion and evaluate situations in an objective and reflective way – can often be difficult and stressful in the classroom, one nonetheless cannot teach in a balanced and accurate way about controversial subjects and groups by pretending to have all of the answers, or by precluding examinations of alternative (or predominant) points of view, if their aim is developing student criticality and autonomy in learning to deal with the tough situations they inevitably will face as citizens in a democratic society. There is no single truth to be held on many of the most important social issues faced, and democratic societies require autonomous citizens, to be sustained. Teachers must therefore not foreclose complicated, contentious conversations, but develop students' skills and personal strategies for engaging in them effectively, elaborating insights from their own experiences and knowledge base. Intercultural educational approaches to difference demand this sort of inquiry as preparation for participating within a democracy where social differences are often sources of controversy.

This discussion has focused primarily on materials and activities of educators with students. However, another important component of interculturalism and intercultural education is to practice dialogue with more diverse others in society, who may not be present in the classroom or school community, namely Muslims, who often are schooled privately when possible in the United States today. American-based interfaith organizations and related Muslim organizations dedicated to promoting positive interfaith relations (including relations with people who are not religious), such as the Council on American-Islamic Relations (CAIR 2013) and the Institute on Religion and Civic Values (previously the Council on Islamic Education; 2013), facilitate events in major cities, which teachers could bring students to, and provide resources for educators online such as transcripts of past interfaith events. Mosques also welcome (Muslim and non-Muslim) visitors who wish to know more about Islam and local Muslim communities, and teachers could contact local Mosques to schedule informational tours. (This could be done as part of a larger tour of local diversity, which might include visiting other religious sites in the area, or cultural centers or meeting places of ethnic or national minority groups.) Finally, teachers could invite Muslim guests into their classroom, whether they are students or educators from elsewhere in the school or district, or other friends or peers, who can help students to recognize Muslims as diverse individuals rather than one homogeneous group.

As with any guest speaker, it may be difficult to arrange time, or find or select someone "representative" (to this end, CAIR and other organizations also facilitate guest speakers and visitors to schools and other organizations, and one can even make the request online [2013]). Ideally, teachers could invite more than one Muslim to their class, or guests of various faiths to class, to develop a breadth of student experience and perspective. However any opportunity to engage in dialogue with a Muslim is preferable to continual conversations about Islam conducted exclusively by non-Muslims. Even when it is not possible to find more than one Muslim classroom guest, there is no better way for students to develop understanding and appreciation for diversity within Islam than to face an individual in real life, which can enable them to see that no two Muslims are exactly alike, just as no two Christians or Jews, etc., are exactly alike. Students may be surprised to find, for instance, that black and white Americans are among American Muslims; that Muslims may be part of religiously diverse families, and that even within a family or small cultural group, opinions may vary on issues such as gender roles and international politics.

On the other hand, one may have Muslim members of their classroom or school community available to call upon. Here, educators face more sensitive issues around treating all students fairly while giving necessary positive recognition to minorities, as discussed in the second chapter. Creating a safe environment while also encouraging lively debate on pressing social issues may be challenging, as Muslim American youth may not want to be treated as representatives of their religion. In this context, teachers should think twice before calling on Muslim students as representatives of their faith, without their prior permission, or before setting up a lesson that encourages peers to focus a great deal of attention on (known) Muslim students. Indeed, there is little reason to treat a Muslim student as an expert on international relations, the "clash of civilizations," or American Muslims as a community. Yet when discussing issues of faith and interfaith, a dedicated educator may find a way to develop engaging classroom conversations that call on classroom members of different faiths or ideologies, to help students better understand each other. There is no trick or recipe to follow here in facilitating such potentially tumultuous classroom discussions, but gaining practice can help, as I will discuss in more detail in the next chapter.

Interculturalism and critical media literacy

Interculturalism and critical multiculturalism are both concerned with how cultures are treated and framed (by media, etc.) unequally in society, and educators following these frameworks want to prepare students in relation as future participants in a democratic community who approach issues of social justice in an open-minded manner. The views are thus linked in their major advocacy of critical media literacy, though for interculturalism, its intention is not to deprogram or build up student critical consciousness, but rather to address the basic need within a democratic society for people to learn how to use media meaningfully and intentionally rather than be passive recipients of media messages. As was touched on in the third chapter, since the mass media and popular culture are seen by many educators as significant influences on personal opinions among American youth, different sorts of critical media literacy that encourage critical inquiries into representations within media and popular culture are valued in assimilationist, pluralist, and critical multicultural orientations.

An intercultural approach for grappling with difference fairly and critically in the classroom incorporates critical media literacy education to encourage students' active and critical, rather than passive, reception of stereotypical and negative media messages about minorities, and to correct for the misinformative effects of much of mass media, when it comes to issues of controversial social difference, such as in the case of Muslims and Islam today. Otherwise, in such a media-saturated climate as contemporary U.S. society, the clear message emerging from media about Muslims is likely to be implicitly accepted by students and effectively undermine or diminish attention to any more complex and nuanced views offered in a course in world geography or social studies, as elaborated in the third chapter. As Lynn McBrien notes, "When youth do not have a space in which they are encouraged to analyze *what is reported, how it is reported,* and *what language is used* in reporting on other nations and cultures, they are less likely to do so themselves" (2005: 29; emphasis in the original). In the case of learning about Islam and Muslims, critical media literacy is essential in order for students to develop a more informed view that does not start with

Saddam Hussein and end with Osama bin Laden. While such a program may surpass that typical today in social studies courses, some form of media literacy is recognized in all fifty states' standards as necessary to informed democratic citizenship today, and in a world where differences (real and perceived) have impacts, as we have explored here, students must be informed about how differences are framed partially by media, in order to meaningfully act autonomously through critical reception of information.

When it comes to specific classroom practice, *modeling* media literacy is fundamental, because the presentation of alternative views illustrates to students that a variety of perspectives exist beyond that (or those) privileged in their textbooks and that each should be considered in turn as one proceeds to developing an informed position. For instance, essays from the *Rethinking Schools* (2001) and Fordham Foundation reports (2002; 2003; 2011) could be used together by teachers, to help students understand how different reasonable people view and treat issues related to Muslims and Islam in U.S. society, and how their reasoning and information related to a given topic differ. Multiple perspectives, both internal and external, should be provided, in order to model for students how effective reasoning is carried out through a thorough examination of sources of evidence. Modeling critical media literacy in this way also enables democratic deliberation as discussed in the last section.

Hijab, or head-covering, is a very common contemporary issue related to Islam for students to consider using multiple perspectives, given that it is connected to negative associations of Muslim societies with gender inequality and female oppression, and also constitutes a norm that is seen as different within a Western context, that many students are ignorant about. Comparing it to other similar phenomena and considering alternative perspectives on it available in various media is one effective way to help students gain more balanced and less partial perspectives, while modeling skills of critical media literacy:

> For her contemporary world problems class, [Hilda] used newspaper and magazine articles and surfed the internet for news that "pushed the button." She looked for current high profile controversial issues that had graphic images and made a deliberate effort to include them in her lessons. She believed that images were really important in telling a story because students could "grasp easily" what was going on. Her students visited a photo bank of images on the internet, showing Muslim women in various degrees of body covering and they compared those images to clothing for traditional Catholic women and explained how traditions influenced fashion and in turn, the Islamic fashion could be seen as a form of political statement.
>
> (Kaviani 2007: 116)

The educator "Hilda" here finds media that is both critical and positive toward hijab, from Muslim women and others, as well as images of religious dress more generally, to provide a wide variety of personal, political, and more large-scale and broad perspectives about this topic in the classroom. By using this method, Hilda helps her students realize that whether one views hijab as a marker of cultural distinction, as an expression of faith common to many belief systems, or as a symbol of female oppression depends on one's frame of reference, what is included in one's lens. Such an approach is clearly preferable to discussing any one of these perspectives on its own, for enabling students to learn to be critical toward media messages rather than passively accepting of their view points.

Yet while many educators use a variety of resources in the classroom for educating about controversial or complicated topics, not all use of media and other diverse resources is effective for modeling and teaching critical media literacy. For instance, some teachers may use media as a reward for students engaging in learning activities, presenting popular films at the end of a term, while others may simply replace historical lessons with documentaries or other televised or film accounts, letting media producers educate their students (Hobbes 2005). While such uncritical uses of media may serve purposes of community building or creating learning incentives, such should additionally include an evaluation of media content and methods to develop media literacy.

> To many social studies educators, the focus [in using media in the classroom] is on content and knowledge acquisition, with an emphasis on the mastery of key ideas, facts, names, and dates . . . since many social studies teachers avoid discussion about controversial issues and as many as half of these teachers lack a BA or MA in history or even a major with "some history" in it. . . . But other social studies educators emphasize instructional strategies that promote critical thinking skills, not rote content-area learning, which is precisely why professional organizations in social studies are urging that media literacy education be integrated into social studies curriculum frameworks, viewing it as a strategy for bringing principles of constructivism to the traditionalist's classroom.
>
> (Hobbes 2005: 78)

In addition to selecting resources encompassing a wide variety of viewpoints, teachers modeling critical media literacy in their classrooms have to be critical about how resources are used, and require their students to engage in critical media literacy education. The sort of media literacy recommended particularly for battling negative media stereotypes of minorities within an intercultural approach should be (1) *thematic,* dealing specifically with the group studied (in this case, Muslims); (2) *analytic,* tracing the path messages take from reality to media; and (3) *critical,* inviting student analysis, comparison, and evaluation of media discourses. In upper-level courses, criticality can also entail developing student understanding of the contemporary political economy of mainstream media production.

There are various foci that can be chosen for media literacy education, from the news, movies, songs, and advertisements, to the companies sponsoring them, to their production methods, to the audience reception. While an approach that analyzes the news as a particular form of media might be best in a class on citizenship education that incorporates lessons involving critical media literacy, or in journalism or communications courses, when teaching about controversial groups, a *thematic* approach is best, which explores various representations: the social group explored in the formal curriculum.

By examining the group as represented in multiple forms of media – from film and television to the radio, music, and so on – students are best able to capture the broadest possible view of existing perceptions and perspectives on the group in question, and therefore best able to develop an informed, critical view of the group for themselves. Additionally, integrating such a thematic approach within the curriculum, intercultural educators can ensure that critical media literacy education is taking place, rather than rely on specialists, for instance, to teach it for them, as Hobbes (2005: 92) observes:

> More and more, media literacy is being taught as a course, often within communication arts, or English, because of an individual teacher's enthusiasm for the subject. Taught as a specialist subject, few students will be reached in a given school or school district. Taught within existing content areas, more students will be reached.

While one challenge identified in teaching thematically oriented critical media literacy lessons is the availability of time or space in the formal curriculum, such lessons are fundamental to learning to understand difference in society, which is often an incidental result of media, in cases when students are not personally exposed to social diversity everyday.

Presuming the *theme* of the lesson to be related to Muslims (though it may be more specific, such as hijab or the "clash of civilizations" view), we can move on to the second characteristic of a critical media literacy education argued for here: It is *analytical*. Whatever aspect or form of media is explored, an *analytic,* process-oriented perspective should be also be basic to the approach taken, which examines media representations as the products of many different individual and group choices. Tracing how a "real life" event becomes a media event is the key lesson here, and students can understand this as a straightforward, linear process, at the outset. Students should understand as choices the creation and reproduction of images, and the words used (and those not used) in discussing an event or group. Additionally, different parts of media production should be understood as discrete acts and choices of message producers.

McBrien (2005) suggests reapplying the traditional journalistic questions of *who, what, where, when, how,* and *why* to critical media inquiries, asking students "Who (source) says what (content/ideology) to whom (audience) in what way (style/conventions/technology) with what effect (influence) and why (purpose/profit)?" By asking such questions, an educator can teach

> that all media are constructed. The top 60-second story on the evening news has been edited down from a half hour, hour, perhaps hours of videotape. In addition, media is a construction of reality, but not the total reality as it happened.
>
> (McBrien 2005: 29)

Asking these basic questions can help students to understand media representations as the results of active processes, and it encourages deconstruction and distance from media messages in the future. Projects involving creating media in the classroom in groups can also be productive toward the end of understanding media as a process of social construction, rather than as a window to reality.

For instance, in comparing textbook treatments of Muslim women with those in other sources – let us return again to *Rethinking Schools* (2001) and the Fordham Institute (2002; 2003; 2011) – teachers can ask students the journalistic questions of *who, what, when, where, why,* and *how* to highlight for students that these information sources are not windows to reality, but interpretations of it, with different aims and methods. Introductory sections of sources can be evaluated, to discover editors' intentions: in *Rethinking Schools,* to help develop toleration of Muslims since 9/11, and in the Fordham Institute's case, to boost patriotism and support for the war on terrorism with elaborations of the threats associated with Islam and Muslims. Such analyses can develop not merely students' critical *media* literacy skills, but their more general critical thinking skills, enabling students to evaluate difference knowledge claims, perspectives, and sources of evidence wherever they may find them, to arrive at more independent viewpoints than they had when they arrived in the classroom.

How textbooks and other sources are produced can also be critically examined with students; texts should not be framed by teachers as tombs of basic, objective social facts. As Kincheloe and Steinberg write, "to be critical in a historical context means to 'de-present' the present; that is, to take the mundane, hold it up to the light and look at it from another angle" (2007: 234). Comparing past textbooks with present ones illuminates the context of the contemporary text that one may have previously held as the official knowledge about history or geography, and about controversial groups such as Muslims. Additionally, bringing in other historical or cultural texts, such as academic texts, alternative historical analyses such as Zinn's (1995) *A People's History of the United States,* or historical or contemporary narratives, such as autobiographical accounts by Muslims living in different places at different times, helps students to further respond to their textbooks with critical distance, recognizing them as the products of individuals' and groups' particular choices, rather than as sources of truth about social difference, or even as accurate reflections of the viewpoints of those whom they discuss:

> John Stuart Mill argued that it is not enough for students to hear the arguments of adversaries from their own teachers.... "Ninety-nine in a hundred

of what are called educated men . . . have never thrown themselves into the mental position of those who think differently from them." . . . Textbooks are written from a point of view, from within a worldview that defines for its author what is true, what counts as a fact, what is normal, what is reasonable, and what is good. . . . Unhappily, most author give their readers no sense of the controversial nature of their basic philosophical commitments.

If we are to take any point of view – secular or religious – seriously, we must let its advocates tell their own stories. . . . True, primary source material is difficult and takes time to work through, particularly when it is historical or from a non-Western culture, but the effort must be made. Students should read Jewish accounts of the Holocaust, fundamentalist arguments against abortion, papal encyclicals on economic justice, and much else.

(Nord 1995: 229–230)

By critically comparing the textbook to primary-source materials, students can learn to view the textbook as a limited source for understanding complex social issues and diverse groups in society. Likewise, the journalistic questions (of *who, what, when, where, how,* and *why*) can be asked in comparative explorations of mainstream media presentations, such as movies like *True Lies,* television series like *24* and *Homeland,* and newspaper editorials, editorial cartoons, and opinion and news articles. By comparing educational resources with mainstream media, or mainstream media with alternative and international media sources, students can see how different groups choose different images, use different words, and quote different people, and evaluate the effects of these choices on their persuasive power. Analyzing how an article about Muslim anti-Americanism in a newspaper compares to one in a textbook can enable students to be more critical about both forms of media as sources of information.

Finally, *criticality* about messages received should be involved in a critical media literacy program. By criticality, I mean here an independent and reflective perspective, which holds others' knowledge claims at a distance, and can be developed in introductory lessons through comparing images, messages, or sources, and asking students to evaluate them in terms of their persuasiveness. For instance, during a presidential election, pictures and information about different candidates provided from different sources can be compared to demonstrate how subjective judgments are involved in presenting images (Hobbes 2005). In the case of Muslims, images of and information about Muslims in mainstream and independent sources, and Western and Muslim news sources, can be compared to uncover how value judgments are made in media production, that convey certain perspectives.

By requiring criticality in media literacy in lessons, students can gain experience weighing in on the meaning, significance, and validity of different media messages, identifying sources they find better and worse about a given topic, issue, person, or group. Students should not be encouraged or asked to respond passively to media even when it is part of the curriculum outside of a lesson on critical media literacy, but expected in all domains to provide informed evaluations of sources:

> Media literacy will provide tools of criticism to help individuals to avoid media manipulation and to produce their own identities . . . This means cultivating the ability to ask difficult questions and the self-confidence to reject easy answers – the two fundamental goals of a critical inquiry and what it takes to be an educated person.
>
> (Semali 2005: 52)

To make media literacy programs critical, students must learn to engage in evaluation activities and debate with others which perspectives on a topic are most compelling and why. Here, teachers may find it useful to incorporate lessons on evaluating sources into research projects, in order to make the insights students can gain from evaluating sources more relevant and important. What makes someone an expert, and what facts or evidence more and less effectively support particular points of view, are key questions for students to explore to get at the critical component of media literacy as conceived here.

Within an intercultural approach, being critical does not mean that one learns to recognize mediated information as susceptible to bias and therefore reject news media or popular culture as a whole, as might be an intended outcome for a critical multicultural educator. Rather, being critical means asking students where they, and their sources, got their information from, and encouraging students to isolate and evaluate independently the information their sources use as evidence for their claims. Comparing two sources on one issue, or multiple perspectives on a more general situation, from one form of media, or from a variety, are all easy ways to add critical media literacy as a component of one's lessons about controversial subjects such as Islam.

Additionally teachers can assign particular sorts of projects that require students' use and presentation of resources embodying multiple perspectives, such as a "structured academic controversy" (Kaviani 2007: 57; Jackson 2014). Similar to a debate, this sort of lesson involves students researching alternative perspectives on one issue – the "clash" view might be a good hypothesis for upper-level students to explore – and presenting their findings to one another. "Public policy deliberation" is a similar method, where students and teachers "uncover and understand the problems faced by various publics, to develop and evaluate policy alternatives together, and to choose a course of action" (Kaviani 2007). Though time-consuming, such research-oriented class projects promote the comparative and critical processes constitutive of critical media literacy better than does reading standard materials and answering questions about their content, as it requires students' active discovery and independent (and collaborative) analysis and critical consideration of different points of view available to them in different contexts. Readings from Said (1997), Huntington (1993), and other mainstream, alternative, and international sources can be used for projects, to broaden student perspectives and enable them to reach better-informed points of view.

A final example represents a typical lesson in critical media literacy, which could be applied in a discussion of hijab or of stereotypes of Muslims, which is thematic, analytic, and critical.

> The students are clustered in small groups. Each group is given a different black and white still image to study. All of the photos relate to the topic they are exploring. . . . The students study their photo and jot down everything they notice. They are asked to consider such characteristics as: the type of shot (close-up, medium shot, long shot); the angle (high angle, low angle); light and shadow; and placement of elements (objects, people, etc.) in the picture (foreground, background, juxtaposition). Then they describe how the images make them think and feel. . . . Students collectively explore questions such as:
>
> - Who do you think took the picture?
> - How are the people in the photos represented?
> - What caption would you write for that photo?
> - What kind of message is the photographer trying to convey?
> - How do the different elements in the image contribute to get that message across?
> - How might the message of the photo change if it were taken from a different angle, or cropped differently?
> - Who might be the intended audience for the photo?
> - How might different audiences respond to the photo?
> - Where do you think the picture appeared?
>
> (Goodman 2005: 212–213; Jackson 2010)

Similar lessons could be created with newspaper clippings, which ask students to understand the points of texts in connection to their use of language, quotations, facts, and so on.

In summary, using resources encompassing a wide variety of views in the classroom, rather than just the textbook, a single supplement, or various sources with similar orientations is more effective within an intercultural approach to education, so long as these materials are accompanied with guidance for students to develop critical media literacy. To engage in projects involving multiple perspectives and weighing alternative viewpoints, students must be encouraged to develop and articulate their understanding of whether knowledge claims are reasonable or unreasonable and why. Teachers need not cull from classroom discussions perspectives and data they view as unreasonable or poorly argued, but they must educate students to evaluate sources using critical media literacy, and actively and critically engage with different viewpoints.

Barriers to such a critical media literacy program (among others) in the course of social studies education in public schools are more related to process than to a critical evaluation of such proposals as put forward here. Given demands to provide for the learning (retention) of numerous strands of content knowledge given in standards, it is likely teachers fail to provide for media literacy even as it is proposed as necessary in social studies education by state boards of education. Additionally, without training in teacher education, teachers may be ill-equipped to encourage criticality toward media messages: uncertain how, for instance, to enable critical distance from curriculum resources, without sanctioning more simplistic student opposition to the formal curriculum (Goetz et al. 2005).

However, when one considers the clarity of media messages about Muslims – their commonplace association of Muslims with terrorism and violence, and nearly defensive stance toward popular stereotypes – it seems essential to include substantial critical media literacy, in a thematic, analytic, and critical way as discussed here, in the formal social studies curriculum, to prepare students to make up their own minds about what differences make a difference when it comes to Muslims. As McBrien (2005: 23) writes, while students may not learn much specific, if anything, from media messages,

> lack of attention does not mean that media messages that students are exposed to every day – television shows, advertisements, radio talk shows, billboards, and more – are not being processed at some level. If, as the studies show, media do influence attitudes that affect health, safety, voting, consumerism, and the like, then we do students a disservice if we do not teach them media literacy skills.

Though it might not be something all schools can easily start doing tomorrow, teaching such critical media literacy is an important part of preparing students to take part in democracy as informed, literate citizens today. In the next chapter, I more fully address the hurdles to critical media literacy and other major challenges with regard to developing and implementing intercultural education as elaborated here.

Conclusion

In this chapter, I have presented an alternative orientation toward difference that departs from the multicultural approaches examined in earlier chapters in its moderate relativism: an optimistic openness on the part of educators with regard to social diversity and its implications for democratic decision making. Unlike assimilationist approaches, intercultural education does not assume that smelting is the best option when it comes to social diversity. And like critical multiculturalism, interculturalism departs from pluralism, in focusing on structural challenges to increasing equality in society through dialogue, understanding that in cases such as that under examination here – learning about Muslims and Islam – the nature of negative representation is systemic and prevalent, requiring a more active response then positive content addition. However, interculturalism departs from the other multicultural orientations altogether in its assumption that the teacher does not have the answer when it comes to questions of social difference – there is no a priori resolution to issues concerning diversity in society – and in its focus on setting the stage for students to participate in democratic deliberation. In order to engage democratically, critical media literacy is required in relation, as a means to train students in gaining the skills needed to consider viewpoints alternative to those most commonly given in the public sphere and mass media.

As discussed here, engaging students in discussions about difference democratically means exploring different points of views with students, rather than disallowing or precluding the sorts of difficult and stressful conversations that are likely to occur, in order to enable students to develop their own more critically informed perspectives, which should be independent from those of the teacher or the text. I argued here that teachers should not represent their view or one approach as most truthful in this context, but allow alternative viewpoints space for exploration, discussion, and analysis. Teachers need not even share their own views, or evaluate whose views are best, as they prepare students to participate in decision-making processes in society, where initial respect and tolerance for others' views is more important than interpreting the information in the best way in any single situation.

In modeling and teaching critical media literacy, teachers must explore with students a wide variety of perspectives within sources, to engage them in viewing the social domain as one marked by a plurality of perspectives, and require their critical attention, rather than passive reception of whatever materials are used, never regarding resources simply as providers of basic facts. Recognizing the processes out of which representations come from, in texts, media, and elsewhere, and gaining experience evaluating sources can prepare students to make up their own minds more independently, with more balanced and accurate information, as is in line with the demands of citizenship within a thick sense of democracy.

In making these recommendations, I do not assume that these changes can be made by snapping our fingers. Many hurdles stand between this ideal situation and the everyday reality of U.S. public schools and schoolteachers. Teachers today are not necessarily well equipped to engage effectively in these practices, based on their training and past experience. There may not be the resources needed, including time in the day, as many teachers may find themselves scrambling in the face of ever-increasing educational standards to teach all the content knowledge required. Indeed, these proposals for intercultural education put educators in a new light, as *facilitators* rather than traditional *knowledge bearers* in the classroom; and though student-centered education is a popular concept in U.S. society today, schools are not structured in line with the practical implications of a more student-centered approach to social studies education. In the next chapter, I consider what is necessary for teachers to be able to teach in line with these best practices, and related hurdles to implementing an intercultural approach.

References

Applebaum, Barbara. "Social Justice, Democratic Education and the Silencing of Words that Wound." *Journal of Moral Education* 32 (2003): 151–162.
Applebaum, Barbara. "Engaging Student Disengagement: Resistance or Disagreement?" In *Philosophy of Education 2007,* edited by Barbara S. Stengel, 335–345. Urbana, IL: Philosophy of Education Society, 2007.

Banks, Cherry A. McGee. "A Historical Perspective on Intercultural/Multicultural Education in the United States." In *Mapping the Broad Field of Multicultural and Intercultural Education Worldwide: Towards the Development of a New Citizen*, edited by Nektaria Palaiologou and Gunther Dietz, 78–92. Newcastle upon Tyne: Cambridge Scholars Publishing, 2012.

Bennetta, William J. "How a Public School in Scottsdale, Arizona, Subjected Students to Islamic Indoctrination." *The Textbook League*. 2005. www.textbookleague.org/tci-az.htm (accessed January 8, 2014).

Besley, Tina. "Narratives of Intercultural and International Education: Aspirational Vales and Economic Imperatives." In *Interculturalism, Education and Dialogue*, edited by Tina Besley and Michael A. Peters, 87–112. New York: Peter Lang, 2012.

Besley, Tina, and Michael A. Peters. "Introduction: Interculturalism, Education and Dialogue." In *Interculturalism, Education and Dialogue*, edited by Tina Besley and Michael A. Peters, 1–27. New York: Peter Lang, 2012.

Boler, Megan. "All Speech is Not Free: The Ethics of 'Affirmative Action Pedagogy'." In *Democratic Dialogue in Education: Troubling Speech, Disturbing Silence*, 3–14. New York: Peter Lang, 2004.

Brooks, Isaac. "Questioning the Answers to 9/11." In *Forever After: New York City Teachers on 9/11*, edited by Teachers College Press with Maureen Grolnick, 31–40. New York: Teachers College Press, 2006.

Buber, Martin. "The Education of Character." In *Between Man and Man*, translated by Ronald Gregor Smith. Boston: Beacon Press, 1995.

Burbules, Nicholas C. *Dialogue in Teaching: Theory and Practice*. New York: Teachers College Press, 1993.

Corngold, Josh. "Egregiously Conflated Concepts: An Examination of 'Toleration as Recognition." In *Philosophy of Education 2005*, edited by Kenneth R. Howe, 265–271. Urbana, IL: Philosophy of Education Society, 2005.

Council on American-Islamic Relations (CAIR). "Request a Speaker." *American Muslims*. CAIR, 2013. www.cair.com/american-muslims/request-a-speaker.html (accessed January 8, 2014).

Emerson, Michael. "Summary and Conclusions." In *Interculturalism: Europe and Its Muslims in Search of Sound Societal Models*, edited by Michael Emerson, 1–16. Brussels: Centre for European Policy Studies, 2011.

Fordham Foundation, ed. *September 11: What Our Children Need to Know*. Washington, DC: Thomas B. Fordham Foundation, 2002. www.edexcellence.net/publications/sept11.html (accessed January 8, 2014).

Fordham Foundation, ed. *Terrorists, Despots, and Democracy: What Our Children Need to Know*. Washington, DC: Thomas B. Fordham Foundation, 2003. www.edexcellence.net/publications/terrorists.html (accessed January 8, 2014).

Fordham Foundation, ed. *Teaching About 9/11 in 2011: What Our Children Need to Know*. Washington, DC: Thomas B. Fordham Foundation, 2011. www.edexcellence.net/publications/teaching-about-911-in-2011.html (accessed January 8, 2014).

Goetz, Sandra K., Diane S. Brown, and Gretchen Schwarz. "Teachers Need Media Literacy, Too!" In *Media Literacy: Transforming Curriculum and Teaching*, edited by Gretchen Schwartz and Pamela U. Brown, 161–190. Malden: Blackwell, 2005.

Goodman, Steven. "The Practice and Principles of Teaching Critical Media Literacy at the Educational Video Center." In *Media Literacy: Transforming Curriculum and Teaching*, edited by Gretchen Schwartz and Pamela U. Brown, 74–99. Malden: Blackwell, 2005.

Gordon, Mordechai. "Engaging Student Disengagement." In *Philosophy of Education 2006*, edited by Daniel Vokey, 246–248. Urbana, IL: Philosophy of Education Society, 2006.

Heller, Agnes. "Can Cultural Patterns Be Compared?" *Dialectical Anthropology* 8 (1984): 269–276.

Hobbes, Renee. "Media Literacy in the K–12 Content Areas." In *Media Literacy: Transforming Curriculum and Teaching*, edited by Gretchen Schwartz and Pamela U. Brown, 74–99. Malden: Blackwell, 2005.

Hochman, Dalia. "Hominid Development: On Being a Social Studies Teacher During September 11." In *Forever After: New York City Teachers on 9/11*, edited by Teachers College Press with Maureen Grolnick, 85–96. New York: Teachers College Press, 2006.

Houston, Barbara. "Democratic Dialogue: Who Takes Responsibility?" In *Democratic Dialogue in Education: Troubling Speech, Disturbing Silence*, 105–121. New York: Peter Lang, 2004.

Huntington, Samuel P. "The Clash of Civilizations?" *Foreign Affairs*, Summer 1993.

Institute on Religion and Civic Values (IRCV). *Initiatives and Events*. IRCV, 2013. www.ircv.org/what-we-do/initiatives-events/ (accessed January 8, 2014).

Jackson, Liz. "Choice Versus Equal Opportunity: What Toleration Requires in the Case of the *Hijab* in French Schools." In *Philosophy of Education 2005*, edited by Kenneth R. Howe, 272–275. Urbana, IL: Philosophy of Education Society, 2005.

Jackson, Liz. "Dialogic Pedagogy for Social Justice? A Critical Examination." *Studies in Philosophy and Education* 27 (2008a): 137–148.

Jackson, Liz. "Silence, Words that Wound, and Sexual Identity: A Conversation with Applebaum." *Journal of Moral Education* 37 (2008b): 225–238.

Jackson, Liz. "Images of Islam in U.S. Media and Their Educational Implications." *Educational Studies* 46 (2010): 3–24.

Jackson, Liz. "Religious Diversity, Multiculturalism, and Representation: The Challenge of Facing Islam in the Classroom." In *Advancing Equity and Achievement in America's Diverse Schools: Inclusive Theories, Policies, and Practices*, edited by Camille M. Wilson and Sonya Horsford, 79–93. New York: Routledge, 2014.

Kaviani, Khodadad. *Teachers' Gatekeeping of the Middle East Curriculum*. Seattle: University of Washington, 2007.

Kincheloe, Joe L., and Shirley R. Steinberg. *Changing Multiculturalism*. Buckingham: Open Court Press, 1997.

Kunzman, Robert. "Imaginative Engagement with Religious Diversity in Public School Classrooms." *Religious Education* 101 (2006): 516–533.

Mayo, Cris. "The Tolerance That Dare Not Speak Its Name." In *Democratic Dialogue in Education: Troubling Speech, Disturbing Silence*, 33–49. New York: Peter Lang, 2004.

McBrien, J. Lynn. "Uninformed in the Information Age: Why Media Necessitate Critical Thinking Education." In *Media Literacy: Transforming Curriculum and Teaching*, edited by Gretchen Schwartz and Pamela U. Brown, 18–34. Malden: Blackwell, 2005.

Nord, Warren A. *Religion and American Education: Rethinking a National Dilemma*. Chapel Hill: University of North Carolina Press, 1995.

Peters, Michael A. "Western Models of Intercultural Philosophy." In *Interculturalism, Education and Dialogue*, edited by Tina Besley and Michael A. Peters, 29–52. New York: Peter Lang, 2012.

Rethinking Schools, ed. "War, Terrorism, and Our Classrooms: Teaching in the Aftermath of the September 11th Tragedy." Milwaukee: Rethinking Schools, 2001.

Richter, Erika. "Intercultural Education as the Responsibility of the School." In *Multi/Intercultural Conversations*, edited by Shirley R. Steinberg, 87–110. New York: Peter Lang, 2001.

Ruitenberg, Claudia W. "How to Do Things with Headscarves: A Discursive and Meta-Discursive Analysis." In *Philosophy of Education 2006*, edited by Daniel Vokey. Urbana, IL: Philosophy of Education Society.

Safi, Omid. "What Fox News vs. Reza Aslan Is Really About (Hint: Not Just Fox News' Idiocy)." *Religious News Service*, July 29, 2013. http://omidsafi.religionnews.com/2013/07/29/reza/ (accessed January 8, 2014).

Said, Edward W. *Covering Islam: How the Media and the Experts Determine How We See the Rest of the World*. New York: Vintage, 1997.

Semali, Ladislaus. "Why Media Literacy Matters in American Schools." In *Media Literacy: Transforming Curriculum and Teaching*, edited by Gretchen Schwartz and Pamela U. Brown, 34–54. Malden: Blackwell, 2005.

Shaw, Robert K. "Intercultural Education Challenges Democracy." In *Interculturalism, Education and Dialogue*, edited by Tina Besley and Michael A. Peters, 369–385. New York: Peter Lang, 2012.

Taylor, Charles. Multiculturalism and "The Politics of Recognition." Edited by Amy Gutmann. Princeton: Princeton University Press, 1992.

Waddington, David, Bruce Maxwell, Kevin McDonough, Andree-Anne Cormier, and Marina Schwimmer. "Interculturalism in Practice: Quebec's New Ethics and Religious Culture Curriculum and the Bouchard-Taylor Report on Reasonable Accommodation." In *Interculturalism, Education and Dialogue*, edited by Tina Besley and Michael A. Peters, 312–329. New York: Peter Lang, 2012.

Zinn, Howard. *A People's History of the United States, 1942–Present*. New York: HarperCollins, 1995.

6 Blazing a path for intercultural education

Introduction

In the last chapter, I discussed why and how to teach from an intercultural perspective, identifying democratically deliberating about difference with students in the classroom, and modeling and teaching students critical media literacy as essential aspects of this sort of education, ultimately providing students with more opportunities to develop richer and more comprehensive understanding of issues related to social difference, particularly necessary in the case of teaching and learning about Muslims and Islam. Grappling with and engaging students in discussions about difference democratically means exploring different alternative points of view with students as active participants, rather than disallowing or precluding the sorts of difficult and stressful conversations that are likely to occur, to enable students to develop their own more critically informed perspectives. Teachers should not represent their view or any one approach as most truthful in this context, but allow alternative viewpoints space for exploration, discussion, and analysis.

In modeling and teaching critical media literacy, teachers must first model the skills by exploring with students a wide variety of perspectives within sources, to engage them in viewing the social domain as one marked by a plurality of perspectives, and expect student critical attention, rather than passive reception, of whatever materials are used, never regarding resources simply as sources of basic facts. Given the predominance of negative messages about Muslims in mass media, recognizing the processes out of which representations come from, in texts, media, and elsewhere, and gaining experience evaluating sources, are final components of education within an intercultural approach that, in the case of Muslims and Islam, can better prepare students to make up their own minds more independently, with more balanced and accurate information, in line with the demands of autonomous citizenship in a democracy.

However, teachers today are not necessarily well equipped to engage effectively in these practices. While some teachers may be conducting the sorts of classroom activities recommended in the last chapter, many are likely to use resources uncritically (Goetz et al. 2005), that put forward only one sort of perspective, or rely substantially on the basic "facts" of textbooks that narrowly represent Muslims among other social groups, lacking training in using supplementary materials or for dealing with social difference critically in the classroom. In this chapter, I therefore turn to issues related to wider mainstream implementation of my proposal for intercultural education. First, I explore current and ideal teacher preparation for facilitating classroom discussions democratically and modeling and teaching critical media literacy. I argue that while the changes required of teacher education to better align it with interculturalism may be substantial, they are necessary for empowering more teachers to effectively educate students for democratic citizenship in a diverse society today. There are other potential challenges and competing priorities that should also be addressed in order to make the educational proposal I have outlined here possible and perhaps more palatable across wider regions of the U.S. public school system. These include the rise in popularity of a certain form of standards-based education and the related conception of educators as content standard-bearers, rather than facilitators of skills development. After exploring the implications of this proposal for contemporary teacher education, I thus consider these competing priorities and discuss a few other potential challenges to broadly implementing an intercultural approach to teaching about social difference in public schools today.

Teacher preparation

As discussed in the last chapter, the intercultural approach to education aims to develop students' dispositions and abilities to think clearly about contentious social issues by engaging in collaborative dialogue and the exploration of different viewpoints and sources of evidence. As an orientation toward considering multiple perspectives, there is no particular method required for discussing difference democratically in the classroom, in line with an intercultural approach. Best teaching styles and lesson planning will vary according to the makeup of the classroom, specific educational goals, teacher style, and so on. Student-led projects, teacher-facilitated discussions or debates, and individual student research studies are just a few of the various formats an educator could employ in an intercultural framework, to engage students in democratic dialogue and deliberation.

Yet while teachers need not learn specific practices in their formal teacher education programs to facilitate democratic classroom discussions, they should be systematically aided in developing (1) insights on their own strengths and weaknesses as a discussant, through experience with controversy and debate in classroom settings, (2) an understanding of the philosophical underpinnings and practices involved in applying an intercultural orientation toward difference in the classroom, and (3) experience meaningfully engaging in inquiries about social difference, all of which go beyond that typically required in teacher education programs today. While some may feel that these charges, when combined, place an unfair burden on pre-service teachers to do and to learn too much in the course of their formal study and preparation, as I indicate later in this chapter, the choice we face in not preparing teachers more as public intellectuals is an important one, and so it is worth considering in some detail what would be needed to make this a serious possibility.

Perhaps the most important things one needs to learn to facilitate democratic discussion in public school classrooms as an educator concern one's own temperament and personal strengths and weaknesses in communicating effectively with others about emotional or complex social issues, about which there are no simply right or wrong answers. It is doubtful one can learn these things from anyone else (i.e., through a lecture or basic teaching practicum); however, through experience with democratic dialogue in educational settings one can begin to reflectively explore and study one's own habits and common tendencies in interacting, and find out what does and does not work for himself or herself as an educator in leading discussions. In the course of developing such reflective teacher practices, educators should also be taught that it is acceptable, if not in a certain sense *obligatory*, to discuss controversial, difficult issues and groups in the classroom.

Though gaining experience with facilitating discussions of controversial issues takes few resources except for time, there is no real place to develop reflective discussion practices in the formal teacher education curriculum of today. While methods courses and classroom practical training may provide suggestions about how to not "lose control" of one's classroom during debates and engaging discussions, discussing controversial groups and issues in the classroom is considered somewhat taboo today – "enter-at-your-own-risk" territory – especially when it comes to religious controversies. There may be a concern here that this is above and beyond what should be required of teachers as educational service providers, charged first with supporting and monitoring student progress in learning knowledge and skills, rather than with structuring debates or psychologically vexing pedagogies in the course of every day practice. This may in turn connect to the deeply held view among some people that education and professional skills development and content sharing should not engage people at an emotional or affective level – that some professional educators cannot "handle" that, or should not be expected to do emotional work, as trained professionals. Yet while concern over the methods used by teachers approaching controversial issues is warranted as it is admittedly no easy or straightforward task to dive into, as Nel Noddings notes:

> Teachers who care deeply for their students, who are willing to engage in continuous inquiry, and who are committed to pedagogical neutrality are probably good enough. It is also possible that teachers, as well as students, will grow from "good enough" to considerable better under a program that allows full discussion of religious and ethical values.
>
> (1993: 138–139)

We shut down possibilities for educators to meet a potential here, if we regard them initially as characteristically ill-equipped for facilitating potentially emotional classroom discussions. There is no better way to enhance future teachers' abilities to grapple with controversy in the classroom, and model critical thinking processes about controversial issues to students, than to allow and to encourage them to practice these activities. Contentious topics exist in the social studies classroom, and are somewhat unavoidable if teachers are dedicated to assisting their students to understand the social world more effectively and productively through their formal education. In this context, teachers should be given space and time to formally prepare for this role in the course of their practical, professional education, so that they are ready to grow and learn as facilitators or discussant-guides, rather than to shut down tricky conversations due to a lack of appropriate expectations, self-knowledge, and self-confidence. They should learn how to not "lose control," perhaps, but they should also learn how to effectively and productively "lose control," in cases where their own or their students' reasonable and relatable "moral distress" (Callan 1997) can potentially guide more enriching and meaningful conversations about important social issues.

A second, more formal way to prepare teachers to engage in reflective classroom discussion practices is to critically explore with them methods and ideologies of multicultural and intercultural education. In learning about the approaches of assimilationism, pluralism, critical multiculturalism, and interculturalism, in U.S. and other contexts, pre-service teachers can consider for themselves the merits and limitations of various philosophies of education and connect these theories to their own ideals of classroom practice. Such philosophical training can assist teachers to be more aware of their own assumptions about the aims of education, enabling their critical self-reflection and more effective, revitalized pedagogies, based on their own clarified views of the social studies educator's professional role. While some teacher education students may not enjoy a very abstract philosophy of education course, about John Dewey or other great thinkers in the field, I have found that many people enter the field of education out of a sense of calling and conviction that education can make a difference in people's lives. Such assumptions, based on students' own educational experiences (good and bad), imply basic philosophies of education, about education's aims and purposes. Encouraging reflection on these "lay" philosophies of education can empower students as future educators in often stifling public school contexts, to engage in meaningful work rather than busy work, based on a more accurate sense of their own working theories they enter into classroom settings holding.

Additionally, intercultural educators should learn of debates regarding religious and moral education in public schools to gain a better understanding of what is at stake, from various reasonable perspectives, in putting forward one view over another in the classroom, thereby learning about the value of educator neutrality, while also exploring how to discuss religion sensitively in relation to social issues. In this context, teachers' right – if not their *obligation* – to discuss religion and ethics in a neutral way in the classroom can be clarified, given the contemporary context where discussing religion in schools is often regarded as taboo, wrongly associated with a breach of the constitutional separation of church from state:

> Professional programs must make it clear to teachers that the study and discussion of religious and existential questions is legitimate. I would even say that such discussion is morally obligatory . . .
> As David Purpel puts it: " . . . we cannot in good educational conscience avoid the serious and volatile disputes on religious and moral matters because they are controversial, complex, and outrageously perplexing. On the contrary: *because* they are so important and *since* they beg for awareness, understanding, clarification, and insight, they are central to significant educational inquiry."
> With such an understanding of our pedagogical obligation, we can at least supply teachers with knowledge of "how to do it." Unfortunately, they will have to acquire much of the content on their own.
> (Noddings 1993: 137)

Future educators must be provided with a clear understanding of the legal context for discussing religion in public schools, as misinformation and fear are stifling influences on the educator's ability to even permit discussions of religious topics in classrooms, let alone to encourage them as an important part of learning about society and the world. This research background can also include case studies of teachers' experiences in teaching controversial religious topics, to prepare educators to know the worst of what they can face, which may be much less terrifying than what one might imagine when such topics remain taboo in teacher education.

As the above quote also mentions, for those comfortable with discussing controversial issues such as religion in the classroom, another challenge specific to exploring topics related to diversity can arise when teachers lack substantive experience with the particular topics, such as Muslims in this case, given their (often minimal) social foundations/social sciences coursework. Educators cannot easily prepare to learn a great deal, systematically, about many groups in society from today's teacher education programs; indeed, it would take no less than a lifetime to substantially study all types of minority groups in the world in-depth! Yet learning about one case of social difference can lend itself to more critical and systematic explorations of other kinds, thereby enhancing teachers' abilities to independently study the situations of stigmatized and disadvantaged social groups in the future in a more objective way. Thus, teacher education programs preparing social studies teachers should require coursework in sociology, cultural or political anthropology, religious studies, or in areas studies (such as Asian American studies, African American or black studies, gender studies, and the like), which requires in-depth, disciplinary exploration of particular cases of difference and/or minority issues, in order to ensure that teachers have the skills needed to approach social difference objectively and systematically.

Pre-service social studies teachers often take a handful of courses in social sciences, but these tend to be lower-level classes in history or psychology, which provide a breadth of knowledge relevant to public school academic subjects, but infrequent opportunities for in-depth exploration of diversity in society. Additionally, while educators may pursue academic majors in social science disciplines simultaneously, these include a wide range of subjects, from economics and political science, to history, psychology, and philosophy; and in many of these majors, diversity is not studied in depth. Students preparing to be social studies teachers are not guaranteed experience dealing with minorities or difference substantively in such contexts, though they may choose to seek them out within their major curriculum or electives.

In the case of educating about Islam, this means that many teachers enter classrooms without any background knowledge about the religion or any others, or even much knowledge about any sociopolitical minority group in the past or today, in his or her society or worldwide. While mandating study of Islam or of world religions would clearly also help in this particular case, more essential from a generalizable view is simply providing pre-service teachers with experience exploring social difference in any particular case in society that interests them, to prepare them to go on to study other diversity issues with a more objective and critical orientation.

This is, in a sense, a call for teachers of social studies to become interculturally competent members of society themselves, who can model inquisitiveness about social difference, rather than reveal cross-cultural ignorance or ethnocentrism, an inability to engage with difference effectively. This is a vital skill for teachers in America's often diverse public schools of today, as Gloria Ladson-Billings writes.

> The average white teacher has no idea what it feels like to be a numerical or political minority in the classroom [and] few teachers (and prospective teachers) know the distinctive histories of Mexican Americans, Puerto Ricans, Cuban Americans, Salvadoreans, Guatemalans, Peruvians, or the countless groups who originate in the Spanish-speaking Americas.
>
> The indictment is not against the teachers. It is against the kind of education they receive. . . . "Helping the less fortunate" can become a lens through which teachers see their role . . .
>
> Culture is a complex concept, and few teachers have an opportunity to learn about it. Most teacher education programs are founded on the social science discipline of psychology (and some sociology). Rarely do prospective teachers examine . . . the discipline of anthropology. And although it is important for teachers to understand their students' culture, the real benefit in understanding culture is to understand its impact on our own lives . . .
>
> Teachers who are prepared to help students become culturally competent are themselves culturally competent.
>
> (Ladson-Billings 2001: 81)

Teachers can hardly teach their students to understand different groups in society in a meaningful, personally enriching way, without some formal experience with such inquiries, themselves. By requiring focused cultural study of human diversity, pre-service teachers can also attain some academic experience with exploring representations and stereotypes, which will doubtlessly aid in their study of other diversity issues, as they gain skills of objectively exploring difference that can be transferred to different contexts.

As Kincheloe reminds (2001: 88–89),

> The well-prepared teacher is not one who enters the classroom with a set of prearranged lessons but is a professional with a thorough knowledge of a subject, a knowledge of what is happening in the world . . . these understandings can [not] be reproduced in a list of specific competencies.

Teaching others how to study the social world does not require that one has prepared for every potential discussion and lesson before they enter in the classroom, but it does require that one has had experience studying the social world successfully for themselves. On the other hand, attempting to learn a small amount about everything, or some token knowledge about Muslims, can be counterproductive, given the emphasis within an intercultural orientation on learning about different points of view in a substantial way, before supposing one or more perspectives about it is best. The point is not to develop token understanding of all "major" social groups in the society or worldwide, but to develop an intercultural view, that involves respect and openness toward other viewpoints, as discussed in the last chapter as goals of intercultural education. One cannot be expected to learn about everything important that may come up in the social domain, but one should have some experience investigating contemporary social issues involving difference, that surpasses the brief attention to difference with regard to multicultural education provided in education social foundations curriculum (which typically consists today of a single class in the course of a teacher education program).

In summary, while there is no single best way proposed here to train teachers to engage their students in democratic dialogue most effectively – practice must depend in reality upon concrete aspects of one's setting, including the characteristics of one's own temperament, rather than upon prescriptive pedagogies (Jackson 2006) – through providing educators with experience facilitating discussions, in public school classrooms or in their college courses, one can help teachers develop more reflective practices for dealing with difference effectively in their future classrooms. Additionally, by learning different educational philosophies for dealing with controversy, including the various multicultural and intercultural frameworks and about debates related to teaching about religion and morality in public schools, social studies teachers can develop an understanding of how helping students to think about complicated and controversial topics is connected to their role of preparing students for citizenship in a diverse society.

However, without gaining experience studying social difference in society systematically themselves, teachers may nonetheless remain ill-equipped to collaboratively guide discussions on such topics and issues in their classrooms, to find appropriate research and classroom resources for studying difference, and to help students conduct their own investigations. Therefore, some area study that focuses on a social group, diversity, or social difference – it need not consist of more than a few lower-level and upper-level courses, but must be more than simple overviews of diversity – can enable social studies educators to teach others about sociopolitical minorities, such as Muslims in the United States today, and about other forms of difference in an informed way, enabling their students in turn to develop critically reasoned understandings, despite the inadequacy of representations provided in their textbooks, the media, and elsewhere in society. Such coursework also helps develop teachers' research and critical media literacy skills, final components of their ideal teacher education as preparation for guiding students using an intercultural approach.

While many teachers recognize that textbooks are inadequate for covering any topic in-depth, particularly any contentious or contemporary one, they may find themselves at a loss in knowing where to look for appropriate alternative sources of evidence and information that can be brought into the classroom, especially when it comes to topics related to religion. Possibly hindered as well by student reading levels and a lack of preparation on how to critically use or complement textbooks with additional resources, teachers risk inadequately modeling critical media literacy to their students, thereby failing to educate them to develop critical media literacy in turn. Because the "decisions that teachers make about their curriculum influence student learning" (Kaviani 2007: 190), teachers must therefore be trained more systematically to model and teach critical media literacy, to ensure they bring forward in balanced and critical ways multiple points of view in their class, and not just interesting, readily available, and/or easily engaging materials.

One particular problem many teachers face in modeling critical media literacy in social studies is their feeling limited in selecting diverse resources by low student reading abilities or, alternately, their ignorance of student reading abilities in assigning readings. Often, reading abilities dictate the materials brought to the classroom, as it makes little sense to require students to read materials they cannot understand. However, students can be aided to understand topics through collaboratively reading materials with their classmates and the teacher, and increasing reading literacy more generally should go hand-in-hand with teaching difficult materials, particularly as primary sources, historical documents, and other alternative resources can be productively used. This means that social studies teachers should be taught as English teachers are (if to a lesser extent) how to track student reading abilities, as well as how to guide students in analytically comprehending materials, as main points, messages, and particular perspectives, rather than merely asking them to extract facts from sentences out of readings, as is often observed:

> Teachers were giving question/answer type assignments (i.e. answer the questions at the end of the chapter, worksheets, study guides, etc.) to accompany textbook reading assignments. Furthermore, most teachers were spending ample time discussing difficult vocabulary found in texts. Yet . . . the above mentioned methods were the only methods used throughout the

course of the school year in order to increase the students' reading comprehension of social studies texts. . . . [L]ittle was being done to actually "teach" students how to improve their comprehension.

(Barker 1992: 111–112)

One cannot gain social science literacy and competency in understanding the complex world they live in today through multiple choice quizzes about secondary sources like textbooks, which have been seen here to obscure complicated realities in favor of overly simplistic views. Rather, to engage in understanding the best research and influential ideas, students need to actively develop their literacy in social science as in English, to develop social studies competency. Because not all perspectives are as easy to comprehend as others from an intercultural viewpoint, it is essential in modeling and teaching critical media literacy to guide students to comprehend the materials. To do this, social studies educators must be taught to aid student literacy more generally, rather than simply instruct and track their capacities for memorizing basic facts or defining terms given in texts. Teaching students to understand the messages of texts rather than just the words and subjects discussed within them also constitutes a basis for teaching critical media literacy.

Additionally, to model and teach critical media literacy skills in the classroom, teachers need to learn critical media literacy themselves, as well as how to impart such to their social studies students at various levels, as they assign materials and provide resources from multiple perspectives in their classroom. While one might imagine that critical media literacy is developed in pre-service teachers' coursework since it is a common element in educational standards, such is not always the case, given that learning of public school curriculum often takes place in education courses rather than in social science or literature coursework and as, additionally, teacher education students frequently fail to take many upper-level courses in social science disciplines (though adding in cultural studies coursework to the required curriculum as discussed here would also help develop educator critical literacy, as well). Additionally, critical reception of textbooks, including even scrutinizing their depth or readability, is not often part of the formal teacher education curriculum, although it may be mentioned briefly within social foundation courses.

Thus, whether as a course within educational studies or elsewhere in universities (such as in a department of English or communications), a class on critical media literacy that teaches pre-service educators the components of critical media literacy as discussed here (its thematic, analytic, and critical characteristics within a social studies context), and how to teach them in turn in social studies classes, is essential to preparing teachers to model and teach critical media literacy. As Goetze et al. (2005: 172–173) note, "media literacy could well enrich the entire preservice teacher education curriculum":

> In a social studies methods course, preservice teachers can study the ways the media interpret history, from film to newspaper to the History Channel,

and how students learn from the media . . . All content knowledge can be influenced by the mass media. Even future teachers' own notions about teaching may have been partly formed by seeing such films as *Dangerous Minds* or *Mr. Holland's Opus.*

Most teachers are interested in gaining critical media literacy skills that can help them to choose resources and develop their students' literacy and critical thinking skills, and such could be easily provided for in one term or less, although critical media literacy is uncommon in social studies teacher education programs today. As is the case regarding the need for experience discussing and academically studying social difference, gaining experience and skills with critical media literacy is fundamental to providing students with the same, and critical media literacy is a basic prerequisite to critically incorporating resources encompassing multiple perspectives in the classroom, for learning how to come to independent positions on important social issues, and for participating in democratic decision making in an informed, effective way.

In sum, to engage students in discussions of different viewpoints democratically in the classroom, teachers must be provided with opportunities to develop reflective practice, including experience with leading discussions, as well as structured study of multicultural, intercultural, and religious educational philosophies. And while teachers cannot be expected to know a great deal about every minority group relevant to or part of our society, learning to conduct research and understand disciplinary orientations toward difference through engagement in some area and/or group studies coursework additionally gives educators transferable practical experience with studying difference in society; this can enable them to guide students to develop better, more accurate understandings of difference in society, themselves. Finally, teachers must be trained in critical media literacy, to model and help their students develop critical media literacy skills, in turn.

While each of these capacities and experiences is necessary for enabling teachers to effectively teach about difference in society, none is fundamental within contemporary social studies teacher education programs. However, if we wish to teach students more than they are typically learning today, from the mass media and usually minimal discussions in the formal curriculum, it would not be difficult to add on to the pre-service teacher curriculum, conceiving the teachers' role as that of a better informed or trained guide, rather than as a manager of student work toward learning standard facts. As such, we would reasonably require of teachers more coursework, and more academic training, than is typically required today. While some may see this as an unreasonable burden to place upon teachers, it nonetheless better enables their preparation to guide the next generation in developing autonomous thinking and decision-making skills about difference in society, which are crucial to preserving democracy in society. As Noddings writes:

> People who are preparing to teach at the high school level need to study the high school curriculum in great depth. Just as physicians must study

anatomy, and lawyers torts, teachers need to study the curriculum. It is the backbone of their work. . . .

The objection might be raised that such preparation would require that people identify teaching as their goal upon entry to college. True. But engineering students are also required to make their choice early, so teachers would not be unique. What if they changed their minds? Lots of people do. . . . It is odd that we worry more about people changing their minds than we do about people "preparing" for careers in ways largely irrelevant to their current choices.

(1993: 135–136)

When difference in society is part of the curriculum, as it is in social studies classrooms, teachers must gain not just the standard, "basic," information about these subjects to impart to students, or skills for teaching students to retain the "facts" of the situation. They must gain intellectual and academic experiences and capacities, which are readily available to them in most universities today, but not required of them as of late. Furthermore, if we perceive the social studies teacher as a guide to students for developing the capacities required for autonomous democratic citizenship – including democratic deliberation and critical media literacy skills – then requiring of them more rigorously academic study is neither impossible, nor unreasonable.

Additional hurdles and possibilities

Interculturalism is an approach to difference that prioritizes critical thinking and evaluating evidence over the ability to accept and retain particular orientations toward a subject matter. As such, it would be hard to implement in educational contexts which favor demonstrations of retention of knowledge claims, over critical thinking skills. In these latter settings, pushes for more critical than basic forms of social studies education such as that implied here are sometimes held as untenable, or as inappropriately politically charged. Additionally, intercultural education has a different conception of the social studies teacher's role and that of teacher education than that approach which embraces standardization of social studies curriculum. However, such an intercultural education may be less partial, or politically motivated, and more effective, than those forms commonly enacted today for teaching about controversial groups and contentious subjects in public schools.

An intercultural approach to social studies education may be precluded in some U.S. educational contexts today that accept the conception of the social studies teacher as a standards-bearer. Since the 1980s, public school teachers in the United States have been seen increasingly as conveyers of key content knowledge, educational standards. As I mentioned briefly in the fourth chapter, the practice of understanding student learning outcomes in terms of consistent standards (standardization) can be useful in fields such as English and math, where there are frequently objective correct and incorrect answers. The spelling of words in a language, or the sum of two numbers, is usually specific, and right or wrong. Thus, stating that the spellings and definitions of commonly used words and basic arithmetic should be systematically taught in public schools, in ways that teachers could be held accountable for, is not implausible and is arguably productive, to ensure equal educational opportunities are being provided.

However, beyond the locations of today's continents, cities, and states and related terminology, one would be hard-pressed to identify many similarly objective and universal facts, or standard knowledge, in social studies, a field dealing with the most complex phenomenon: human social relations. As discussed in the fourth chapter, diverse perspectives have developed on the causes and effects of the rise of the "Islamic empire" – there is no single, correct position on such a complex subject matter, or any sound way to choose one answer over another as official school knowledge. To understand politics in the Middle East, should teachers concentrate on Saudi Arabia, or Jordan, or Lebanon? Considering all of them might be ideal; however, given the typical quantity of state social studies standards, time does not allow for a substantial lesson or discussion of many different perspectives or foci, or for students to develop nuanced points of view on such very general topics as the rise of Islam or Middle Eastern politics today. Recall also, the way that religion was explored in many textbooks, in line with a standardized approach to understanding religion, in painted maps depicting homogeneous religious spaces across the world, of Buddhists, Hindus, Christians, and so on. To teach that Europeans are Christian or that Middle Easterners or Egyptians are Muslim – presenting such information as standard knowledge (e.g., "identify the global distribution of the world's major religions") – obscures as much as it explains a world in which heterogeneity, not homogeneity, is often the rule.

Thus, standardization of social studies curriculum directly opposes the intercultural approach advocated here by framing as series of facts popularly accepted contemporary perspectives about societies. Even if critical understanding is also encouraged in state standards, it can hardly be emphasized, as Kincheloe observes (2001: 596), when mainstream interpretations regarding the Islamic empire (and the Roman Empire, and China, and the rise of Europe) are what teachers are held responsible for teaching:

> Even teachers who encourage interpretation, reflection, and exploration of the historical process are pressured into teaching history as isolated facts by the tyranny of tests and standards. . . . Fragmented, content-driven history programs often run students through a series of memorizations, barring them from a deeper exploration into an event or a period of history. Excluded from such experiences on the basis that they take too much time, students fail to learn how to understand the flow of a stream of events, construct a compelling picture of life in a specific historical era, or conceptualize the complex and subtle nature of social, cultural, political, and economic change.

To implement intercultural education in social studies classes more broadly, then, expectations of social studies teachers need to shift to enable more teachers to focus on methods in social sciences rather than "facts," and share these with students, engaging them in critical social inquiry. Teachers need to be seen as skilled workers, and students as future skilled participants in society, rather than as retainers of standard facts chosen by someone outside the classroom, who has been given authority over the curriculum and thus over both the students and the teachers' daily practices.

> Deskilling has involved taking jobs that demand skill and decision-making and dividing them into simplified actions. In this manner, less skilled, less costly, and more controllable workers and teacher can be employed. . . . [This logic] precludes the need for teachers to analyze the materials that should be taught, understand the backgrounds and needs of individual students, or adapt certain subject matter and certain methods of informational delivery. . . . The job of teaching is reduced to merely executing plans that are made elsewhere.
>
> (Kincheloe 2001: 192)

Resistance to such ideas often involves arguments such as that problem-based, critical approaches to social studies knowledge such as interculturalism are unsound educationally, or inappropriately political, aiming to show students negative things about their society and wrongly influencing them to fight for internal social changes. As we have seen previously, assimilationists regard the status quo and popular knowledge about political subjects such as Islam in the United States today as superior to alternative views, arguing for instance that teachers must prepare "knowledgeable and patriotic citizens" that know "why the United States is worth preserving and defending," rather than "'civics' as consisting largely of political activism and 'service learning'" (Finn 2003: v, i). That students need to learn to walk before they can run is also additionally suggested sometimes in this context, by educators who feel that "basic" facts, or "what one needs to know," must precede education for critical pursuit of different understandings. There is an idea that "critical thinking" can only follow from learning the "facts."

Yet few deny today that social studies education must *engage* students to be effective, and that rote memorization of popular ideas or basic facts fails to inspire or develop students' critical abilities. Theorists of many different orientations, from assimilationist to critical multiculturalist, understand today that the method of teaching social studies as a series of important abstract facts neither enables effective student retention of information in the United States today, nor engages students in study, and is therefore as a whole inadequate for deep student learning. Additionally, while teaching facts uniformly to students may increase test scores, it results in "deskilled students" who can collect "technical skills and atomistic bits of knowledge which can be measured," but have been discouraged from thinking about "the relationship of one fact to another, the connection between what one learns and how such knowledge might affect his or her fellow human beings, the kinship between the school curriculum and what constitutes a good society" (Kincheloe 2001: 51). The latter is clearly more appropriately the end of social studies education, for independent thought and action within a liberal democratic society.

Indeed, at a general level, no educator or critic of education favors a social studies education on disconnected facts over more personally meaningful materials in social studies classrooms. Even Fordham Institute reviews of U.S. world history education conclude that neither an assimilationist (European focused, Western based), nor pluralist ("treat-all-stories-and-cultures-as-equal") approach is preferable to one that focuses on select elements and groups within world history, in order to not "cover everything and pass judgments on nothing," but instead make lessons memorable and personally meaningful to students (Mead 2006: 16). The latest assimilationist project of developing common core standards also focuses significantly on skills rather than content, a substantial departure from state standards that usually focus on the latter, though not all are pleased with this project generally (Ravitch 2013). A social studies curriculum shaped by content standards is neither ideal for educating students as autonomous decision makers, nor is it politically unbiased or impartial, precluding the inclusion of material and points of view not regarded by policy makers as worthy of standardization (or as easily standardized).

Furthermore, social studies education will always remain political, in one sense, as there is always a choice made about what to cover and how, and what not to cover. Yet in the case that content standards supersede a focus on civic *skills* development in social studies, disingenuous depoliticization of curriculum takes place, as such education can never be entirely without bias. For example, in the case of religion, social studies education that relegates religious beliefs and people to a facts-only domain strips religion of its practical significance to students as learners who live in social world made up by and large by diverse, interrelated religious believers. As discussed in Chapter 4, because of standardization practices and controversies surrounding religious difference and Islam, very few standards among states consider Islam or Muslims since the medieval ages, despite its tremendous growth and influence on civilizations worldwide since. However, by aiming to avoid controversy or sensitive, subjective content, the minimally religious curriculum is unimportant and irrelevant in today's world, where it is widely recognized as crucial "in a democracy to help children and young people gain the capacity for interpretation and critique by examining the beliefs" of others around them (Kincheloe 2001: 61). Students can hardly learn to weigh in effectively and productively on important policy issues regarding religion, such as religious expression in public settings (like wearing hijab), when they do not learn anything interesting or complex about it, or regarding relevant faiths and points of view, in school.

In summary, while some may suggest that an education that critically investigates major beliefs and perspectives and focuses significantly on skills is less educationally effective, overly political, or fails to teach students patriotic values when compared with other methods and approaches, to develop skills to participate in democratic society students must gain exposure to alternative points of view and their knowledge sources, and learn how to *think* rather than *memorize*. Such preparation of students, to make up their own minds on important social issues, fundamental to citizenship education in a democratic society, cannot be achieved by basing the curriculum on standard sets of social studies "facts." As Kincheloe (2001: 61–62) writes:

> The basic difference between democratic and totalitarian social studies education is that democratic social studies education allows students to step back and examine social assumptions. Unfortunately many social studies programs . . . provide students little opportunity with uncertainty. If social progress and empowerment are possible, we must get beyond this discomfort with uncertainty.

Additional major barriers to enacting an intercultural approach to social studies education throughout U.S. public schools include (1) challenges related to the implications of intercultural education for elementary education and (2) concerns related to the possibility that intercultural educators would teach for relativism. First, having examined and discussed practices in social studies education primarily – the major domain where Muslims and other controversial groups are discussed substantially in the curriculum – I have not yet here considered the implications of intercultural education for lower levels of education and the potential disconnect that may occur when students are asked, perhaps for the first time in the course of their education, to think for themselves about social difference in the classroom setting. It is possible that students might have a hard time learning effectively with an intercultural approach to difference at the middle-school or high-school levels, without prior experience at lower levels. Students may be unaccustomed to democratic deliberation about serious issues, and to their teachers not knowing all the answers, for instance, and this may hinder the effectiveness of such an educational approach.

However, implementing intercultural education at lower levels introduces new challenges, as Nord and Charles Haynes (1998: 62) observe: "objections to the inclusion of religion are loudest if elementary schools are involved . . . Leave religion to the family and faith communities, goes the familiar argument, and wait until students are older to discuss the role of religion in history and society." Elementary school teachers also often lack understanding of what is and is not prohibited when it comes to teaching about religion in public schools. Those who are not nervous about teachers' capacities to handle religious and political issues in the classroom may still fear that *students* are not emotionally and cognitively mature enough, in elementary school, for such topics. However, as Nord and Haynes go on,

> Far from being a way to usurp the role of parents or clergy, study of religion in the elementary grades is part of the core of the schools' mission to provide a good education and to prepare students to live in a democratic society. Properly considered, the study of family, community, various cultures,

the nation, and other key themes and topics important in the early grades all require some discussion of religion . . .

The fact that it isn't easy to achieve a fair and balanced elementary curriculum is no reason not to try. Silence about religion can also be a form of indoctrination – however unintentional. The notion that individuals can understand all of human life and history without reference to religious is itself a view of life that is antithetical and hostile to religious claims.

(1998: 63)

Philosophers of education for children (Laverty 2004; Splitter 2006) and dedicated elementary teachers find that there are ways to engage students in discussions of religion as well as ethical issues in society from early ages, debunking ideas that children simply cannot examine complex or emotional issues. On the other hand, if we obscure big-picture questions from elementary school curriculum, we risk teaching students implicitly that they should not engage in controversial investigations in public places like schools – potentially disabling some students from feeling comfortable with democratic dialogue at later stages. In order to teach for intercultural understanding at secondary education levels, there must be some preparation for students to do so at earlier age levels, too. This indicates that elementary teachers, who are responsible for teaching broadly across the curriculum, may also need to be reconceptualized more as highly skilled professionals with changes made to their pre-service training. Additionally, as students are often tested on their social studies knowledge at lower levels by state boards of education, revising the tests or diminishing their significance would likely be required to make implementing an intercultural approach at lower levels successful. However, in today's dynamic elementary education context, high-stakes testing is increasingly becoming commonplace, though reversing this trend is far from impossible. These are important issues to explore in continuing to evaluate the need for, tenability of, and optimization of, intercultural education in the social studies curriculum.

A second potential pitfall of applying an intercultural approach to difference has to do with concern about the possibility of educators promoting moral or cultural relativism (that is, the view that all orientations are equally valid and true), in place of a consideration of all perspectives as initially worth pursuing with an optimistic, pluralist intercultural attitude. As one educator put it in the last chapter, one does not want to appear "wishy-washy"; yet educator neutrality, as advocated for here, seems to indicate, at least a *toleration* of all perspectives, which may border on, if not cross the boundary into a relativistic orientation, where all perspectives are considered equal, or equally valid. Indeed, a type of "moderate cultural relativism" was also promoted in discussing the intercultural perspective generally, which was defined and recommended as a way to compare cultures in the areas that really matter, such as those related to social justice, violence, and oppression, but to also aim at the same time to reserve judgments when possible, in an effort to better understand, with appropriate distance and respect, before evaluating others' actions and views.

To students who are only beginning to learn about how to consider and weigh out different sources of evidence, it will likely appear that intercultural educators are treating all views as approximately equal in merit when exercising such neutrality and moderate cultural relativism.

This is particularly problematic when it comes to religious education, as mentioned in the second chapter, as schools should be neutral toward the plurality of religiosity in U.S. society. Yet many scholars who emphasize the importance of learning about religion in public education regard moral relativism in education as comparable to teaching for secularism, for how can you take all religions seriously as sources of truth, at the same time? Distinguishing between educator neutrality and toleration of religious pluralism in society, and educator endorsements of moral relativism as if all religions are "correct," is challenging for educators to do in practice. Eamonn Callan describes this as the problem of pluralistic dialogue as "values clarification," which, in the aim of making discussions as pleasant and harmonious as possible in classrooms marked by diversity, "invites children to think of rival moral judgements as no more than so many different preferences to be tolerated as we tolerate the odd tastes of people who do not share our own" (1997: 207). Acknowledging that "pluralistic moral dialogue is a difficult and delicate endeavour," Callan observes, however, that "ethical avoidance is a blindly regressive social tendency that pulls us away from the dialogical conditions that would enable us collectively to distinguish the pluralism that deserves our respect from the pluralism that does not" (1997: 220). One can only develop his or her skills to teach such practices through experience – and avoidance is no better option, potentially obscuring even the possibility for pluralist toleration as distinct from moral relativism from some students' minds.

As mentioned in the last chapter, intercultural education does promote a kind of moderate relativism, where all views are considered worthy of initial examination, yet all are regarded as evaluable, in terms of their implications for the avoidance of undue harm to individuals and groups. Additionally, it demands tolerance that, as an ideal, "surely extends to beliefs and values that we find misguided, untrue, perhaps even offensive, but neither tolerance nor neutrality commits us to the claim that all beliefs or values are equally true or good" (Nord 2010: 181). This problem can only be resolved through taking care in teacher education and in public school teaching, so that students can realize that there are tough, complicated issues in society, and that teachers have the responsibility to be neutral and encourage tolerance but not to support all beliefs. This is also a vital if tricky task of citizenship education, connecting the right to free speech to a toleration of diversity, which in liberal democratic societies enables new possibilities for more just, flourishing communities. Through careful design, intercultural approaches need not encourage or imply relativism toward different views, knowledge claims, and behaviors. This is a pluralism that takes the views of others seriously, but not a mandated acceptance of all views, or a mandated lack of evaluation of these views upon careful examination of their practical implications.

The problem of relativism in education takes us back, in a sense, to the way we conceive of teachers, increasingly in the United States, as social workers employed to teach content and standards, but not as highly skilled professionals, with the capacity to develop students' intellectual capacities. Educators who are trained and empowered for the task can surely better navigate the seas, in elementary education and in discussing contentious religious and non-religious beliefs, to maintain neutrality without promoting relativism or secularism. Educators have a role to play not only to impart content knowledge but to facilitate an environment of intellectual flourishing of students in the context of their interpersonal and intergroup socialization. This important role in U.S. public schools as "common schools" is worth maintaining today. Regarding ordinary teachers as valued intellectuals in society and preparing them for their professions as such are not impossible tasks. They are crucial if students are going to graduate from public schools with the ability to participate in democratic discussions and decision making in society, as critical thinkers who are able to understand others' viewpoints as well as media messages, in open minded, but not relativistic or "wishy-washy" ways. Revising popular conceptions of public school educators, which are increasingly negative and disempowering today, is crucial if we regard their work as important in children's lives.

Conclusion

In the last chapter, I elaborated an intercultural approach to education and illustrated ways social studies teachers can use an intercultural approach to difference to help students develop better informed understandings of diversity in their classrooms, lacking ideal classroom resources for educating students substantively and objectively. Teachers need not have ideal textbooks, for instance, to counter prevalent, harmful views of minorities in media, if they can guide their students to grapple with difference constructively and democratically in the classroom, rather than regard one perspective as official curricular knowledge, and if they can model and teach critical media literacy as recommended here, thereby developing more accurate, critical understandings of difference, that do not rely on stereotypes, in the case of Muslims.

These ideal practices require specific teacher preparation and training that goes beyond that typically provided, however, for teachers to effectively facilitate such challenging democratic discussions, and model and teach critical media literacy. Most teachers are not required to study minorities and difference, critical media literacy, or reflective pedagogy themselves today, making them ill-equipped for teaching others to think about difference in society in an intercultural way. What is required in addition hardly constitutes a dramatic change to the curriculum of teacher education, however, as more practice with discussions and multicultural and intercultural theories can be integrated with currently required coursework; while experience in critical resource use, literacy, and area studies need not require more than a handful of additional courses.

And without teachers well prepared for these tasks of democratic deliberation and critical media literacy education, intercultural education cannot be more than a rarity in public schools, and a mere possibility for the future. Without practice with democratic deliberation and critical media literacy, students will have little opportunity to critically consider predominant, biased, harmful media messages about different groups in society, such as Muslims, with critical distance. Instead, many will be likely to passively receive media messages, as if they are sufficient as the "whole story," given textbooks' similar association of Islam and Muslims with terrorism and conflicts in the Middle East and Western Asia.

In this chapter, I also considered a few other challenges to the intercultural approach. I noted that the way that some people in society view the teacher's general role should shift, to empower teachers to dynamically produce and revise knowledge with students, rather than oversee their retention of facts, as is often their charge today, given current practices for educational accountability, particularly standardization. Some may see such a shift in focus as overly or inappropriately political; however, social studies education can never be reduced to just learning factual content – the "basic facts," despite some people's hopes and assumptions. It must also involve development of *skills* in a liberal democratic (and religiously plural) society. Teaching that is relevant and engaging to students is more effective, furthermore, and although there is no way to avoid controversies, they can be approached with sensitivity and respect, by educators who are role models of active participation in diverse, democratic public life.

More work remains to be done to enact the proposals put forward here. The largest hurdle to implementing intercultural education in public schools after the consideration of teacher professional development is the standards movement in social studies education. Standardization, I have argued here, challenges teachers to explore with students the breadth of the social world, while also teaching skills for critical thinking and analysis. The standards themselves at the state level tend to focus on facts, although in social studies, the facts are often quite open to interpretation. To ignore this situation in favor of teaching toward standards is to teach against critical thinking skills development, treating preferred answers as truth in an arguably more subjective space. In this context, social studies standards should be reoriented toward skills and with greater faith and trust in educators, as experts who have the specialized knowledge and abilities necessary to balance breadth with depth, and not sacrifice the latter for the former.

Other pitfalls to implementing an intercultural approach to classroom practice that require some careful thinking through include the risk of teaching for relativism, and the challenge of introducing greater intercultural approaches at the elementary level. No doubt these are tricky issues in today's public sphere, although research is increasingly on the side of teaching philosophical issues to children, while issues over relativism can be alleviated through greater educator training as recommended here. Yet we harm students as future citizens in the case of learning about Islam and Muslims, by enabling the narrowest margin of minority experiences held as exceptional in mass media and in educational standards to represent the whole, a grossly inaccurate rendering. Bureaucracy need not preclude educational interventions that aim to enhance democratic citizenship and personal autonomy of the U.S. citizenry, as these are vital to the continued flourishing of this political liberal democratic society.

References

Barker, Rod Philip. *The Frequency and Extent of Textbook Usage Among Arizona High School Social Studies Teachers*. Flagstaff: Northern Arizona University, 1992.

Callan, Eamonn. *Creating Citizens: Political Education and Liberal Democracy*. Oxford: Clarendon Press, 1997.

Finn, J., Chester E. Foreword. In *Where Did Social Studies Go Wrong?*, edited by the Fordham Foundation, i–vii. Washington, DC: Thomas B. Fordham Foundation, 2003. www.edexcellence.net/sites/default/files/publication/pdfs/ContrariansFull_7.pdf (accessed January 8, 2014).

Goetz, Sandra K., Diane S. Brown, and Gretchen Schwarz. "Teachers Need Media Literacy, Too!" In *Media Literacy: Transforming Curriculum and Teaching*, edited by Gretchen Schwartz and Pamela U. Brown, 161–190. Malden: Blackwell, 2005.

Jackson, Liz. "Dialogue as a Good for the Disadvantaged." *Philosophical Perspectives on Educational Practice in the Twenty-First Century*, edited by Padraig Hogan, 161–167. Malta: Allied, 2006.

Kaviani, Khodadad. *Teachers' Gatekeeping of the Middle East Curriculum*. Seattle: University of Washington, 2007.

Kincheloe, Joe L. *Getting Beyond the Facts: Teaching Social Studies/Social Sciences in the Twenty-First Century*. New York: Peter Lang, 2001.

Ladson-Billings, Gloria. "Teaching and Cultural Competence." *Rethinking Schools* 15 (2001). www.rethinkingschools.org//cmshandler.asp?archive/15_04/Glb154.shtml (accessed January 8, 2014).

Laverty, Megan. "Philosophy for Children and/as Philosophical Practice." *International Journal of Applied Philosophy* 18 (2004): 141–151.

Mead, Walter Russell. *The State of State World History Standards*. Washington, DC: Thomas B. Fordham Institute, 2006.

Noddings, Nel. *Educating for Intelligent Belief or Unbelief*. New York: Teachers College, 1993.

Nord, Warren A., and Charles C. Haynes. *Taking Religious Seriously Across the Curriculum*. Alexandria: Association for Supervision and Curriculum Development, 1998.

Ravitch, Diane. "The Upside Down World of Common Core." *Diane Ravitch's Blog*, August 21, 2013. http://dianeravitch.net/2013/08/21/the-upside-down-world-of-common-core/ (accessed January 8, 2014).

Splitter, Laurance. "Teaching teachers to 'teach' philosophy for children in the US and Australia." *Critical and Creative Thinking: The Australasian Journal of Philosophy for Children* 14 (2006): 15–31.

7 Conclusion

As a society, the United States faces important questions today about the aims of education. Multicultural education has traditionally conceived the school as a melting pot or salad bowl, where diverse individuals come together. Yet increasingly, public schools as individual entities are becoming demographically homogeneous (Kozal 2006). The moral role of public education remains suspect, as religious parents fear the moral influence of secular teachers on their children, while secularist parents challenge historically common religious features of schools. Standardization of curriculum nationwide is becoming a popular goal (Common Core 2012), as the United States looks to evaluate schools competitively to make funding decisions, and compete with other countries worldwide. From this perspective, sound education in public schools about Islam and Muslims may not be the most crucial issue the society faces with regard to the educational system. As charter schools, privatization, and other choice models are increasing in popularity today, saving the public educational system, with its multicultural civic aims, may seem prerequisite to any component of teaching within it!

Yet no matter how education is facilitated – by public funding or otherwise, in the future – within a liberal democratic society, schools must prepare students as future citizens with sufficient skills for civic participation. This includes, at the most basic level, sharing of the laws of the land and the principles undergirding them, which inform interpretation in practical disputes. It includes understanding how to participate in democratic decision making: how to vote, and how to engage in processes related to having one's views represented or heard in policy making domains, at local, regional, and national levels. And it includes learning about the society, and the world of which it is a part: its diversity, and its serious challenges. As students at early elementary levels learn to understand their neighborhood and local community, students at higher levels should identify the characteristics and social composition of their society and those of others around the globe.

In relation, democracy requires toleration of diversity for its survival. Debate and deliberation over social issues and challenges depends vitally on the rights and abilities of individuals and groups to communicate freely. By implication, schools that support a liberal democratic society must enable students to learn how to exercise their rights and protect those of others actively, including the rights of others who are different from them. Part and parcel of learning the meaning of personal freedom, then, is to learn the importance of respecting others' rights, which entails recognizing that people deserve equality to speak, act, and believe, regardless of whether their views, accent, or skin color are similar to one's own. Schools should not promote nor condone discrimination, intolerance, or prejudice, but instead sanction acceptance of religious, racial, cultural, and other forms of pluralism, in the classroom and in society.

When it comes to educating about Islam and Muslims in U.S. public schools, much more can be done. Muslims do not necessarily see public schools as safe places, because some students and teachers display ignorance, prejudice, intolerance, and overt hostility in some instances (Elnatour 2005; Rizvi 2005). Teachers, who are responsible for intervening in such cases, can also face a significant upward battle. In the first place, they may not know much about Islam and Muslims themselves. Not all communities in the United States are religiously plural, though the country as a whole is; so teachers may not know any Muslims firsthand. The ones they are likely to see on television are not usually ones they would like to meet. Many media representations of Muslims, as we have seen here, are of terrorists, anti-American Muslims, or others framed in a threatening way, as members of combustible social groups, as in Arab Spring media coverage. In the public sphere, there is an active battle taking place today between Muslims who demand equal rights to speak and represent themselves within the media and popular culture and those who argue that such equality conflicts with liberal democracy, conflating commitment to Islam with fascism, barbarity, and terrorism. In this setting, even ordinary Muslims are cast commonly as bad guys, by news media that aims to cover debates in a provocative, alarming, and/ or mesmerizing way – not to discuss commonplace, reasonable people acting in rational ways.

Many teachers see through this smokescreen and recognize that tolerance of Muslims and Islam in the United States is not anti-American in any way. Rather, it is among the most patriotic of acts to fight for greater democracy and equality across diverse groups in the United States, a country founded in individual liberty of speech, and free action and belief. Yet such teachers face further barriers. Organizations of private groups and parents actively scrutinize educators and educational resources in some parts of the country and conflate promotion of tolerance in the case of Islam with anti-Americanism or Islamic religious indoctrination (Bennetta 2005; Finn 2002; Hochman 2006; Sewall 2008). Counting lines of textbooks discussing Christianity and Islam, the Texas State Board of Education (2010) has threatened to stop buying textbooks that say too many nice things about Muslims, at the apparent cost of Christians. Some parents and politicians want to focus on *right* and *wrong*, in relation to American foreign policy and the war on terrorism. They do not want teachers confusing students, sympathizing with "the enemy" in the classroom, or teaching political attitudes, when basic facts are also necessary.

Some arguments put forward by such groups as the Fordham Institute and the American Textbook Council are well founded. As in the Texas State Board of Education Resolution, I strongly agree that in a religiously diverse country as the United States, with a proud heritage of religious tolerance, students should learn to understand great world traditions informing diverse people's lives today. Among these are Islam and Christianity, and other spiritual, religious, and/or ethical orientations that are often needlessly avoided and wrongly excluded in public schools. In a recent review of state world history standards for the Fordham Institute, Walter Russell Mead's (2006: 16) arguments are strikingly similar to my own here: history curriculum must share the rich cultural heritages of majority and minority groups in U.S. society and around the globe; students must learn about the complex social domain; and curriculum should focus on critical issues of global importance today – not of either a Eurocentric model, nor a multicultural, "treat-all-cultures-and-stories-as-equals approach." And I concur with Sewall (2008) that textbooks can be exasperatingly cryptic in their attempts to avoid controversy today, painting stories (of Muslim women's lives, or the root causes of 9/11) as simple, though they are quite complex in reality, and editing over time, in new editions, to remove partial content, when no content can be entirely value-neutral. As Fitzgerald wrote (1979) decades ago, the textbooks sometimes seem to be edited for readability in such a way that they *become* unreadable – they can become useless to students who want to know helpful information for their everyday lives.

However, when it comes to teaching and learning about Muslims and Islam in public schools, many solutions that have been provided are unhelpful and may actually have a detrimental impact on student understanding. One cannot promote tolerance in society and American foundational religious pluralism while at the same time dismissing Muslims in America or Western societies as unimportant, as Sewall argues (2008: 13, 25). Though educators I have discussed here from Finn (2002), Schlesinger (1998), Hirsch (2003), and Ravitch (1990; 2004) have asserted that educational tolerance of Islam in public schools is less important than teaching for patriotic pride in the United States and for assimilation to a common culture, these are not exclusive options – teachers do not have to choose between minority cultural integration or celebrating and/or tolerating diversity. They can do both.

Teaching about diversity in society and worldwide is made quite difficult in this context. Earlier models for managing difference in classroom settings are not up to this new task since 9/11 to teach about Islam and Muslims in an effective way. As discussed here, assimilation is a problematic stance in relation to religious pluralism in this case. Muslims can (and do) integrate into U.S. society – that is not a problem. However, emphasizing American exceptionalism over democratic tolerance, as some educators discussed here recommend, is unhelpful in this case, as Muslims experience intolerance and prejudice in society. Though assimilationism assumes that society is sufficiently just, the case of Muslims in the United States suggests otherwise. Resolving this conflict does not require us to "blame America" or promote moral relativism, as some fear (Finn 2002; Schlesinger 1998). But it requires us to look beyond a discourse that presents tolerance and sociopolitical minority integration as mutually exclusive options.

Yet pluralism and critical multiculturalism are also not ideal models when applied to the case of learning about Muslims and Islam in public schools. As a religion and not a racial or ethnic identity, Islam should not be subject to substantive educator endorsement and recognition within a religiously plural society, though a more minimal tolerance is necessary. Pluralism's basis in celebrating cultural difference is also not helpful when discussing a large cross-section of the world's population – Muslims who include Indonesians, Canadians, French citizens and residents, South Africans, etc. There is no best way or single way to be a Muslim, and teachers should not suggest otherwise. Romanticizing Islam is also too superficial to be effective in this context (Kincheloe & Steinberg 1997). Students can ignore what teachers say in favor of newscasters or others in their community. Muslims may not significantly benefit from such educational practices, themselves, which are not effective ways to ameliorate larger systemic issues impacting people's attitudes toward diversity in society (McCarthy 2003; Parekh 2000). Critical multiculturalism goes too far in its practical implications, by suggesting teachers as moral and ethical authorities in the classroom, guiding students to preferred orientations about dichotomous groups of oppressed and oppressors: in this case, good Muslims and bad non-Muslims (Kincheloe & Steinberg 1997; Peters 2012). Reality is not so black and white, or good and bad. Though critical multicultural educators mean to empower students, conflating racial groups with "power blocs" does not help students understand why inequality exists, and how to best address it in society.

Interculturalism has been raised here as an alternative approach to thinking about diversity in public schools. As argued here, interculturalism implies that we cannot decide before entering a particular situation how to navigate issues of social diversity. Ideally, such decisions should be made through dialogue and deliberation within and across groups in society. Education, by implication, should prepare people to enter in to these dialogues. This requires that people approach difference in society with an attitude of respect and trust, an initial optimism that people are well-intended, and do not mean them harm (Burbules 1993; Taylor 1992). However, in the United States, such dialogue about Islam can be precluded by ignorance developed from gaining information from television, which suggests (by omission) that Muslims leaders condone terrorism, for example (Council on American-Islamic Relations 2005). Thus, to enable students to engage in dialogue in this case, students and teachers should develop critical media literacy skills, so that they are able to research issues, identify and discuss alternative perspectives democratically, and come to independent judgments. Students should have access to a range of sources and perspectives, and learn how to investigate and revise their own viewpoints by evaluating information, alongside their teachers and peers. Teachers in turn must be regarded as responsible for developing student skills, not just disseminating facts and assessing student retention of them. Within intercultural education, teachers have an important role to play in sustaining a liberal democratic society. Such a role requires further, different preparation as I have discussed here; but such requirements are not extreme or unreasonable, given the value of preserving an effectively liberal democratic nation-state.

Educators have a moral role and responsibility in this case, to develop student skills, but not to tell the students what the right answer is, to any question about navigating and managing dilemmas related to diversity in society. This is an important, but difficult job to do. The teacher does not have the right answer. But this does not mean there is no right answer. Some may fear that teachers should not have this role: that it is too tricky to walk the line between neutrality and moral relativism, the idea that all answers are right or equal. In this case, some people think it is better to avoid religion in public schools, to not get caught up in controversy or taboos of the public sphere. However, this communicates a message that there is no place in the public sphere for religion, which is not quite right (Nord 1995). Rather, the public sphere should be seen as a meeting place for all members of society, religious and non-religious.

In a nation-state with a proud heritage of religious toleration and pluralism and liberal democratic freedom, education has a duty to continue this tradition in an open, productive environment. Yet in the case of teaching and learning about Muslims and Islam, we risk allowing ignorance to prevail without an active intervention, because of the prominence of negative stereotypes in the mass media and popular culture. Though all religions face harmful dismissal in public schools, for Islam this is particularly intolerable, as messages that are negative and harmful prevail outside the classroom. Education can and should do more in this case. Though education does not have a role of celebrating any religion, to celebrate American toleration, schools must tolerate Islam and encourage tolerance among students despite media messages. Without such an intervention, education harms both Muslim and non-Muslim students, enabling ignorance to prevail over knowledge and disabling skill building vitally needed for critical thinking and democratic dialogue. Interculturalism and the active pursuit of genuine democratic citizenship should guide education about diversity in U.S. society, not media coverage of the war on terrorism or other extraordinary, alarming events.

References

Bennetta, William J. "How a Public School in Scottsdale, Arizona, Subjected Students to Islamic Indoctrination." *The Textbook League*. 2005. www.textbookleague.org/tci-az.htm (accessed January 8, 2014).

Burbules, Nicholas C. *Dialogue in Teaching: Theory and Practice*. New York: Teachers College Press, 1993.

Common Core. "English Language Arts Standards: Speaking and Listening, Grade 9–10." 2012. www.corestandards.org/ELA-Literacy/SL/9–10 (accessed October 18, 2013).

Council on American-Islamic Relations. *Unequal Protection: The Status of Muslim Civil Rights in the United States, 2005*. Washington, DC: Council on American-Islamic Relations, 2005.

Elnatour, Mohamed. *Perceptions of Muslim Students' Needs and Challenges in a Public High School in the Midwest*. Aurora, IL: Aurora University, 2005.

Finn, Jr., Chester E. Introduction to *September 11: What Our Children Need to Know*, edited by the Fordham Foundation, 4–11. Washington, DC: Thomas B.

Fordham Foundation, 2002. www.edexcellence.net/publications/sept11.html (accessed January 8, 2014).
Fitzgerald, Frances. *America Revised: History Schoolbooks in the Twentieth Century.* New York: Atlantic Monthly Press, 1979.
Hirsch, Jr., E. D. "Moral Progress in History." In *Terrorists, Despots, and Democracy: What Our Children Need to Know,* edited by the Fordham Foundation, 72–73. Washington, DC: Thomas B. Fordham Foundation, 2003. www.edexcellence.net/publications/terrorists.html (accessed January 8, 2014).
Hochman, Dalia. "Hominid Development: On Being a Social Studies Teacher During September 11." In *Forever After: New York City Teachers on 9/11,* edited by Teachers College Press with Maureen Grolnick, 85–96. New York: Teachers College Press, 2006.
Kincheloe, Joe L., and Shirley R. Steinberg. *Changing Multiculturalism.* Buckingham: Open Court Press, 1997.
Kozal, Jonathan. *The Shame of the Nation: The Restoration of Apartheid Schooling in America.* New York: Random House, 2006.
McCarthy, Cameron. "After the Canon: Knowledge and Ideological Representation in the Multicultural Discourse on Curriculum Reform." In *Race, Identity, and Representation in Education,* edited by Cameron McCarthy and Warren Crichlow, 289–305. New York: Routledge, 2003.
Mead, Walter Russell. *The State of State World History Standards.* Washington, DC: Thomas B. Fordham Institute, 2006.
Nord, Warren A. *Religion and American Education: Rethinking a National Dilemma.* Chapel Hill: University of North Carolina Press, 1995.
Parekh, Bhikhu. *Rethinking Multiculturalism: Cultural Diversity and Political Theory.* Cambridge: Harvard University Press, 2000.
Peters, Michael A. "Western Models of Intercultural Philosophy." In *Interculturalism, Education and Dialogue,* edited by Tina Besley and Michael A. Peters. New York: Peter Lang, 2012.
Ravitch, Diane. "Multiculturalism: *E Pluribus Plures.*" *American Scholar* 59 (1990): 337–354.
Ravitch, Diane. *The Language Police: How Pressure Groups Restrict What Students Learn.* New York: Vintage, 2004.
Rizvi, Fazal. "Representations of Islam and Education for Social Justice." In *Race, Identity, and Representation in Education,* edited by Cameron McCarthy and Warren Crichlow, 167–178. New York: Routledge, 2005.
Schlesinger, Jr., Arthur M. *The Disuniting of America: Reflections on a Multicultural Society.* New York: W.W. Norton, 1998.
Sewall, Gilbert T. *Islam in the Classroom: What the Textbooks Tell Us.* New York: American Textbook Council, 2008.
Taylor, Charles. *Multiculturalism and "The Politics of Recognition."* Edited by Amy Gutmann. Princeton: Princeton University Press, 1992.
Texas State Board of Education. Resolution. September 24, 2010.

Index

Abrahamian, Ervand 60–1
Afghanistan xi, 68–9, 79, 90, 95–7, 119
Africa 81; Christians 91; descendants in U.S. society 11; Northern xi, 79; public school standards 79; South Africa xiv; 79, 170; sub-Saharan 81
African Americans: curriculum 30; enslaved 11; equality 29; ethnic group, as 30; identities 33; ideological constructs 41; inequalities 11, 29; media 67; Methodist 66; minority 35; non-Western 41; racism 35–6; slavery 11; studies 151
Aladdin 55
All-American Muslim 64, 66, 71
"Answer to the Question: 'What Is Enlightenment?' " 3
agnosticism 91
agnostics xiv, 2
Akpinar, Unal 116
Albright, Madeline 105
"American" 17; cultural superiority 19; "everyday life" 21; "generic" xii; norms 15
"American Indians" 18; *see also* Native Americans
Americanization 19; *see also* "American"
American Muslims 23, 28; *see also* Muslims
American Textbook Council 107, 168
Amiri, Abid 59
Amish 38
Anderson, Benedict 43
Anglo-Saxon 14; culture, maintenance of 17; men as originally dominant group 14; minorities and 30; Protestants 15; "race suicide" of 15
Applebaum, Barbara 128–9
Arab American Institute 28

Arab culture 62, 95, 102
Arab-Israeli conflict 61
Arabs: "clash of civilizations" 62; dress 130; media, in the 54, 67, 130; textbook, in 83
"Arab Spring" 59, 62, 71, 95, 168; Tahrir Square 62
Arab "world" 24; *see also* Islamic "world"
Arnold, Matthew 41
Asia: conflicts 94; culture 33, 95; East xiv; religions in 81; South 3; Southeast xi, 3, 79; Western 76, 79, 165; terrorism 108; U.S. interventions in 105
Asian Americans 33, 151
Asians 67
Aslan, Reza 65, 71
assimilationism 6, 13, 14, 19, 20, 23, 33, 39, 43, 47; conservative assimilationism 12; cultural oppression 16; diversity and 40; failure of 29; immigrants resistance to 17; importance of 48; liberal assimilationism 12; multicultural education 12; Poles, of 21; risk to national security 17
atheism 91, 97
atheists 2
"Attacks Draw Mixed Response in Mideast" 60
Australia 8, 91, 114

Babel xiv, 67–8
Baghdad 90
Bahrain 80
Bangladesh 104, 124
Banks, James 1, 12, 29, 30, 31, 33, 35
Barber, Benjamin 27

Bednarz, Sarah Witham 90
Bennetta, William J. 104
Besley, Tina xiv, 117
bias viii, 24–6, 34, 39, 45, 54
"Biblical nation" 27; *see also* "Christian nation"
black Americans 12, 13, 21, 28–9, 34–5, 41, 47; diverse population, part of 4; enslavement 16; integration 28; in the media 4, 57; stereotypes 36; *see also* African Americans
Blair, Tony 61
Blanchett, Cate 68
Boehm, Richard G. 96
Boler, Megan 127–9
Bourne, Randolph 17, 29
Brown vs. Board of Education 29
Buber, Martin 129
Buddhism 81, 90–1
Burbules, Nicholas ix, xiv, 117–19
burka 92, 115
Bush, President George W. 47, 59–61, 66

Cairo 62, 83, 95
California 81, 84
Callan, Eamonn 163
Canada 36, 90–1, 113–14
Canadians 170
Catholics 2, 16; integration 28; private schools 28
chador 92
China: Buddhism in, 91; media 55; public school standards 81, 158; women 94
Christianity xiv, 2, 16, 27, 29, 81, 85; classroom, in the 28, 124; compared with Islam xiv, 7, 125, 127; foundation for U.S. public schools 16; generalizations 88; media 66; morality 85; politics 85 ; pluralism 2–3; private schools and 28; society, in 27, 29; textbooks 7, 85, 89–91, 119, 168; world religion 169
"Christian nation" 2; from historical perspective 2; United States as 1, 27
Christians xiii, xiv, 1, 2, 27–8, 65–6, 85, 87, 91–2, 98–9, 125, 133, 158, 168
Civil Rights Movement 29
"clash of civilizations" view 26, 33, 45, 117; controversy 127–8; culture 62; history of 23–4; intolerance vii; media 59–60, 63, 76; stereotypes 3, 54, 108; textbooks 77; themes 137

CNN 59, 71, 102
Comedy Central 58
common core educational standards 23, 57, 77, 160, 167
common schools 1–2, 39, 164; assimilation 15; compulsory 16; morality 16; national identity 44; national unity 44; *see also* public schools
Confucianism 91
Connections to Today 92, 96
conservative assimilationism 6, 12, 14, 19, 20, 122
conservative multiculturalism 12; *see also* multiculturalism
Control Room 67
Council on American-Islamic Relations (CAIR) 4, 63, 133
Council on Islamic Education (CIE) 32–3, 86, 133
Crash 67–8
critical multiculturalism 6, 12, 13, 14, 34, 40, 48, 102, 105, 114; assimilation 47; classroom, in the 127, 132; controversial subjects 129; difference in society 41–2, 104, 116, 121, 128, 142; educators 77, 120–3; faith 58; media 49, 54, 57, 134, 140; morality 121, 129; nation state 43; national allegiance 44; oppression 46; power blocs 45; public awareness 48; social norms 40, 105; textbooks 108; tolerance of Islam 63
Crockett, Davy 84
Crusades, the vii, 81, 97–8
Cuban Americans 152
"cultural amnesia" 17
cultures: broad categorization of 33; division of 45; groups 38; "imagined" 43; interchangeability 41; interdependence 46; racist 36; relativism 6, 22, 81, 120–1, 125, 127, 142, 161–5, 169, 171
curriculum i, vii, viii, 1, 7, 29–30, 35, 42, 81, 137, 153, 161–2, 169; diversity in 30; minorities 30, 35–6; Muslims in 1, 7, 142, 161; reform 42; standardizations 167
Curtis, Jamie Lee 67

Daily Show with Jon Stewart, The 58
Dangerous Minds 156
Declaration of Independence 156
democracy 104; Arabs 62, 95; citizenship 143, 147; controversy

133; diversity 167; equality 168; Iraq 60; Israel 80; morality 132; personal freedoms 3, 127–8; public education 54, 132; public schools 11, 31, 37, 44, 123, 130, 142; students' participation 45, 134, 160; symbol of 11; teaching 22, 122, 130, 132, 156; thick sense 20, 119, 122, 143; tolerance 119; U.S. society 20, 48–9, 54, 156; Western Europe 20; worldwide 117
Dewey, John 150
difference as deficiency; *see* assimilationism 12
Disney, Walt 55
diversity xi, 40–1; "clash of civilizations" 26; Dr. Martin Luther King 32; education in 6; equality xii, 3, 7, 8, 11–14, 17–22, 24, 26, 28–9, 31–2, 35–40, 45, 48–9, 80–1, 93, 105, 114–6, 118, 121, 127–8, 142, 158, 160, 162–3, 168–9; inequality 11–13, 15, 18, 20–1, 25–6, 28, 35–6, 45–7, 116, 129, 134–5, 170–1; Islam, within 133; multiculturalism 22; of Muslims 24, 32–3, 124; racial 30; religious expression and 39; school reforms 29; social advancement 4, 15; in society 123
Dixon, Marion 62
Downey, Jr., Robert 68

Eastern religions 3, 91, 158
educator neutrality 6, 36, 39, 118, 149–50, 162–4, 171
educators 1, 2, 22, 31, 33–4, 36–7; censorship of 77; classroom strategies for success 29, 122; difficulties 130; finding good information 4–5; empowerment of 6; evading criticism in teaching diversity 5; fallacies in 21; inadequate education 136; mass media 42, 136; misunderstanding Muslim students' needs 28, 48; modeling ix, 122, 124, 126, 130, 132, 135–6, 143, 147–8, 150, 152, 154–6, 164–5; morality 46; need to intervene in anti-Muslim climate 6, 29; neutrality 40; power blocs 47; religion 39; responsibilities under pluralism 13; role 46; supplementary material vii; teaching controversial issues 4–5, 132, 137; thematic approach 7, 137, 162; tolerance 40; *see also* teachers
Egypt xi, xii, 62, 83, 95; history 47; Muslim clothing 92; Muslim majority 89; Orientalism 25; politics 102; public school standards 81; religion 158
equality: citizens 12; classroom 15; Declaration of Independence 15; democracy 48–9; gender 7, 80, 105; individual 13; minority 18, 29, 31–2; misrecognition 36; Muslims 22, 24; political guarantee 15; society 20–1; students 40; tolerance 19
"ethnic cheerleading" 2, 21
Europe xiv, 8, 15–17, 20–1, 24–5, 33, 41, 43, 79–82, 90, 93–5, 108, 114–17, 158, 160; anti-Semitism 80–1; assimilation 16–7, 21; conflated with U.S. 41; educating about 158; educators 116; interculturalism 8, 114, 117; leaders 115; minorities, as 17; model for curriculum 169; Muslims in xiv, 24, 90, 93–4, 108, 115; politics 43; public school standards 79, 81–2; religions 158; Social Darwinism 15; source of liberating ideas 20; Zionism 80

Fahrenheit 911 69–70
Family Florida Association 64
Feinberg, Walter xiv, 22, 24, 26, 37, 38, 44
Finn, Chester 22–4, 34, 64, 103–4, 108, 169
Fitzgerald, Francis 83, 169
Florida 64, 84
Fordham Foundation 22, 102, 105, 135
Fordham Institute 22, 57, 103, 106–7, 138, 160, 168–9
founding fathers 2, 11, 14, 15
Fox News 58–9, 63, 65–6, 71
France: hijab 114, 117; Muslim integration 115; social diversity 113
Frankfurt School of Critical Theory 13
Freedom House 80
French: citizens and residents 117, 170; culture 37; language xiii, 37–8; public schools 114; society 114; state 93; Tunisians xiii
Fulbright Program 117

Galal, Ehab 62
Georgia 79–80

Germany 113, 115–16
Global Gender Gap Index of the World 80
Goetze, Sandra K. 155
Greece 81
Green, Lauren 66
Greenblatt, Miriam 89
Griswold, William J. 82
Guatemalans 152

Hale, Everett 15
Hall, Stuart 56
Hamilton, Alexander 11
Haynes, Charles C. 161
head covering 106; *see also* burka; chador; hijab; veil wearing
Heller, Agnes 121
hijab: "covering" 92; educating about 135–7, 160; France, in 93, 114, 117; meaning of 117; media, and the 137, 141; Qur'an, in the 92; religious custom 39, 106; textbooks, in 87
Hinduism: public school standards 81; textbooks 91, 158; world religion 91
Hirsch, E. D. 23–4, 31, 169
Hispanics 30
History Channel 155
Hobbes, Renee 137
Hollywood 6: Arabs' portrayal 54; Muslims as scapegoats in 57; Muslims, demonizing of 69
Hollywood Reporter, The 64
Homeland 70–1, 139
Houston, Barbara 132
Houston, Sam 84
Human Heritage: A World History 89, 93, 96
Huntington, Samuel 23–6, 42, 45, 61, 88, 98, 101, 117, 128, 131, 140
Hussein, Saddam 59, 60, 86, 135

Iftikhar, Arsalan 63–4
"I Have a Dream" 32
India: Islam in 89; public school standards 81; *see also* Indians
Indians: Muslim 24, 87; women 94; *see also* Native Americans
individual, the 116; ability to succeed 19; equality 13; identity 35, 43; liberty 20; meaning makers, as 33; minority groups 114; pride 35; prioritization of 37
Indonesia 91, 104
Indonesians 24, 87, 170

inequalities: of African Americans 11; homeless, of 11; landless, of 11; poor, of 11; power 36; within textbooks 86; of women 11
Institute on Religion and Civic Values 133
integration of Muslims with non-Muslims 8; *see also* interculturalism
"intercultural" framework 7, 13; *see also* interculturalism
interculturalism viii, xiv, 7, 31, 113; binary thinking 116; classroom, in the 5, 6; "critical thinking" skills 41, 47, 85, 98–9, 101, 122, 124, 126, 131, 136, 138, 150, 156–7, 159, 165, 171; cultural relativism 121, 125, 127, 162–3; democracy 119, 130; European 117; free speech 122, 127, 163; integration 115; justice 121, 139; model, as 116; morality 16, 46, 85, 121, 131, 153; multicultural perspective, as one 122; Muslims and Islam 8, 109; outcomes 123; social injustice 118, 121, 124; social justice 31, 35, 46, 54, 121, 132, 134, 162; students 120, 122; summary 122; teaching 114, 125; textbooks 119
Iran: women 81; extremist groups 87; Iranian Americans 65; leaders 117; Muslim majority 89; *see also Shahs of Sunset*
Iraq xii, xiv, 60, 67, 69, 79, 90, 95, 97, 105
Iron Man xiv, 6, 67–9
Islam i, vii, viii, xi, 40; Allah 69, 78, 82, 106; assimilation 13, 29; bigotry 55; compared with other religions 82; culture 28; curriculum 1; diversity within 24; ethnocentrism 48; extremism 54, 60, 87, 96, 98, 105; fascism 103, 168; fears about 28; five pillars 78, 90; fundamentalism 23, 27, 103; Gabriel, the angel 90; gender equality in 7; hajj 90; identity crises 23; ignorance about 4, 8, 28; indoctrination 39, 81, 168; inferior tradition 28, 36; interculturalism 8; "Islamic empire" 78, 158; jihad 58, 60, 69, 85–9, 92, 103–4; Koran, the (Quran) 66, 78, 90, 92–3; "lionizing" of 7; Mecca 90; "militants" 97, 103; mosques 4, 90, 133; Muhammad 78, 82, 87, 90; Muslim countries,

in xiv; negative stereotyping 28; in news media 4; number of worshippers 81; other religions 3; perspectives on 1, 2, 24, 26, 45, 76; popular culture, in 4, 48; positive portrayals of 39; public school standards 81; public schools 14, 32–3; "radical" 66, 97, 115; rhetoric xiii; seclusion of women 87, 93; sexism in 7; *sharia* law 103; in social studies 4; social reproduction 22, 81; Taliban, and the 96; textbooks 82–4; toleration 23, 31, 49, 115; violence 82; women 39
Islamic civilization i, vii, viii, xi, 23, 78, 89, 90
Islamic extremists 89
Islamic fashion 95, 135–6
Islamic "world" 24
Israel: educator modeling, and 126; Palestine, and 94, 8; public school standards 79–80; U.S. relations 14, 61
Italian-Americans: curriculum 30; threat to national security 17

Japan 68, 81
Japanese Americans 63
Javidi, Manoocher N. 55
Jesus 65–6
Jews xiv, 15, 16, 17, 28, 57, 65, 87, 92, 125, 133, 139; anti-Semitism 79–80; in the media 4; "Jewish connection" 79; *see also* Judaism
jihad 58, 60, 67, 69, 85–8, 92, 103–4
"Jihad vs. McWorld" 27
Jordan 80, 98, 158
Judaism 3, 85; contrasting with Islam 124; generalizations about 88; public school curriculum 81; textbooks 85, 90–1; *see also* Jews

Kallen, Horace 17, 19, 29
Kant, Immanuel 3
Kaviani, Khodadad 100, 102, 106, 124
Khatami, Seyed Mohammed 117
Kincheloe, Joe 7, 34, 42, 45, 47, 99, 138, 153, 158, 161
King, Dr. Martin Luther 32
Kuwait 80

bin Laden, Osama 59–61, 90, 96–7, 135
Ladson-Billings, Gloria 152
Latinos 12, 13, 29, 33
Lebanon 80, 98, 158

Lemmo, Peter S. 89
Lewis, Bernard 23, 65, 101
"liberal assimilationism" 12, 14, 39, 117
"liberal democratic" society 2, 3, 8; cultural groups 38; diversity 163; education 72; independent thought 160; morality 126; politics 114, 123, 166; religious toleration 171; skills development 165; teachers 170; U.S. schools 167
"lionizing" of Islam 7, 86
Locke, John 3
Louisiana 106

Mann, Horace 2, 16
Mayo, Cris 129
McBrien, Lynn 134, 137, 142
McCarthy, Cameron xiv, 34, 36, 41–2, 46
McGee-Banks, Cherry 1, 30–1
McVeigh Timothy 96
Mead, Walter Russell 169
media i, viii; Arab Spring 62, 71; Catholics 57; challenged alternative views 66; classroom, in the 43; construction of reality 135; critical inquiry 140; educational, as 6, 54–7, 72; influential, as 42; Islam 60, 135; Jews 4, 57; journalistic method of teaching 137–9; literacy 58; meaningful, as 134; Media Research Center 66; messages 48, 55–7, 58, 62, 66–7, 69–72 108, 134, 136, 138–9, 142, 147, 164–5, 171; Middle East xiv, 55, 60, 65, 67–8, 70; models 56, 102; moralizing 55; Muslims at disadvantage in 6; Muslims since 9/11 xiii, 4, 36, 48–9, 59–62, 71–2; nationalism 43; obscuring perspectives 6; pedagogy 8; politics 136; popular culture 6, 42, 53, 59; profit, for 54, 58–9, 63–5; propaganda 70; race 40; reality television 65; religion 36; representing minorities 42; research 56; shaping behavior 54–6; social diversity 4, 56, 113, 121, 137, 142, 170; sponsorship 137; students' understanding 137; suggesting framings for ethics 6, 57; teachers and 53, 58; terrorism 57, 69–71; young people 42, 53, 55, 70–2
melting pot viii, 14, 17, 18, 167; *see also* assimilationism
Melting Pot, The 14

Mexican Americans 152
Mexican War, The 84
Middle Ages: Islam 92; public school standard 81
Middle East: 9/11 61; actions against 101; Arab world 55; civilization 82; conflict 79, 165; democracy 62; integration 32; interfaith 65; leaders 60; media xiv, 4, 55, 68; Muslims in 3; National Association of School Psychologists 104; oil 98; politics 80, 158; stereotypes 67–8; terrorism and 70, 76, 86, 98, 165; textbooks 89, 94, 96, 100, 108; U.S. interests in 3, 79; U.S. intervention 105
Mill, John Stuart 3, 16, 138
"minoritization" 13
"minority groups" 12, 13; alienation of 35; conformity 17; controversial traditions 39; in the classroom 35; curriculum 29, 169; disruption 15; emerging 5; English literacy 19–20; equality 18; girls' and women's rights 38; Iranian Americans 65, 67; Japanese Americans 63; limitations 36; mainstream society 38; maintaining cultural identity 18; in the media 42, 134; Persian Americans 64–5, 67; public schooling 37; recognition of 30, 32; respecting 38; self-esteem 33; stereotyping 134; students 120; teachers 133, 151; textbooks 99; *see also* sociopolitical minorities
"mixed salad" society as 18
monoculturalism 12; *see also* conservative multiculturalism
Moore, Michael 69
Mozambique 91
Mr. Holland's Opus 156
MSNBC 58
Mulan 55
multicultural education i, vii, viii, 12; assimilationism 12–29; curriculum 137, 153; democracy 122; diversity 12; educating about Muslims and Islam 5, 31; hindering patriotic education 3; history of 6; inequality 12; justice 32, 8; limitations 14, 36; media and popular culture 53; minority groups 5; pluralism 12, 29–48; public school 167; religion 1; solving today's challenges 3; world groups within the United States, 5; *see also* interculturalism

"multiethnic" education 30–1; *see also* multicultural education
Muslim community 3
Muslims 76–7, 120, 160: 9/11, after 1–3, 6, 22, 49, 59, 66–7, 100, 107, 138; American Muslim relations 86; anti-American 168; Arab 24, 62; assimilation 13, 22, 27–9, 114; "bad guys" 3, 55, 59, 63, 71, 104, 108, 113, 168; "clash of civilizations" view 24, 134; concerns in ethics 4, 107; contrastable positions 12; critical multiculturalism 48, 170; curriculum, in 1, 7, 142, 161; dietary needs 28; discrimination 28, 31–2, 40, 71–2, 106; diversity of 24, 58, 62, 71, 105, 124, 133, 170; educating about ix, 1, 5, 72, 87, 101–3, 107, 114, 118, 122–4, 131, 134–5, 137, 147–8, 153–4, 167, 169, 171; enslavement 103; equal rights 168; ethnocentrism 48; exploration of 44; faith 98; fallacies regarding xi, xiv, 8; fundamentalist groups 59, 96; hate crimes 22; hatred 4; hijab 39, 114, 117, 141; ignorance about i, 4, 151, 170–1; inequality 28; integration of 8, 32, 42, 113; interculturalism 8, 109, 147; jihad 86–8; leaders 4, 87, 170; media, in the xiii, viii, 4, 6, 42, 55, 99, 102, 108, 127, 134, 136, 139, 142, 147, 168; media source 102; Middle East 124; military 92, 105; minority group, as i, 154; misconceptions 4; moderate 27; monotheists, as 125; new Nazis, as 69; norms 23, 63, 135; numbers of 24; offensive terms for 82–3; out-of-school youth 38, 49, 54, 56–7, 63–4, 68–71; outsiders, as 23; peaceful 27, 98; popular culture vii, xiv, 65, 67; positive portrayals 39; prejudice 4, 40, 71–2, 100, 103, 106, 114, 119, 131; private schools 28; public schools xiv, 5, 8, 14, 23, 32, 107, 168–70; Qur'an 31; religious intolerance 4, 6, 66, 97; September 11, 2001 1; Shiite 91; significance 78; social differences 14, 29; social reproduction 22; society 1, 2, 4, 6, 23–4, 33, 44–5, 53, 165, 169; stereotypes of vii, 4, 36, 45, 53–4, 71, 85, 99, 119, 136, 141, 164; students in public school 28, 31, 36, 78; Sunni 91; teachers i, 100,

107, 127, 168; teachers intervening on behalf of 36; terrorism and 3, 8, 36, 48, 57, 59, 63, 67–70, 87, 96–7, 99, 106, 108, 123, 125, 128, 138, 142, 165; textbooks 7, 31, 39, 76, 82–5, 87, 89–90, 92, 94–6, 99–101, 107–8, 119, 138, 154, 168; threat to U.S. society 27, 103, 125; tolerance 27–8, 104; "traditional culture" 31, 36; U.S. citizens 27; violence 4, 54, 59, 64, 68, 83, 106, 142; West, the 98; women and girls 38–9, 93, 106, 169; *see also* Muslim community

"Muslims *Rip* '24' for Renewed Terror Role" 64

Muslim world xi, 3; America and 32; "Arab spring" 95; diversity within 105, 133; hijab 117; inaccurate portrayal of 3; *Iron Man* 68; stereotypes 3; textbooks 89; women 92, 94; *see also* Muslim community

National Association of School Psychologists (NASP) 103–4
National Education Association (NEA) 103–4
Native Americans: assimilationism 16, 28; real culture and exotic others 34; in "white civilization" 18; *see also* American Indians
Natural Advanced Geography 82
NBC 64
NCSS 103
Neavel, Geordi Cortez 84
New England 84
New York City 95, 97, 101
New York Times: editorial about Disney 55; as liberal 58; regarding 9/11 59–61
New Zealand xiv, 114
9/11 i, vii, 1–4, 6–7, 106; classroom, in the 103–4, 108, 169; culture clash 98; educators 5, 108, 130; emotional context 101; ethnocentrism 48; fear 28; Islam 125; bin Laden, Osama 96–7; media 49, 96; Muslims 99–100, 106, 138; patriotism 44; pedagogy 22; pluralist approaches since 23; protest of positive information 3; terrorist attacks 42, 56, 113; textbooks 83, 85, 89–90, 94–5, 97, 169; *see also* September 11, 2001
Noddings, Nel 149, 156

No End in Sight 67
Nord, Warren 1, 82, 161

Okin, Susan Moller 38
Oregon xi, 65, 80–1
O'Reilly, Bill 63
Ottoman Empire 90

Pakistan xi, 87, 104
Palestine 61, 94, 98
Parekh, Bhikhu 36
patriotism 44; advice for victims of hate crimes 44; civic values 32; cultural heritage 21; multiculturalism 84; teachers 104; tolerance 104; war on terror 138
Patterns of Interaction 92–3
pedagogies 7, 131, 149; affirmative action 128; democracy 107, 123; empathy for minorities 22; morality 129; neutrality 149; pluralism 46; power blocs 47; politics 104; recommendations 123; self-esteem 33; social studies 77, 107, 123, 135, 150; student-centered 8, 122; substantial 29; teachers' beliefs 61, 150–1, 153; teacher training 164
pentagon 86
People's History of the United States, A 138
Persian Gulf War 79, 94
personal freedom: of Americans 11; respect 168; roles of citizens 80–1, 107, 132, 135, 148, 157, 166, 171
Peruvians 152
Peters, Michael xiv, 45, 116–17, 120
Pitt, Brad 68
pluralism 19, 21, 114, 123, 163; critical multiculturalism 12; diversity 40–1; equal toleration 13, 142, 169, 171; ethically deficient, as 20; founding fathers 2; groups 31; integration 115; interculturalism 113; limitations 114; moral relativism 81, 121, 163, 169, 171; multiculturalism, as 13; Muslims in public schools 108, 168, 170; neutrality 118; politics 120; pride in cultural origins 17, 34; self-esteem 33, 36; social injustice 118; strengths 48, 170; students 47; teachers 150, 163; traditional 12; U.S. history 8; world religions 88
Polish-Americans: assimilation 19; Jews 15; personhood 19; *Polonia Americana* 18

politics 17; campaigns and media 58; commitment to individual freedom 11; culture 34; divisiveness 21; education 103; international 133; Islam 61; liberty 80; media 118; Middle East, the 80, 97, 105, 158; minority, as 35; Muslims 100; national security 17, 97; partisan 3; poor, and the 47; recognition 36; religion 53; U.S. foreign policy 61, 76, 86, 97, 105–6, 168; U.S. history in 3; white males 14
Portland xi, 65
post-9/11 climate 6, 20; events 20
problems in education vii, 2: bias 25–6; controversy 99, 135; public policy 140; terrorism 89
Protestantism 1; Social Darwinism, and 15
Protestants: Anglo-Saxon 15
public education: alternative views 135, 159; assimilation of diverse populations 2, 4, 12, 38; Christian foundation 16; classroom inequalities 36, 129; controversial subjects 107–8, 120, 122, 125, 127–32, 135–7, 140, 148–51, 153, 165; democratic flourishing 3, 125; disadvantaged 12, 82; exclusion of by religious groups 39; harmful tendencies 3; liberal tradition 3; main role of acculturation 2; minority culture 37; multicultural 3; Muslim community, and 3; nation building 22; preparing students to encounter diverse society 2–3; problems 2, 78; promoting neutrality 6, 125; prejudice 31; purpose of 2–4, 11; social roles of 1; standards 7, 107; stereotypes 4; student's responsibilities, and 4, 133; tolerance 32, 38; Texas State Board of Education "situation of textbooks" 7; value of 5
public schools: assimilation 15, 19, 28; Christians 1, 27–8; civic values 32; controversial issues vii, viii, 1, 4, 5, 53, 58, 130, 157, 160, 171; curriculum i, 30, 42, 161–2; education 165, 170; educators' influence 149, 152–3; enabling good decision making skills 45; ethics 121, 126, 129, 153; hijab 114; limitations 6; media literacy viii, 8, 42, 53, 57–8, 123, 134–43, 147–8, 154–7, 164–5, 170; morality 150, 153; multicultural 14; multiculturalism 48, 167; and Muslims in i, vii, 1, 4, 5, 22, 27–8, 32, 36, 76, 106, 108, 167–80; politics 21, 37, 157; productivity 120; Protestant foundation 16; religion in 5, 36, 39, 81, 106, 115, 151, 161, 169, 171; right of exit 121; rules 129; since 9/11 54; in socializing role 11, 164; standards 72, 77, 79, 148, 150, 155, 157–8, 161, 163; subjects 78, 152; as symbol of democracy 11; textbooks 83; treatment of students 12; *see also* common schools
Puerto Ricans 152
Purpel, David 151

al-Qaeda (al-Qaida) 59, 86, 90; *see also* Terrorism
Quakers 38
Quebec: different societal groups 36–7, 118; French culture 37; intercultural education 118; right to exit 38

race: acceptance 168–70; bias 34; biological differences 20; categorization 33; classroom 30–1; collaboration between 113; complication of factors 34; differences 123; diversity 30; equality 29; identity 34, 40–2; inequality 47; inferiority 15; injustice 34; job market 36; labels 46; learning 31; media 56; Muslim women 93; oppression 46; pluralism 33; power blocs 47, 170; pride 35; segregation 29; self-esteem 22; "suicide" 15
Ravitch, Diane 13, 21–3, 33–45, 64, 169
religion in schools 133–4; "clash" view 26; debate about priorities 1; diversity 8; exclusion of in classrooms 1; law, the 151; indoctrination 162; interfaith; 133–4: perspective 125; society, in 3, 150; source of conflict, as 79; toleration of 3, 6; truth, as 125; unconstitutionality of 16; within a primarily Christian context 1; *see also* agnosticism; atheism; Christianity; Confucianism; Hinduism; Islam; Judaism; Protestantism; religious toleration
religious toleration: arguments against 3; heritage of 171; history of in the U.S.A. 2; individual rights 38; public

education about Muslims and Islam and 6
religiously plural country 2, 163, 169
research xiv, 1, 5, 34, 165; bias studies 25; classroom 55, 124, 153; consumer 56; educators 151, 154, 156, 170; inequality of power 25; media 42, 58, 71, 108; misunderstanding of cultures 26; political 61; power blocs 47; textbooks 100; projects 140–1, 148
Rethinking Schools 104–7, 102, 113, 135, 138
Richey, Amanda B. 95
Richter, Erika 116, 121
Rizvi, Fazal xiv, 106
Rome 81
Roosevelt, Theodore 15
Rosaldo, Renato 25–6
Rousseau, Jean-Jacques 3
Russia 21, 91

Said, Edward 6, 25–6, 51, 58, 105, 131, 140
Salaita, Steven 62
Salvadoreans 152
Saturday Evening Post 15
Saudi Arabia: "clash of civilizations" 95; extremist groups 87; politics 158; public school standards 80; Taliban, the 96; textbooks 88; women 80
Schrag, Robert L. 55
Schwartz, Stephen 103
Schwarzenegger, Arnold 67
secular humanist 1
secularism in schools 1
separation of church and state 2, 27
September 11, 2001 xi, 1, 59, 61, 95–6, 104; see also 9/11; post-9/11 climate
September 11: What Children Need to Know 22, 102–3
Sewall, Gilbert 86–7, 89, 103–4, 169
Shaheen, Jack 6, 54, 58
Shahs of Sunset 64–5, 70
Shanker, Al 22
sharia law 103
Shaw, Robert 119
Sidky, H. 25
slavery 11, 16, 85, 103
Social Darwinism 15, 19
social problems: inequality 45; oppression 46; power blocs 46; unresolved 12
societal goals, U.S. 11; equality 11, 13; mainstream 19; minorities 15–16; norms 27; reproduction and nation building 22, self-image 47; survivance 37
sociopolitical minorities 13, 84, 114, 152, 169
South Africans 170
Southeast Asia xi, 79, 81, 91
Southeast Asian Muslims 3
South Harlem 130
Southwest Asia 79, 95; *see also* Middle East
Spain 90, 98
speech: banning words 13; famous 32; free 122, 127, 163; liberty of 168; prohibition of 129; reactive 131; silencing 128; students 129
Spencer, Robert 66
Spielhaus, Riem 62
Spielvogel, Jackson J. 112
Springfield Plan of 1939 31
standards 166: availability 77; California 81; citizenship 135; common core 23, 160; Common Core State Standards Initiative 57, 77; Georgia state 79–80; Illinois 78; Islam and Muslims 5, 7, 76, 78–81, 92–4, 107, 160; learning outcomes 77; moral 15; Oregon 80–1; public education vii, 5, 148, 157; social sciences 7, 76–7, 80, 158, 160, 165; teachers 77, 141, 143, 155, 158, 164–5; Texas 84, 123; textbooks vii, 80, 84, 90, 107, 124–5
Steinberg, Shirley 34, 38, 42, 45, 47, 138
students 1, 12, 39, 42, 44, 47, 77, 89, 108, 122, 124–5, 136–7, 148–9, 153, 159–63, 170; abilities 154; active learning 124, 134; backgrounds 38; becoming teachers 157; Christian 28–9; comparing resources 137, 140; comprehension 155; critical thinking 41, 85, 98–9, 101, 122–3, 126, 131, 136, 138–9, 150, 156–7, 159, 164–5, 171; democracy 6, 8, 132–3, 143; development of understanding 125; diversity 40, 105; English literacy 19, 38; ethics 4, 120–1, 129, 162; intercultural education 120; learning about Islam 6, 7, 23, 32–3, 39, 49, 55, 78, 81, 88, 92–4, 101, 103–4, 107, 113, 123, 127–8, 133, 168; media, and the 137–8, 140–1, 143, 147–8, 156; minorities 31–2, 34–5, 152–4, 169; Muslim 28, 31, 33,

39, 133–4, 138; Muslim cultures vii, 3, 5; personal autonomy 45, 165; politics 53, 79, 118, 131, 158; popular culture 43, 135; prejudice 106; preparation 77, 154, 161–2; public school distinction 21; religious representative 133; responsibilities 40, 44, 46, 123–4, 129, 132, 167; right of exit 121; role of public 2, 3, 77–8; self-esteem 22, 33, 35, 40; special needs 31; textbooks 7, 91; understanding controversial issues, and 5, 23, 36, 39, 46, 93, 98–9, 125, 139, 140–7, 150, 164 ; understanding norms of country 30, 45, 48, 132
survivance 37
Sutherland, Keifer 63

Taliban 89, 96; *see also* Islamic extremists, terrorism
Taxi to the Dark Side 67
Taylor, Charles 36–7
teachers i, viii, ix, 1, 7, 22, 37, 48, 109, 124, 127, 131, 136, 140, 149, 153, 156, 158–9, 169; content knowledge 76–7; difficulties 143; education 148, 156–7; emotions 100–1; empowering of 2, 148; "ethnic cheerleading" 21; ignorance 2, 161, 168; insecurity of 5; Islamic educating 2, 31, 78, 82, 103–6, 124, 133–5, 138, 168; media education 6, 140–2, 154, 156, 164–5, 170; modeling 135; moralism 130–1; nation building 21, 159; neutrality 125–6, 130, 143, 147, 150, 156, 163; pedagogy 128; politics 58; power blocs 49; preparation 100, 108, 132, 148, 154, 156–7, 164, 170; punishment 5; respecting students' backgrounds 37; religion 28, 80–1, 107, 149, 151, 161–2; roles 5, 121, 125, 129, 157, 164, 167; social studies 151–3, 155–7; specific challenges 5, 8, 43, 107, 132, 170–1; success 77; supplementary resources 76, 96–7, 99–102, 105–8, 124, 141, 148; textbooks 84, 88, 99, 100, 108, 154, 164; training 2, 36, 101, 152, 155; understanding controversial issues 36, 53, 101–2, 122, 136, 149–51, 170; *see also* educators
Teaching About Islam and Muslims in the Public School Classroom: A Handbook for Educators 33

Team America 69–70
Terrorists, Despots, and Democracy: What Our Children Need to Know 102
Texas 104, 113, 119; law 86; politics 98; textbooks 7, 84–5, 88–9, 93, 103, 119, 123
Texas State Board of Education 7, 85–8, 94, 119, 168
Texas State Textbook Committee 84
Textbook League, The 105
textbooks 2, 84, 105, 125, 138, 155, 168–9; Arab world 54; biases 83, 139, 147; classroom use 100; controversy 99–100, 108, 138–9, 169; inequality 47; limited source 139; mainstream 38; media and social relations 42, 82, 104, 135, 154, 164; minorities 99; orientation toward Muslims and Islam, and vii, 6–7, 23, 82–4, 92, 94, 96, 99, 101, 107–8, 119, 124–5, 127, 165, 168–9, 187–9; political content 83; power blocs 45; publishers 77, 93; religions 88, 91, 99, 124, 158; social studies 7, 76, 84–6, 100, 103, 108, 134, 142, 155, 157–8, 160–2; standards 90, 158; teachers 155; Texas State Board of Education 85–6, 119; terrorism 87, 96, 107; women 138
Thomas B. Fordham Foundation 22
Thomas, William 18–19, 21, 35
To See a World 89
True Lies xiv, 139
Turkey xi, 98
24 educational media, as 139; Muslims and 64; treatment of Muslims 63

United 93 66
United Arab Emirates 81
United Kingdom xiv, 113, 115
United Nations 117
United Nations Educational, Scientific and Cultural Organization (UNESCO) 117
United States 159; Afghanistan, invasion of 96; American identity 28; black people in 16; "Christian nation" as 1, 27; Christians in 91; "clash of civilizations" 26, 62, 95; common schools 16; diversity 3, 8, 126, 168–9; educational aims 167; educational standards 62, 79–80, 157; equality 11, 22; freedom 11; Hussein, Saddam 60; immigrants

15; inequality 20; interculturalism 7, 8, 31, 114, 117; Iraq xii; Islam in xiii, 6, 23–4, 32, 159, 168; liberal democratic society, as a 2, 125; bin Laden, Osama 60; media 4, 57, 62, 67–9, 71; Middle East, and the 98; minority groups i, 22, 37, 154; multicultural nation, as 1, 5, 6, 12; Muslim nations 97; Muslims in, i, 2, 4, 28, 32, 38, 54, 58, 60, 63–4, 66, 68, 71, 87, 89–90, 105, 113, 108, 118–19, 124, 154, 168–70; national foreign policy 97; politics 3, 47, 61; private school 16, 38, 133; public education 1–2, 12, 48; public schools 38, 89, 169; religion 1, 2, 8, 38, 82, 90, 119, 124, 168; religious intolerance 4; religiously plural country, as a 2–3; "secular humanist" nation, as 1; September 11, 2001 95; Social Darwinism 15; stereotypes in 4; teachers 5, 164; terrorism 63, 68, 95, 98, 115; textbooks 86; women 38; young people in 72, 113

USA Today 96–7

U.S. society 14, 21–2, 48, 77, 82, 95, 113–14, 143, 163, 171; Christianity 27; diversity 11, 169; Islam and Muslims 23, 27, 28–9, 32, 48, 53, 60, 63–5, 76, 88, 90, 104–5, 114, 123, 125, 127, 134–5; media 134; multicultural challenges 5; educator's role 8; minorities 20; multiculturalism 13; patriotism 44; personal freedoms 11; power blocs 45; success in 19

veil wearing 39, 93–4, 106; *see also* burka; chador; head covering; hijab
Venerable, Penny 84

Waddington, David 118–19
Washington D.C. 95
Washington Post 59, 64
Western Asia 76, 79, 81, 94, 105, 108, 165
Western civilization 20, 23, 80; contrasted with the Islamic world 24, 88, 103; diversity 41; textbooks 82

Western Europe: anthropologists 25; interculturalism 114; leaders 115; Muslims in xiv; Social Darwinism 15; source of liberating ideas 20

Western liberalism, 23, 27–8
Wilson, Woodrow 17
women: Islam 89, 92–4, 96, 99, 103, 114, 117, 135–6, 138, 169; media, in the 65; oppression xi, xii, 3, 80, 87, 135; struggle for equality 7, 11, 29, 30, 38, 105, 135

World Adventures in Time and Place 89
World and Its People, The 82
World Cultures: A Global Mosaic 89
World Cultures and Geographies 90
World Cultures and Geography 91
World Geography and Cultures 96
World Geography Today 91
World History 92, 97
World History: A Global Mosaic 87, 92–3, 95
World History: Patterns of Interaction 91
world religions: Buddhism 5, 81, 90–1, 158; Eastern Churches 91; educating about Islam, and 152; diversity 118; fundamentalism 23, 27, 31, 38, 59, 96, 99, 103, 139; "Mixed/Traditional" 91; "Other Christian" 91; pluralism, and 88; Protestant Christianity 1, 16, 91; public school standards 78, 81; Roman Catholic Christianity 91; "Sparsely inhabited" 91; symbols 115; textbooks, in 91; "Traditional" 91; *see also* Christianity, Confucianism; Hinduism; Islam; Judaism; religion in schools

xenophobia 17

Zagumny, Lisa 95
Zangwill, Israel 14
Zinn, Howard 14, 138
Znanieck, Florian 18–19, 21, 35
Zogby, Jim 28